Telling Stories That Matter

Other Books of Interest from St. Augustine's Press

Telling Stories That Matter: Memoirs and Essays

MARVIN R. O'CONNELL

Edited by William G. Schmitt

Foreword by Wilson D. Miscamble, C.S.C.

Afterword by David Solomon

ST. AUGUSTINE'S PRESS
South Bend, Indiana

Library of Congress Control Number: 2020944814

St. Augustine's Press
www.staugustine.net

TABLE OF CONTENTS

Foreword
Marvin R. O'Connell: Master Historian

When I was an undergraduate at the University of Queensland, now quite some decades ago, I read an essay by a noted Australian historian, Manning Clark, on "Writing History." Clark traced the etymology of the word "historian" to the ancient "*histor.*" Clark's *histor* was "the wise man who told a story about the past, vouched for the accuracy of the events he described, and used those events to communicate his vision of life." The *histor* had to "choose a subject that touches men deeply, [and to] write about things that matter." Furthermore, he needed to engage and entertain his readers by writing in the way that all great stories are told. My friend Father Marvin O'Connell was a true embodiment of the *histor.*

Born in St. Paul on July 9, 1930, O'Connell grew up in small towns of southern Minnesota and northern Iowa during the Depression years. He early discerned a vocation to the priesthood and studied first in the minor seminary, Nazareth Hall, and then at St. Paul Seminary, the major seminary of the Archdiocese of St. Paul. Fr. O'Connell traveled to Notre Dame in 1956 to study for his doctorate under the direction of the renowned Church historian, Monsignor Philip Hughes. O'Connell had been ordained a priest that very year. His notable talents as an historian were already in evidence as he had published a well-researched book, *The Dowling Decade in St. Paul* (1955), a version of his Master's thesis at St. Paul Seminary, which examined the Church in the Twin Cities in the 1920s. It would not be the last time that O'Connell would explore Catholicism in Minnesota.

Under the astute guidance of Msgr. Hughes he turned his attention to the history of the Reformation and the Counter-Reformation. He wrote his dissertation on Thomas Stapleton, a prolific figure of the English Counter-Reformation and, when revised, Yale University Press published this in 1964. By this point Fr. O'Connell had returned to St. Paul and begun his distinguished tenure as priest, teacher, and scholar at the (then)

College of St. Thomas. His reputation as a brilliant lecturer and demanding teacher were clearly established during his years at St. Thomas. He also wrote his wonderful account of John Henry Newman and the Oxford Movement — *The Oxford Conspirators* (1969) — which culminated in Newman's reception into the Catholic Church in October of 1845.

In 1972 O'Connell received Archbishop Leo Binz's permission to return to Notre Dame to assume the position previously held by his now-deceased mentor, Philip Hughes. So began well over two decades of exemplary service. His teaching at both the graduate and undergraduate levels was especially noteworthy and challenging. His rather intimidating physical presence guaranteed that undergraduate students maintained high standards of decorum and commitment in his classroom. From 1974 to 1980 Fr. O'Connell chaired the history department and proved a capable administrator who recruited talented faculty.

During his first year as chair of the department, Fr. O'Connell published *The Counter Reformation, 1559–1610*, a volume in the prestigious Rise of Modern Europe series edited by William L. Langer. This book was well received and even named as a History Book Club selection. O'Connell took special pride in Langer's description of the book as so balanced and fair-minded that a reader could not tell whether it was written by a Catholic or a Protestant. Langer rightly noted that this was a "tribute to the author's depth of understanding and truly unusual objectivity."

While carrying his administrative responsibilities and leading the history department in a characteristically firm way Fr. O'Connell sought a new vehicle for his always lucid prose and chose to write a novel. He published *McElroy* in 1980, his fictional account of the trials and tribulations of a post-war Minnesota politician who some readers thought bore a certain resemblance to Senator Eugene McCarthy, whom O'Connell had known during his years at St. Thomas. Writing history, however, remained his true passion as the remarkable books he published over the following three decades clearly illustrated.

First came his masterful biography of the great American churchman and first archbishop of St. Paul, John Ireland. *John Ireland and the American Catholic Church* (1988) was not a narrow study but a true "life and times" portrait which cast essential light on the Americanist movement and the place of Roman Catholics in American political life in the late nineteenth and early twentieth centuries. Upon reading this splendid book Fr. Theodore Hesburgh reached the firm conclusion that he must enlist O'Connell to write the life of Notre Dame's founder, Fr. Edward Sorin. He knew that O'Connell could do justice to the experience and accomplishments of that notable figure. Father O'Connell found that possibility of interest but knew he had other projects to complete. The first of these he published in 1994, the year he retired from full-time teaching, as *Critics on Trial: An Introduction to the Catholic Modernist Crisis.* This beautifully written multiple biography offered sympathetic portraits of an array of Catholic modernists and assessed their significance as a movement.

Soon thereafter came *Blaise Pascal: Reasons of the Heart* (1997), which tracked not only Pascal's spiritual journey but also the religious turmoil of seventeenth-century France. On completing that book Fr. O'Connell observed correctly that his various works had allowed him to engage "many of the great issues that have confronted the Church during modern times: the English Reformation, the Counter-Reformation, the Oxford Movement, Modernism, Americanism, and finally, French Jansenism." He was telling stories that truly mattered. His scholarly work revealed his broad interests covering compelling topics from the sixteenth century forward and on both sides of the Atlantic. Yet, especially for those fascinated by the history of Notre Dame, the best was yet to come.

Fr. O'Connell's magisterial account of the life and times of Edward Sorin, C.S.C., appeared in 2001. *Sorin* made no genuflection in the direction of hagiography. O'Connell was too gifted an historian to succumb to that temptation. The book recounts in riveting detail the deep clash between Edward Sorin and his religious superior, Basil Moreau, the beatified founder of the Holy Cross Order. In revealing the contest between these two complex personalities, Fr. O'Connell addressed the larger issue (as the historian Gerald McKevitt noted) of "the struggle of European institutions — in this case, a religious congregation — to adapt to the American environment."

The book garnered high praise from reviewers, one of whom described its thirty chapters as "thoroughly researched and beautifully crafted with rhapsodic descriptions of place, complex character development, and a fine sense of pacing. It reads like a good novel, partly because Sorin was such a character." O'Connell surely captured the essence of that Sorin character in this memorable description: "Whether sad or happy, however, he simply refused to entertain the possibility of failure. So confident was he in his own powers, so sure of the ultimate righteousness of his goals, and so deep his faith that God and the Virgin Mary had summoned him to America to accomplish a great work, that no obstacle could confound him. He was no saint. He was capable of duplicity and pettiness and even ruthlessness. But for sheer courage and for the serene determination that courage gives birth to, he was hard to match."

Fr. O'Connell might have been expected to rest on his laurels after the completion of this major work but his passion to write history remained undimmed. He fulfilled a promise first made to Archbishop John Roach of St. Paul to write a history of his home archdiocese, and so his *Pilgrims to the Northland: The Archdiocese of St. Paul, 1840–1962* was published in 2009. It allowed him to tell the story of the Church which had received his immigrant ancestors from Ireland and which had helped shape him.

Marvin O'Connell utilized his striking talents as an historian as an integral part of his fundamental vocation as a priest. He once described the historian as a veritable "midwife to our faith," who must capture, as best the evidence will allow, the truth of the past. His work recognized both that God revealed himself "in an historical person who, at a particular time and place, went from town to town, doing good, who was like us in all things but sin," and that "the life of Christ is extended into the life of his people, the Church." He made the latter his special subject and understood "the special role in the life of the Christian people" of history and the historian. He notably filled this role and contributed much to our understanding of the Church's journey over the past five centuries.

In his late retirement years O'Connell next set about to craft a narrative history of the presidents of Notre Dame from Sorin to Hesburgh. As his health deteriorated, however, his capacity to undertake the necessary archival research diminished. He had always "subscribed cheerfully," as he once put it, to Monsignor Hughes' definition of the discipline, namely: "History is the reconstruction of the past by the mind from sources." Sources were essential for him and without access to them he laid his Notre Dame presidents project aside.

He had long resisted the urge to write his memoirs even though he admired the fine autobiographical reflection that his oldest and closest friend

Ralph McInerny had written. Yet, when increasingly confined to his apartment at Holy Cross Village he began to reconsider the matter. The urge
within him to tell stories was irresistible. He decided that the final story he
would tell would be his own.

He wrote it primarily from memory and without access to sources as
conventionally understood. He normally regarded "personal reminiscences"
as suspect because he discerned that they were usually self-serving. But as
he crafted his own story, which I had the privilege to read as each chapter
was completed, I observed him avoiding that pitfall. His memoirs were not
some exercise in self-promotion but rather were self-revealing and also rev-
elatory of times, places, people, and experiences worth remembering. Those
recollections added to the complex picture he painted of the past in his
books and articles. His final search through memories and their context
was yet another effort on his part "to chronicle that tangle of mind and
emotion, of pride and passion and sentimentality, of providence and
chance, of cruelty and compassion, of the good and the bad, that has been
the human story." Readers of these memoirs won't see a forced or exagger-
ated portrayal, but instead they will learn of the Church and the world
through the lens of a priest's training and ministry in the period surrounding the Second Vatican Council. Additionally, they will witness the education and emergence of a master storyteller and of all that he encountered
along the way.

Marvin O'Connell died on August 19, 2016. His final illness forced
him to put his memoirs aside before he completed the full story of his
earthly journey. Still, having some sizable part of the account of this mod-
ern-day *histor* more than suffices, especially when complemented here by
selected materials through which he engaged and entertained many. This
volume will be especially valuable as a tool of inspiration and enlightenment
for all those who practice the challenging art of writing history, as well as
for those who appreciate learning from it. May the reader draw a variety of
benefits from surveying the life of a priest-historian who wrote about what
really matters.

Wilson D. Miscamble, C.S.C.

Preface

The structure and contents of this book have been guided by several basic principles depicted by the words on its cover: "Telling Stories That Matter: Memoirs and Essays," by Marvin R. O'Connell.

Most importantly, this is a book by and about Marvin R. O'Connell, a premier Catholic historian whose life as a priest, scholar, author, and teacher made him a formidable force in the lives of countless truth-seekers. The story of his life of 86 years deserves to be told in his own words, from his own perspective, because seeing the sweep of Church history he studied so masterfully, through a unique lens, offers an abundance of insights that should not be missed.

Therefore, readers will find here O'Connell's voice, enhanced only by supplemental commentary from friends and touched only by occasional editing for readability, clarity in references, and format continuity, lest the insights lose any of their power to reflect the author and instruct the audience. Ralph McInerny, a friend since boyhood who joined O'Connell among the important figures in the history of the University of Notre Dame, describes the value of this historian's words: "Few writers have the ability to locate the reader more surely in place and time, to give a sense of the human beings whose deeds and antics are the stuff of history. The historian dotes on the particular; the great historian makes it shine with a more than particular import."

McInerny, in his appreciation of O'Connell, included here as an addendum, also offers what might be called "a word to the wise" for those who would impose substantial editing upon the expression of the historian's rigorous, comprehensive research. "An editor at *Notre Dame Magazine* presumed to cut a commissioned article in half," McInerny recalled in his 1998 essay. O'Connell determined he would "never again appear in those benighted pages. He is, in a word, Irish." There is no desire in these pages to provoke that insistent professional ire again, this time from beyond the grave.

The second guiding principle for this book is found in the title's reference to "telling stories." O'Connell was a master story-teller whose passion for compelling content and context about people and circumstances was sparked in his youth while enjoying the genre of historical fiction. Again, McInerny's reflections from 1998 are relevant: "An historian like O'Connell becomes perforce a bit of a biographer, and there is always a *soupçon* of the novelist in his style now."

This project is grounded in the fact that, in the last years of his life, O'Connell took up the project of telling his own story. The memoirs he began writing constitute Part One — the impetus, validation, and anchor of this book. Although he died before he could advance his biography beyond a glimpse of the 1970s, he suggests in the first chapter the delightful complexity of the task he is undertaking. He refers to a book from his childhood, *George Washington's World* — this time, a work of non-fiction. But it is a feast of "language and imagery suitable for a clever youngster," with "notable events and personages that flourished outside the United States," opening up "a wonderful new insight into the human story." He observes, "It is well if the schoolboy recognizes that the world is a vast place and that the human family includes a dizzying number of components. History therefore brings forward a myriad of stories and stories within stories, and parallels, and distinctions, all of which must be taken into account if one is to grasp something of the past. An integral, multi-faceted history is the only satisfying variety."

The title of this book spotlights "stories that matter," pointing out its third guiding principle. In his story-telling, O'Connell sought out not only the multi-faceted but the deeply meaningful. This priest-scholar is not patient with wasting his or others' time. Indeed, in Chapter 12 of his memoirs, he looks back over a lifetime of scholarship and recalls the statement of Pilate from the Scriptural account of Christ's passion. Referring to the words placed on the cross of Jesus which declare him to be the King of the Jews, Pilate says, "What I have written, I have written." O'Connell launches from that statement of bold resignation to a reflection applying a touch of wit and humility to "the sheer bulk of what I have written over a long career. I'm startled when I contemplate what I've asked readers to accept from me: books (some very long), articles (some serious, some trivial), columns, reviews, sermons ... and now even memoirs." He asks for "forbearance" from the audiences who have consumed all that text, concluding: "Yet I must say that, like Pilate, I'm pretty satisfied with what I have written."

One must conclude he believes in the meaningfulness of the immense body of his work assessing people and developments that shaped the Catholic Church, society, and people's lives, past, present, and future. His stories matter because people matter — an appreciation aligned with his dual vocation as priest and historian. The Church and the pursuit of truth matter. If the central question is whether the Christian religion is true, O'Connell says the question is "essentially an historical one." Pondering this in a funeral homily whose text is included here, he notes that God chose to reveal himself as an historical person "at a particular time and in a particular place." The Christian religion is first a subject for the mind to comprehend before it can engage the emotions, he says. History may have its "humdrum" aspects, but it "has a special role in the life of the Christian people, and so does the historian." He describes the historian as a "midwife" because "our faith is stillborn" without the facts which relentlessly emerge from history. An historian's "obsession with objective facts" saves humankind from a subjective religion of "self-consciousness and sentimentality."

This means O'Connell took the discipline of history, with all its protocols and canons, seriously. He respected the past — every story within a story and every point in the timeline — as a subject revealing its own gift package of distinctive and integral qualities. The past, with all its fascinating and multi-dimensional stories, seemed so worthy of attention that he also appreciated other ways to spread its lessons, such as novels and plays, although he insisted upon properly practiced historical research as an independent guarantee of solid interpretation.

In a critique of Robert Bolt's play, *A Man for All Seasons,* he demurs with a reminder that Saint Thomas More's one season "is all gone now." That fact does not take away from the brilliance of the drama or the holiness of the martyr. But O'Connell cautions against imposing generalized, present-day interpretations that may diminish the past. The embrace of a particular "season," exactly as it was, enlightens an audience; they learn how the context of circumstances and viewpoints made More so special for his time and place.

Such applications of O'Connell's passion for the big picture, plus his insistence on precise focal points when making judgments about everything, from plays to presentism to the role of an historian, point to one final guiding principle of this book. As captured in its title, the phrase "Memoirs and Essays" identifies the special endeavor here to bestow upon O'Connell's story the same kind of comprehensive, broad yet deep, treatment he gave to others' stories throughout his career. His memoirs cease at the point where he accepts a journalistic position he was to hold until 1973, when he was on the threshold of a capstone career at the University of Notre Dame. But the team that assembled this book saw in his additional decades of writing in magazines and journals a way to expand his biography, extend his voice into specific timeframes and circumstances, and examine his diverse analyses as a consistent model. He still speaks to his readers today through essays he wrote while pursuing the work of teaching and authoring acclaimed books.

Thus, Part Two comprises essays of various sorts O'Connell wrote between 1978 and 2001. The selections presented here are only a sampling of subjects he explored, commentaries he published, and contributions he made to Church history. But they do allow the reader to get to know this remarkable historian better in light of the principles discussed above and the narrative arc begun in Part One. Each essay was selected because, in some way, it elucidates how his talents and traits are applicable to a particular topic and how his viewpoints can inform new generations teaching and learning history. Each essay is presented with its own brief introduction, but the following roadmap will connect certain themes of the reader's encounter with O'Connell.

Two essays regarding Cardinal John Henry Newman, an Anglican convert to Catholicism and perhaps the dominant force in the religious history of nineteenth-century England, constitute a natural follow-up to the memoirs. They include a discussion of O'Connell's stance as an academic at the intersection of faith and historicity, as well as his launch into writing newspaper columns between 1966 and 1973. O'Connell's columns, reflecting a more conservative mind frame transformed from his earlier inclinations toward the views of a more liberal Catholic journal *Commonweal* (making him a "Commonweal Catholic"), were titled "Tracts for the Times." That phrase memorialized the name of the series of essays co-edited by Newman at the helm of the Oxford Movement. O'Connell sympathized with the effort to establish the small-c catholicism of the Anglican Church and keep faith-informed values alive in public conversation at Oxford University and elsewhere. The essay, "Newman and the Ideal of a University," describes O'Connell's experience at the University of Notre Dame in terms of challenges to the vibrant dialogue integrating faith and reason for which Newman had fought.

"Defenders of the Faith" goes deeper into O'Connell's argument that history and Christian religion are inseparable. He uses examples from the Doctors of the Church in positing the need for historical insights in order to cultivate a mature faith. A disregard for history leads to a privatization of faith that does not enable sound judgments, he warns.

The value he placed on the role of history helped O'Connell to appreciate authors who could communicate essential messages of faith alive in the public sphere over time — even authors who could not technically be called historians. One such contributor, spotlighted in the next essay on "the uses of history," was Hilaire Belloc, the outstanding English polemicist whose passion and Catholic imagination O'Connell found "exhilarating."

Nevertheless, concerns could arise from a "slippery slope" between the rigorous canons of historiography and lesser forms of story-telling. O'Connell saw the danger from what today's audience might call disinformation rise to distressing levels in defamatory, hyperbolic legends about the Spanish Inquisition. In an essay reflecting the breadth and depth of his knowledge — embracing theology and culture along with history — O'Connell quashes notions of the Inquisition as a weapon of mass murder wielded by the Church.

The next two essays transport the reader to another front, along which O'Connell battles the slippery slope he sees in the historical scholarship of controversial Notre Dame theologian Richard McBrien. O'Connell sharply derides what he sees as injections of opinion and selective use of sources, as well as carelessness in research and writing, in two McBrien books — one on the history of the papacy and one called *Caesar's Coin: Religion and Politics.*

But O'Connell consistently exhibited a balance between staunch advocacy of responsible Church history and an interdisciplinary openness to descriptions of the life of faith served up in different genres. Not surprisingly for a man who had a fondness for historical fiction and variety in

explorations of religion, his next two essays — on the historian and literature — discuss the ability to humanize religion evinced in the novels of J.
F. Powers and in the famous play about Saint Thomas More written by
Robert Bolt. The everyday insights into the lives of priests in the Midwest
offered by Powers resonate with O'Connell and draw only restrained cri-
tiques. However, as discussed above, the assessment of More as a model of
the faithful conscience transcending "all seasons" receives a mixed review.
O'Connell acknowledges "the play's the thing" that can laudably reach new
audiences with worthy displays of religious zeal, but he wants to shed more
light on the story. He defines the understanding of conscience dominant
during More's unique "season" of challenge and boldness. An unwavering
skepticism toward the use of history to make generalizations or predictions
prompts O'Connell to push back against the claim of timelessness in Bolt's
title.

His next essay, "An Historical Perspective on Evangelization in the
United States," takes readers on a tour through a timeline of religious history close to home. Assessed through O'Connell's panoramic but precise
observations, each period in the American Catholic immigrant experience,
from the "survival" phase of early arrivals to the "assimilation" phase of later
generations to the new challenges driven by secular culture, yields its own
lessons. He concludes with a bold suggestion that Catholics return to a
"ghetto" of sorts. This is not a presentism that imagines repeating the past,
but a call for Catholics to return to their own identity, to "recapture a sense
of ourselves" as separate from the "consumerist" society: "We need to find
again the spirit of community and fellowship we have lost."

Just as a review of the past in the "Historical Perspectives" essay of 1991
spawns a fresh idea presaging twenty-first-century proposals for a "Benedict
Option," the next essay presented here traces different steps in the development of modernism and extracts fundamental principles. These prompt
O'Connell to issue another clarion call to the Church. This time, he pre-
scribes what might be called a preferential option for reality. Seeing the
seeds of relativism planted, he says current cultural tendencies among many
people to create customized realities and abstract notions of progress must
be resisted. The strategy he recommends is taken from the historian's play-
book — judging the tenor of the times objectively and standing by the evidence found in faith and reason, not drifting with tides of personal taste

or popular opinion. His strategy gains credence from the fact that in 1994 he wrote a history of modernism titled *Critics on Trial: An Introduction to the Catholic Modernist Crisis.*

The last two essays found in Part Two are reminders that O'Connell's perspectives and prescriptions are rooted not in coldly analytical research, but in the exhilaration of real-life relationships. In a lecture to the American Catholic Historical Association, he is the consummate educator whose credibility is that of a witness sharing personal experiences. He recalls developing his passion for history through the power of teachers and authors who captured the complex stories of people and places, sparking a sense of wonder. In a homily he delivered at a funeral, he is the consummate priest, appreciating the gifts of an incarnational God whose revelation emerges not in mere sentiments, but in our human relationships and communities over time — essentially in one's enduring connection to the historical figure of Jesus Christ: The practice of exploring our past, present, and future, when conducted with sensitivity, is "at once human and divine."

This is a good point at which to refer one last time to the appreciation written by Ralph McInerny. Perhaps O'Connell's own sensitivity as an educator and priest, in creative tension with the "Irish" irascibility cited earlier, helped shape his friend's observations, including a recommendation of *Critics on Trial.* McInerny says this: "Rare is the writer who can combine compassion for his subjects and judgment on what they did and said. There will never be a better book on the modernist crisis."

O'Connell's lifelong respect for the impact of relationships in real time has informed the approach taken in these pages. The "Memoirs and Essays" of Part One and Part Two are bracketed by recollections from three of his closest friends. The Foreword by Rev. Wilson D. Miscamble, C.S.C., and the Afterword by David Solomon, along with McInerny's Addendum, provide the reader with valuable extensions of Marvin O'Connell's voice. These scholars saw him persevere to draw conclusions that served the truth in the context of community as well as personal integrity. They testify that he can enlighten audiences today — about the two vocations that jointly shaped him; about the way he championed the art and craft of Church history as a gift to others; about his own experiences amid the complexities of collegiality and accountability; and about challenging trends now manifest in the Church and society. These friends of O'Connell deem the historian's passion for truth-in-context to be foundational for shaping stories that matter, including his own story.

The editor of this book, who has learned a great deal from seeing O'Connell at work in his words, offers sincere gratitude to friends Miscamble and Solomon for their invitation to participate in the project. Their entrustment of stewardship for details of a respected colleague's life story provided great inspiration and encouragement, as well as opportunities to interact with ideas and insights that truly do matter. Now it is the editor's privilege to offer readers a taste of these interactions in the sure hope that excellence in the academic discipline of history, modeled by O'Connell, will continue to yield rich meaning and understanding. The editor is also thankful for the exhilaration found in the academic community and in a loving family, especially wife Eileen and daughter Mary, where reality truly does show itself through relationships of both content and context, where everything has its season and every season offers its own abundance of joys and lessons.

William G. Schmitt

Part One
Memoirs

Chapter One
Initium

Of course, I had heard of Notre Dame, but in the small Minnesota towns where I grew up during the 'thirties and early 'forties I never met an alumnus or indeed anybody familiar with the place. As a Catholic I guess I took some remote pride in the institution and its famous football teams, but my childish loyalty in the latter regard, such as it was, lay with Coach Bernie Bierman and the Golden Gophers of the University of Minnesota, winner of half a dozen national championships during those years. I never saw a game — the reality of the Great Depression made such a venture unthinkable — but on Saturday afternoons during the season my Dad would stretch out on the kitchen table a long piece of plain brown wrapping paper, and draw on it the lines of a football field, and then, as we listened to the account of the game on the radio, he would mark the location of the ball after each play. Such a procedure sounds pretty primitive today, but it did allow free rein to a child's imagination. As far as fidelity to my religion was concerned, I felt especially satisfied when in 1941 Gopher halfback Bruce Smith won the Heisman Trophy, and Bruce Smith was a Catholic.

In 1944 my Dad was promoted into the main office of the *Minneapolis Star Tribune*, for whose country circulation department he had worked for some years in Pipestone, Owatonna, and Mankato. And that autumn I enrolled at Nazareth Hall, the preparatory or minor seminary of the Archdiocese of St. Paul. This was the training program for those aspiring to the secular priesthood that prevailed under the old ecclesiastical regime before the Second Vatican Council (1962–1965): four years of high school and two of college at the minor, followed by the completion of college as a philosophy major, plus four years of theology at the major seminary, twelve years in all. The percentage of those who partook in this system at whatever level and who were ultimately ordained was, for all sorts of mostly good and appropriate reasons, small. But I was, so to speak, a lifer; I did the whole twelve years.

Nazareth Hall, about twenty years old when I first went there, was a large and exquisitely beautiful building located on a peninsula jutting out into Lake Johanna, on the northern outskirts of St. Paul. It was a boarding school with about 250 students who ranged in age between fourteen and twenty and who, except for a fairly lengthy vacation at Christmas time, spent the nine months there from Labor Day to Memorial Day, all the while carefully preserved from worldly distractions (like radios, telephones, secular newspapers and magazines, and, I need hardly say, girls). In retrospect Nazareth Hall seems to me to have been a combination of the French *petit seminaire* and the English public school. Emphasis was on classical and modern languages, history, basic mathematics, and a smattering of physical science. The faculty was composed entirely of diocesan priests, and their instruction was, with a few notorious exceptions, at a high level. Leaving aside personal spiritual considerations, for me the place had a special charm, and this for two reasons. As an only child, I had inevitably suffered a measure of loneliness; now and through the years that followed I took my place amidst a band of brothers.

Also, as one who had attended five grammar schools over the eight grades — itself a testament to the uncertainties of employment during the Great Depression — I found here on the shores of Lake Johanna a stability and a predictability that were a daily solace.

Along with the accumulation of debts any fourteen-year-old boy would have to acknowledge, I brought with me to the Hall an additional trio of them. The first was to the philanthropist Andrew Carnegie, who during the late nineteenth and early twentieth centuries spent vast sums of money to build libraries across the United States, indeed across the world, more than 2500 in all. In Minnesota alone sixty-five Carnegie public libraries were constructed, at a cost of nearly $1,000,000, including the one I rejoiced in in Pipestone when our little family lived there. A great reader himself, and a Christian committed to putting his vast wealth to use for the common good, the open-handed steel magnate's largesse acted as a spur and an inspiration to other private persons of means and to enlightened political leaders as well. The overall result has been the magnificent library system that prevails to this day. And for me, in the towns I lived in when I was a sometimes lonely boy, the public library was a second home.

I suppose the first serious piece of literature I read was Robert Louis Stevenson's *Treasure Island.* The tale still holds a golden place in my memory. But before that I encountered the works of a much less well-known writer called Joseph Altsheller. A journeyman American newspaper reporter, Altsheller, until his premature death in 1919, turned out scores of adventure stories designed to appeal to precocious lads like me, all of which were set in the American past. The first one I found in the stacks of the local public library was titled *The Horsemen of the Plains,* a rousing tale about the Indian wars of the 1870s. I next discovered that Altsheller had a particular gift for creating multi-volume series of books with continuing characters; there was one, for instance, to cover chronologically the American Revolution, another for the Civil War — the latter with titles like *The Guns of Shiloh* and *The Sword of Antietam.* The violence which these subjects suggest was carefully tempered; the good guys won, and the bad guys were really not all that bad and, like the Cheyenne chieftains and the Confederate generals depicted, not without honor.

Thus was I introduced to history, to the *story* of the past, an idealist account, to be sure, or, if you like, a fanciful one that consciously appealed to an immature mind and imagination. Many years were to pass before I became able to discern precisely what was the intimate process I had undergone thanks to the prolific Joseph Altsheller, and even to put a name to it. I did not simply relish the tales he told; in some sense he allowed me to march up the Shenandoah Valley with Stonewall Jackson and then, a few years later, to ride back down with Philip Sheridan. The adventures of the gallant figures Altsheller wrote about I came to share, without departing from my ordinary life. Indeed, that ordinary life was enriched because of them. And though as I grew up I had to set aside the simple unsophisticated exuberance of those boyish days, I never, even as a professional historian, could deny that the attraction of history for me always involved vicarious experience.

The third debt I owed on the eve of my departure for Nazareth Hall was to a lady named Genevieve Foster. A book she published in 1940 I received a few years later as a Christmas or a birthday present — after seven decades I'm not certain which. In any case, *George Washington's World* it was called, and it laid out, in language and imagery suitable for a clever youngster, notable events and personages that flourished outside the United States during the lifetime of the first president (1732–1799). *World* in the title is something of a misnomer, since the book confined itself pretty exclusively to western Europeans. Even so, it opened for me wonderful new vistas and a wonderful new insight into the human story. The same time as Washington was living out his remarkable career, J. S. Bach and Mozart were composing unforgettable music, Samuel Johnson was the presiding savant in the London coffee houses, Voltaire became the fierce herald of the Enlightenment, and Captain Cook nudged *HMS Endeavour* out of Tahiti and across the blue western Pacific till he reached Botany Bay. The Franciscan friar, Junipero Serra, born in Majorca, transformed wild California through the host of missions he founded there; moreover, since after 1776 Father Serra sympathized with the rebels 3000 miles to the east, he collected $137 and sent that sum to General Washington. I'm not sure I believe that last anecdote, nor was Mrs. Foster concerned with citing precise source material. But that was not the point of her book, and that point was not lost on me. It is well if the schoolboy recognizes that the world is a vast place and that the human family includes a dizzying number of components. History therefore brings forward a myriad of stories and stories within stories, and parallels, and distinctions, all of which must be taken into account if one is to grasp something of the past. An integral, multi-faceted history is the only satisfying variety.

On the eve of departure on my first trip to Europe in 1964, I resolved to keep a diary. That intention I fulfilled for a couple of days, and then, like so many of my good resolutions over the years, this one went whistling down the wind. So what I write here is entirely from memory, which means of course that the narrative's accuracy is often suspect. And, no doubt, it bristles with oddities. For instance, I can remember clearly how thrilled I was when I realized that in the conjugation of a Latin verb the presence at its ending of the letter "n" denoted a plural; thus, *amat*, he (she, it) loves, but *amant*, they love.

This moment of truth occurred during my early weeks at Nazareth Hall, in Walter Peters' first Latin class. Father Peters, whom I came to know well later on, was given to severe swings in mood which deprived him of much stable contentment; still, in his field of expertise, modern German literature, he was deeply learned, and always an excellent teacher. Many of his colleagues exhibited similar pedagogical skill. Edward Gleason possessed real genius in the way he opened the mysteries of mathematics to a roomful of squirming adolescents. William Nolan, who had the reputation of being a particularly tough guy, was in any event a marvelous English teacher. He had wide literary interests combined with a dramatic flair, so that in his rich bass voice he could bring to life texts as various as *The Green Pastures,* Marc Connelly's lilting African-American evocation of the Old Testament, and Browning's *Andrea del Sarto:* "But do not let us quarrel any more/ No, my Lucrezia, bear with me for once." Most significant for me in the long run, however, was the essay Father Nolan assigned the class every Monday morning, due the following Monday. This exercise gave me my first sustained challenge to produce readable prose, my first chance to develop a disciplined literary style. I experienced a great deal of exhilaration when Nolan approved of some of these writing assignments, but no doubt I profited more from his sharp criticism of their shortcomings.

Our history professor was Father James Cecka — "Butch" we called him behind his back. (I don't know why; all the faculty had nicknames that antedated our arrival in 1944.) He was a corpulent man with slicked-back, thinning black hair, and like the proverbial fat person he was for the most part quite jolly. But he was serious about history and expected his students to be the same. Sources, he kept telling us, documents, witnesses to past events, these are what matter. I remember especially a unit on the English Civil War, the contest between Roundheads and Cavaliers. My instincts told me to side with the Roundheads because they were — weren't they? — the agents of nascent democracy. But were they really, Butch asked, and sent me scurrying off to our (very limited) library to seek out the available collection of pertinent documents. There I discovered the grim Oliver Cromwell, dictatorial warts and all, and ever since I have been something of a cavalier.

It may be argued that Father Cecka's methodology delivered me from the boyish romanticism of Joseph Altsheller. There is certainly some truth in this assertion, but, even so, I prefer to come to a different, a perhaps more nuanced, conclusion. The engagement of my imagination, the stirring up of my sense of vicarious experience first aroused by the exposure to juvenile historical fiction, was not squelched by following Butch Cecka to a more serious level of inquiry into the past. Indeed, if anything the original feeling was enhanced. Now I could find myself sharing in the lives and endeavors of real people, like Prince Rupert, the archetypal cavalier, rather than made-up cowboys and Indians.

The six-year program at Nazareth Hall ended for me in the spring of 1950, a few weeks before my twentieth birthday. In the fall I took up residence at the St. Paul Seminary, located within the city on a bluff overlooking the Mississippi. I took many friends with me, some who were ultimately ordained priests, some not. Most of them are dead now, and anyway once I settled permanently at Notre Dame in 1972, I met them only occasionally. With one notable exception. When I was a high school freshman, Ralph McInerny was two classes ahead of me. I scarcely knew him then and thought little of it when he left the Hall at the end of that academic year. His departure was not unusual or in any way disreputable; it was a common — indeed, healthy — instance of discernment. As a seminarian matured, he might very well decide that in fact he did not want to be a priest or that he was not ready to adopt the required life-style. So Ralph finished high school in the city and then joined the Marine Corps — remember, it was 1945. Two years later he came back to Nazareth Hall, now as a college freshman, or, to use the preferred terminology, as a fifth-year man. Clearly the idea of the priesthood, or at least some aspects of it, still appealed to him. Over the next two years I came to know him very well indeed. He graduated from the Hall in 1949, and so when I arrived at the seminary a year later, Ralph was already there.

This institution was a collection of singularly ugly red brick buildings dating back to the 1890s. The atmosphere, as one might expect in a major seminary, was much more visibly ecclesiastical than that at the Hall. The ordinary student garb, for instance, was the black cassock topped off by the white Roman collar. For generations an amiable Jewish tailor named Zolly Witoff had kept his shop on the edge of the campus, where he specialized exclusively in crafting quite handsome cassocks for the young men nearby. My Grandfather O'Connell, nearing ninety in 1950, insisted on paying for my first one; he wanted Marvin, he told the family, to have a proper "coat," for such was the designation he gave to the long black formal garment the priests wore in the country church he had attended all his life. He was very pleased with Zolly's work, and so was I.

The first two years at the seminary completed the collegiate course begun at Nazareth Hall, which brought with it the bachelor's degree. It amounted to a tightly constricted philosophy major; there were a few classes in auxiliary subjects but no electives. The quality of the teaching — once again handled entirely by diocesan clergy — was uneven, as was the case also, unsurprisingly, within the four-year theology curriculum that followed. I must testify, however, to the fact that when I went to graduate school and mixed with those who had attended other seminaries, I discovered that my alma mater compared quite favorably to them.

One reason, quite accidental, why the St. Paul Seminary in those days scored relatively well in the measurement of the intellectual preparation of its students was largely due to the temper of the times. The early and mid-1950s marked the climax of the great Thomistic revival within the Catholic community worldwide. That movement, which had been growing and maturing since the end of the nineteenth century, had various strands associated with the names of luminaries like Maritain, Gilson, Bernard Lonergan. Perhaps less known but in his way no less significant was Professor Charles de Konnick of Laval University in Quebec. In St. Paul we were fortunate enough to have two of his students on our faculty, and they set a scholarly tone in the institution that was felt far beyond the classroom. William Baumgaertner taught us logic and metaphysics, and I, with my unphilosophical temperament, found it hard going. But I came gradually to appreciate the value of studying the very texts of St. Thomas Aquinas and Aristotle rather than the tired manuals with their synopses based on disconnected quotations that for generations had been the ordinary coin of seminary education. Similarly, the theologian David Dillon — tall, redheaded with matinee-idol good looks — led us with Aquinas through the thickets of formal dogma; the tough tracts he taught on the Trinity and on the Seven Days of Creation were a kind of tribute to the Laval methodology.

There were, to be sure, other effective professors: Gerald Baskfield on natural theology, for instance, and Eugene Moriarty on canon law. On the other hand, the course in Scripture, six semesters of it, was an utter waste of time, while that in fundamental moral was little better. Even worse was the ordinary course in the history of the Church, four semesters. The professor was William Busch, the eminent liturgical reformer. Indeed, that eminence may have been the root of the problem. Of course, it could be argued that his scholarly contribution to the Liturgical Movement as it emerged out of the 1920s was much more important than the instruction in the long history of Catholicism which he oversaw for several generations of St. Paul seminarians. But his indifference to this obligation remains indefensible. Class after class Father (later Monsignor) Busch, his wispy figure wrapped in a black cloak, sat on the stage in the *aula maxima* and chirped away at the restless crowd of bored students on the floor below him.

And perhaps even more pernicious than these vapid, barely audible lectures was the textbook assigned for the course. There was nothing wrong in itself, I hasten to say, about Philip Hughes' three-volume *A History of the Church*; quite to the contrary, the book was an excellent, up-to-date survey (published in the late 1940s and early 1950s) of the life of the Church from the earliest times to the eve of the Reformation. And there, as the poet might say, was the rub, the chronological rub. Busch chose to harmonize the conclusion of the fourth and last semester of his course with the end of Hughes' third volume, at the historical moment, that is, *just before* Martin Luther nailed the Ninety-five Theses on Indulgences to the door of the castle church in Wittenberg. The unhappy result was that young men representing as many as twenty Midwestern dioceses entered their assignments as teachers of the Catholic people with black holes in their intellectual preparation. Unbelievable as it may seem, they remained uninstructed about the context of the Reformation and Counter Reformation, about Jansenism and Josephism and Modernism and Americanism, about the Oxford Movement and, yes, ironically enough, about the liturgical movement, about Philip Neri and Sixtus V, Teresa of Avila and Therese of Lisieux, Pascal and Newman and Lacordaire; about John Ireland and Mother Cabrini and Dorothy Day.

Here was a travesty indeed, and the seminary administration, given the clerical realities, could not censure or interfere with Busch's conduct of his course. Yet it did shrewdly find a way to make positive use of it. An initiative to put together a master's program was undertaken in the late 1940s, the purpose of which was to equip graduates with a higher degree and thus widen their usefulness in whatever ministry they might be assigned to. The project combined the credits gained from the four semesters of Busch's general history, together with those of several allegedly related courses, plus two semesters of historiography, followed by a written thesis, and, *voila,* there was a Master of Arts in history. Even though this program was of great benefit to me, I must say that in retrospect it looks pretty rickety, the sum of several dubious parts. Still, it was approved by the appropriate accrediting agency, and over the long term it produced in its theses an accumulation of very respectable scholarship.

Its overall success was almost entirely the accomplishment of a man to whom I owe, professionally and personally, the greatest debt.

Chapter Two
In Medias Res

Patrick Henry Ahern, a trim man of medium height with a graying crew-cut, was thirty-four years old in 1950 when he assumed direction of the St. Paul Seminary's fledgling master's program. He had served as a chaplain during the final stages of the Second World War, and as such he was eligible to take advantage of that truly revolutionary piece of federal legislation, the Servicemen's Readjustment Act of 1944 (the G. I. Bill of Rights). Upon demobilization, with the archbishop's approval, he enrolled in the church history course of study at the Catholic University of America in Washington D.C. The dominant figure in that graduate program then, and for many years after, was John Tracy Ellis, who became at this time mentor to a goodly number of young priests around the country, including Father Ahern. Ellis' own research concentrated on the history of Catholicism in the United States during the nineteenth century, and unsurprisingly he steered his doctoral students in the same direction. Ahern's dissertation, a study of the career of John J. Keane, first rector of Catholic University, who died as archbishop of Dubuque in 1918, was published in 1953.

Pat Ahern was a straightforward sort of fellow. To invoke the overused bromide, what you saw in him is what you got. From the average student's point of observation, he did not quite fit the conventional persona of a seminary professor. Not that he was not a good priest or that he did not work as hard and conscientiously as his colleagues — indeed, in this latter regard he could put many of them to shame. Rather he disdained to assume any of the mannerisms of the professional intellectual. And he knew how to relax. He appreciated good cuisine — in fact, he was himself an accomplished cook, specializing in salads and in the exotic preparation of shellfish — and he always knew which wine was appropriate to serve with this or that entree. He had a dry sense of humor, which played out over a wide array of friends, both lay and clerical.

Students in first theology who had attained a certain grade-point average were automatically enrolled in the master's program. I don't remember how many in my class participated, but the number was not large. Several of them — especially those from rural dioceses without many high schools to staff — did not take the matter very seriously. Others resented the program on the grounds that it interfered with their theological education. For my part, I found the opportunity challenging, involving as it did the composition of a piece of original research. With Father Ahern's strong encouragement and helpful direction, I wrote my thesis on the tenure of Austin Dowling as archbishop of St. Paul (1919–1930). I found it to be a gratifying experience, so much so that I completed the essay ahead of schedule and so got my degree in the spring of 1955, a year before my ordination. Looking back sixty years, I can see that "The Dowling Decade" has plenty of youthful defects, and yet I remain proud of it.

At the same time that I began my master's work, I was harboring a bitter disappointment. In the summer of 1952, the announcement was made that four of my classmates — Walter Cullen, John Gilbert, James Moudry, Francis Ostrowski — were to be sent for their theological studies to the Catholic University of Leuven — or, more familiarly to English speakers, Louvain in Belgium. To complete one's seminary training in this world-famous institution of higher learning was an honor indeed, but it was also a public acknowledgment of one's academic prowess thus far. Humility has never been my strong suit, and it wasn't then. I had not the slightest doubt that only one of this quartet — Ostrowski — could possibly have claimed to be my intellectual equal; the other three certainly could not. Moreover, none of them, except Moudry, had endured with me the rather bleak social life of high school at Nazareth Hall; the other three matriculated there only after graduating from a fashionable (in Catholic circles) military academy in St. Paul, and so had enjoyed the adolescent amenities I had missed. All of them came from relatively well-off families, and all from roughly the same neighborhood, the solidly bourgeois midway district of the city. Their square shoulders, good posture and white teeth apparently impressed one influential cleric, who promoted their appointment on the grounds of their "manliness." And so out of such superficial judgments, combined with a certain class-based prejudice, I was deprived of what by the record of talent and academic achievement I deserved. I was deprived of a chance to experience the world abroad, to share in the exciting milieu of a real university, to live and travel in Europe, to see for myself those monuments, from the Arc de Triomphe to St. Peter's Basilica, I had yearningly read about, to learn to speak French and maybe German, to widen, in short, my horizons beyond the corn fields and iron mines of Minnesota. I had to wait twelve years to cross the Atlantic.

The resentment I felt then ran deep, and after all this time it still does. Not directed, to be sure, at the fortunate foursome, but rather at those authorities who played such favorites. And yet as things turned out, had I been appointed to Louvain I would have missed out on the greatest good fortune that ever befell me. What happened was a kind of after-the-fact fulfillment of that old saying: Beware of what you hope for, lest you get it and it fails to live up to its promise. I had not had a chance to hope for Louvain, but once the decision had been made and announced I regretted bitterly having been passed over. Little did I realize then that another door to a better place might open for me. And had I been appointed, I wonder how much those four years abroad would have contributed to my happiness or, more importantly, to my worth as a man and a priest? After all, three of the four who did their theology at Louvain ultimately resigned from the priesthood. Only Jack Gilbert remained; Jack seemed happy and productive and was overall a very good fellow.

One day in the autumn of 1955, Father David Dillon without any notice came to my room. Dillon was Pat Ahern's great friend on the seminary faculty. In quite general terms he described a scholarship program that the history department at Notre Dame was about to announce, designed to support graduate study under the direction of Father Philip Hughes — the same Hughes whose three-volume *History of the Church* was the required text in Busch's seminary course. Hughes was an Englishman, and so the grant, to be awarded to two mature students, was appropriately called the Lingard Fellowship, in honor of the distinguished nineteenth-century English priest-historian, John Lingard. In the ordinary run of things the course would end with a doctoral degree. The program was scheduled to begin in the fall semester of 1956, three months after my ordination. If such a fellowship were offered to you, Dillon asked me, would you accept it? Surprised as I was, I don't recall in detail how I answered this question; I'm sure having been programmed through twelve years of seminary life I said first that I would do cheerfully whatever I was assigned to do. But I must have added that studying with an historian of Hughes's stature certainly had its attractions.

Some context is needed here. In the mid-1950s the archdiocese of St. Paul ministered to a Catholic population of about 450,000 in perhaps 250 parishes; the number of secular priests in service totaled a little over 400. These numbers would appear to mesh quite neatly between needs and professional personnel available. St. Paul, however, unlike most ecclesiastical jurisdictions of middling size, supported a high-quality high school, a minor seminary, a major seminary, and a diocesan college This meant that as many as 60 or 70 priests had to be assigned full-time to staff these all-male institutions. And it meant too that these teachers and administrators by and large needed post-ordination education and advanced degrees. The upshot was that the seminary faculty were necessarily on the look-out for students who were interested in, and capable of, further training.

In my case, and perhaps in others, the process had a comic-opera flavor. Final permission to accept the fellowship, or even to apply for it, had to be secured from the archbishop of St. Paul. John Gregory Murray had come to Minnesota from Portland, Maine, in 1931. He was a small man with courtly manners, tireless in attending to the duties of his office, immensely popular among the people at large, but somewhat ambivalent in dealing with his priests. They in turn tended to try to keep a step ahead of him. Father Dillon explained that Ahern would recommend me to the archbishop as one who was capable of doing the work at Notre Dame, and as one who would thus benefit the archdiocese in the long run by bringing to it a Ph.D. free of charge. Murray would most likely respond by saying, "Have you spoken about this to the young man?" or something akin to that, because he was habitually suspicious in situations like this; might not the "young man," in collusion with his professor-sponsor, use advanced study as a way of avoiding the basic commitment to the parochial ministry? On this matter of priorities the archbishop was adamant, and rightly so; indeed, care for the parishes was (and is) almost the secular priest's *raison d'etre*. Father Ahern would reply that he had not spoken to me. Not that Pat would thereby deny the principle involved, Dillon observed with a smile. It was just that in dealing with some mistrustful people a tactical deniability can be of use.

And so it proved to be in this instance. Archbishop Murray gave his approval, and over the succeeding months I saw to the prior requirements. All was hush hush, all carried out under the rubric of strictly confidential, and so my journey across town to the University of Minnesota to take the Graduate Record Exams seemed like a small conspiratorial act. In the spring of 1956 came a letter from the Dean of the Notre Dame Graduate School informing me that I had been awarded a Lingard Fellowship.

But there was one more act in the small drama to be played out with the archbishop. During the week leading up to the annual priestly ordinations — for my classmates and me the date was Saturday, June 2, 1956 — Murray came to the seminary and interviewed each of the men to be ordained for his diocese. When my turn came on that day in late May, I found the old man — he was 79 — huddled in a chair too big for him. Visible on his neck was a lump that testified to the throat cancer that would kill him a few months later. His voice, however, was strong, still exhibiting the twang he had brought with him from New England. "I understand you are going to study history," he said. In accord with the clerical culture of the time, I replied, "If it please your Excellency," or words to that effect. Now tell me — I paraphrase — what is your notion of the discipline of history? Is it the gathering of discrete pieces of information about events during eras gone by? Or is it an account representative of the overall political, economic, and religious culture of the past? I have no idea how I answered. He went on: You will go to the University of Notre Dame ("Dahm") in the fall. I shall tell no one about this, and I strongly recommend that you do the same. Otherwise, the pastor to whom I assign you next week perhaps will not treat you well if he knows he is to lose you in September.

I left the audience trembling and went straight to Father Ahern's rooms. "I blew it," I told him. "Ten seconds after he posed the question to me, I was so nervous I didn't have the faintest idea what I had said." Don't be concerned, he replied with a chuckle. You were simply having your first experience of the Murrayesque method of keeping his clergy off balance. He put that dilemma to you, because you could not solve it. If you said the accumulation of isolated facts, he would have countered, where will you locate them? If you had said the general overview, he would have asked, how can you construct it? A couple of days later, in the sanctuary of the St. Paul Cathedral at the conclusion of the long and moving ordination service, we new priests knelt in a row of fourteen prie-dieus. As was then the custom, the chancellor passed down the line handing each of us the formal letter of assignment. Mine read that I was to be "acting pastor" of the Church of St. Mathias in Wanda, Minnesota. So Archbishop Murray had after all decided not to send me to a large parish from which my departure in the autumn might have occasioned some unpleasantness. Still, the rule of silence he had imposed had to be abided by, with the result that there was considerable puzzlement about my appointment. This did not lessen the joy of that day or of the festivities culminating in my first Mass on the Sunday following, when my family and friends rejoiced with me. It was a dazzling and yet humbling experience all round.

Wanda was (and is) a village about a hundred miles southwest of the Twin Cities. According to the latest census its population numbered eighty-four people. It boasted of a tavern, a filling station, a general store, a grain elevator and, most importantly, a bank which dealt with all the financial matters of concern to the farmers throughout the region. Most of these farmers, who each year harvested tons of corn and soy beans out of the rich, black soil, were Catholics of German descent, and it was for them that St. Mathias had been founded. Unhappily, the parish now needed a temporary replacement for its pastor, an amiable and yet undisciplined man who drank too much and who therefore required institutionalized supervision.

I was nervous as I drove my brand new two-door Chevrolet Biscayne — an ordination gift from my ever-generous parents — west down U. S. highway 71 on Saturday, June 9. When I arrived, I found a handsome, well-appointed church, a large brick rectory, and — something of a surprise in so small a community — a trim school house serving pupils in grades one through eight, all set together on a gentle hill overlooking the village's single street. I had been informed — I forget by whom — of the traditional sched-ule at St. Mathias on Saturdays after supper. So at half past seven I presided for the first time at Benediction of the Blessed Sacrament, and afterward I walked out of the sacristy and down the center aisle to the confessional in the back of the church. I remember as though it were yesterday the lines of those waiting to receive the sacrament, women on one side, men on the other, all dressed simply, the women with kerchiefs over their hair and in flowered short-sleeved dresses, the men in faded but sparklingly clean blue overalls, most of them of both sexes with their bronzed, powerful forearms folded over their chests. In contrast, I remember nothing of what had been murmured to me in the intimacy of the confessional box, nor did I within minutes of leaving it — a special grace of God for which I continue to be grateful.

The next morning I celebrated two parish Masses and preached my first two sermons — or rather the same sermon twice. I have little doubt that I was more favorably impressed by what transpired than my parishioners were. Nineteen fifty-six marked the chronological middle, so to speak, of the movement toward liturgical reform that would in time alter the worship patterns of Catholics everywhere. But it was still the era of the Tridentine Mass, and I was startled and edified how the people in the pews recited all the common parts, including the long bits like the *Gloria* and the *Credo,* in impeccable Latin. This was the so-called *missa recitata* or dialogue mass, a sort of halfway house on the way to a vernacular liturgy. So began my happy three months of parochial ministry, among a people the memory of whose kindness to me still, after all these years, warms my heart.

A couple of weeks later, like all the priests in the area, I was invited to participate in the dedication of a new social hall built by the parish in Sanborn, about ten miles from Wanda. Archbishop Murray presided at the celebration and, as was his wont on such occasions, he almost seemed bent on flooding the edifice, sprinkling holy water relentlessly in its every nook and cranny. Just before the festive dinner that followed, he picked me out of the crowd.

"How did you find Wanda?" he asked.

"Wonderful, your Excellency," I replied.

"That's not what I meant. I meant, *how* did you find it?"

"Well, it's on the map."

"Oh. I wasn't aware of that."

I never saw John Gregory Murray again. He died with great fortitude on October 11, 1956.

I had no notion of how deep darkness can be till I spent a moonless night in Wanda. It could have been, I suppose, a depressing experience for a city-dweller like myself, accustomed to an endless variety of distracting lights and noises, but in fact it had an opposite effect on me. I found the dark and the accompanying silence soothing and comforting, an occasion for quite cheerful reflection. I came to believe that up till now I hadn't appreciated the tradition that a strong union exists between peace and quiet. And when the clouds cleared away, there was happy confirmation of all this in the brilliantly star-studded sky.

Every evening at dusk, before the fullness of nightfall, Hattie Hammerschmidt, a tiny unwed lady who lived at the bottom of the hill, made her way up to the church. She was for all practical purposes its sacristan, though I don't suppose she ever used so formal a title. Once satisfied that all was well and in proper order, she walked back down to the house she shared with her father to prepare supper for them both. Thanks to Hattie, all the proper paraphernalia needed for the various services were always ready at hand. There was no full-time janitor at St. Mathias, nor much call for one, especially in the summer; I could do the simplest chores myself, and for tasks more difficult I could count on plenty of volunteers.

I had no housekeeper either; I cooked a few primitive meals, mostly out of cans. But *die Hausfrauen* of the parish took pity on the young Irish priest and saw to it that he was supplied with many a tasty casserole; the ladies arranged as well to have the rectory cleaned every week or so. I also found occasional sustenance at St. Raphael's parish twelve miles away in Springfield, a town of 2500 and the birthplace — one claim to fame — of the great University of Minnesota football coach, Bernie Bierman. St. Raphael's was large enough to require the services of two priests: the assistant my classmate and close friend, Merle Monnens, and the pastor, the kindly Father Eustace Frederick. Their housekeeper, Catherine, was a marvelous cook, who, whenever I appeared, smilingly put another plate on the table.

There were no funerals at St. Mathias that summer and only one wedding at which a priest-friend of the bride's family presided. But it was up to me to do the paperwork and to give the lovers an ill-defined "instruction" about the dignity and responsibility of married life. I recall how awkwardly I, knowing so little, skirted around the sexual aspects of the subject. Indeed, more generally I felt uneasy about how to deal with certain matters of sexuality when they came up in the confessional, so I turned for advice to Father Frederick. The custom at St. Raphael's was that after dinner the priests made a brief "visit" to the Blessed Sacrament. One evening, as we emerged from the church, I took Frederick aside and presented him with my problem in unspecific terms. He had the habit of screwing his eyes shut tight when he intended to speak seriously, and he did so on this occasion. He answered my query directly and with appropriate discretion, and then added, "You must remember, Father, these people live very close to the stock" — by no means a derogatory remark but rather a simple observation of a man whose priesthood of forty years had been spent exclusively in the rural parishes of western Minnesota, including a stint at St. Mathias of Wanda.

Meanwhile, events elsewhere moved on as they always do. In mid-June the announcement came that William Otterwell Brady had been appointed coadjutor archbishop of St. Paul with right of succession. He was only a name to me, but I did know that the Massachusetts-born Brady while a seminarian had been recruited by Austin Dowling to serve as a priest in the archdiocese and, specifically, to teach theology at the St. Paul Seminary. After due academic preparation, much of it in Rome, so he did until 1939 when he was named bishop of Sioux Falls. Given his wide-ranging talents and his somewhat imperious temperament, it is not presumptuous to suppose that after seventeen years in South Dakota Brady was more than ready to play a role on a larger stage. Nor did he have to wait very long to do so. Within weeks of the new coadjutor's arrival in St. Paul, Archbishop Murray entered the hospital, destined never to leave it.

These happenings in the upper reaches of the local hierarchy had no particular effect on the church of St. Mathias, Wanda. Still, they left its "acting pastor" in something of a quandary. Murray had laid down the rule that both of us remain silent about me and Notre Dame. What would happen now that the poor man was so desperately ill that the administration of the archdiocese had necessarily passed into other hands? Through most of July and early August I tried to put together some plan of action, and finally on a very hot day when I was mowing the grass in the Catholic cemetery a mile or so outside the village — odd what snippets of memory persist over many years — I decided that it was up to me. It may seem peculiar to a later time that I fussed over reaching so obvious a conclusion; let me simply observe that in the clerical culture of those days juniors like me were not encouraged to assume initiative.

When I got back to the rectory, I placed a phone call to the chancery in St. Paul. I spoke to the veteran vicar general, Father Hilary Hacker. He knew nothing about the Lingard Fellowship or Notre Dame or my assignment there as sanctioned by Archbishop Murray, whose right-hand man he had been for many years. You had better come in and talk to the archbishop, he said — meaning Coadjutor Brady. The old chancery was a squat two-story building at 244 Dayton Avenue, directly behind the cathedral. Much of the ground floor was taken by the Catholic Cemeteries Authority, which left only cramped space for the archdiocesan central bureaucracy, which of course was much smaller then than it is now. Upstairs a waiting room had long been dubbed by the clergy "the trembling room," because there priests waited for an audience with the archbishop. And there was I on an August day in 1956 when William Otterwell Brady swept in.

He was dressed in a black house cassock with purple sash and buttons and a cape of the same color over his shoulders. I genuflected and kissed the ring on his right hand. It is difficult to mention this customary gesture without calling to mind the semi-feudal rigmarole that then marked the relationship — lord and vassal — between a bishop and his clergy, now happily passed away. As I rose Brady regarded me with kindly impatience — clearly, he had other business to attend to. I handed him the letter from the Dean of the Graduate School at Notre Dame with the announcement that I had won a Lingard Fellowship. The archbishop turned and read it quickly, turned back to face me, and said with a nod and a smile, "I'll honor this." He handed the paper to me, and then he was gone.

The next couple of weeks must have been preoccupied with preparations for the move to Indiana, but I have no memory of any details. Surely I experienced a measure of sadness in leaving the good people of St. Mathias. Still, I had known all along that my time among them had been temporary by definition; the alternative to Notre Dame was a curacy at a big parish in the city, not Wanda. And besides there was as much hopeful anticipation as curiosity in what lay ahead of me. Was I really going to be an historian? By no means an unpleasant prospect.

Said prospect, however, did not at the moment eliminate the resentment I still felt at having been passed over for the chance to do my theological studies at Louvain. Little did I realize then that I was about to embark upon the most fulfilling, most exciting, most gratifying intellectual experience of my life. Only later, therefore, did I come to appreciate how richly ironic it was that my replacement at St. Mathias until the appointment of a permanent pastor was Father James Moudry, fresh from Louvain.

Chapter Three
Discipulus Iterum

I have no memory of my arrival at Notre Dame that September day in 1956. I felt no flutter of the heart at my first sight of the golden dome, or, if I did, the rapturous moment passed away quickly. Once arrived, there was much confusion associated with formal registration of more than 8000 students and with everybody simultaneously trying to get physically settled. The campus was so much larger an institutional setting than I had experienced before that it took me a while to get my bearings. But soon enough I found myself ensconced in the Howard Hall Annex, a single corridor attached to the first floor of the Hall which was reserved for graduate student priests and religious brothers. There must have been a dozen or so of us altogether. The venue, while serviceable, assuredly lacked glamor. Each of us had a single room (I had had two, a study and a bedroom, my last year in the seminary), and we shared the lavatory at the end of the hall. Two larger rooms also were made available to us, one as a kind of furnished lounge, including a television set and a public telephone, and the other, outfitted with four or five simple plywood altars, intended as a makeshift chapel where Mass could be offered each day. I don't recall that in that era before concelebration we had any difficulty working out a mutually agreeable liturgical schedule.

To my shame — or perhaps you may kindly attribute it to the vicissitudes of old age — I cannot remember all the details about my companions in the Howard Hall Annex. Some were readily forgettable, like the tall Christian Brother from Philadelphia who habitually confused Michigan and Minnesota with "somewhere out there." In several cases, however, the names of people I grew close to then elude me now. A Canadian Oblate of Mary Immaculate who combined social science smarts with a keen and discerning sense of humor. A monk from St. Meinrad's Abbey in Indiana, a man of about my own age, pursuing a degree in physics; the deep joy he felt in his Benedictine vocation spilled over into all his human relationships. Another Benedictine, this one from Alabama, whose jocular charm could not save him from failing the language qualifying exam which required him to translate from German into English all the parts of a camera.

Robert Brooks, a Norbertine priest from Green Bay, lived next door to me; he was perhaps ten years my senior and assumed a kind of guardianship over me, which, though kindly intended, was not always welcome. Tom Wood was a Sulpician studying American history, a gentle, soft-spoken man when sober, but drink revealed in him an almost pathological hatred of authority, especially that exercised within his own religious community in Seattle; and drink finally and tragically did him in. Perhaps the most intriguing of my neighbors in the Annex were Vincent Lonergan and Emmett O'Neil. Father Lonergan, of the Archdiocese of New York, was a veteran Navy chaplain, and as such he had the right to a year's expense-paid leave to devote to higher studies; he decided to spend it at Notre Dame and earn a master's degree in philosophy.

Father O'Neil hailed from Helena, Montana, and, after a varied career in parochial ministry, sought a graduate degree in political science to prepare him to teach at Carroll College, his alma mater. Both men were in their late forties, and though very different in temperament — and in outward appearance too: Lonergan burly with a sailor's deliberate step, O'Neil thin, tall, and wispy — they obviously got along well. And they got along with us younger men too, always cordial and never condescending toward us. We may have felt a twinge of envy once in a while, for both of them were relatively well-off; Vinnie Lonergan, for example, dined most evenings at Eddie's Steak House in South Bend, where the end cut of the roast beef au jus was always reserved for him.

And then of course there was Gene, my fellow Lingard Fellow. Eugene Vincent Clark was four years my senior, a strikingly handsome man of middle height and build, who displayed the physical properties my grandmother used to call characteristic of the "black Irishman": dark hair, creamy complexion, a beard that though shaved in the morning was by dinner time a dusky shadow on the chin. The old saying, that you can take the boy out of the Bronx, but you can't take the Bronx out of the boy, certainly applied to Gene, though not with the negative connotation usually intended. He had indeed exchanged the working-class borough of his birthplace — in

23

St. Raymond's, the first Catholic parish founded in the Bronx, still going strong at 1759 Castle Hill Avenue 170 years later: Gene's widowed mother still lived there — for the glitter of Manhattan, but he never forgot his roots, even as increasingly over the years he mingled with an ever more sophisticated society.

Like me, Clark prepared for the priesthood through the traditional six-and-six administrative arrangement. The New York version, however, differed from St. Paul's in one important respect. The minor seminary, Cathedral College, was a day-school located on the Upper West Side of Manhattan — at West 90th Street and West End Avenue to be precise. I have often thought in retrospect that this experience of a great city during such impressionable years added much to Gene's natural astuteness and *savoir faire*. After completion of the course there, he moved on to St. Joseph's Major Seminary in Yonkers, known popularly as Dunwoodie, the name of the neighborhood in which it was situated. Ordained in 1951, he was assigned first as curate in the up-scale parish in suburban Mount Kisco, and then for a couple of years as an instructor at Bishop Dubois High School in Harlem (long since closed). Meanwhile, demonstrating a good deal of energy and initiative, Father Clark used his spare time to earn a master's degree in history from Fordham University, and thus returned, so to speak, to the Bronx.

At the moment we met in the Howard Hall Annex, Gene Clark and I began a very close friendship that lasted for fifty years. The first (and as things turned out the last) Lingard Fellows we were, but that never sparked in either of us any sense of competition or rivalry. We joked between ourselves that he was the Lingard Fellow who drank and I the one who smoked — which in fact was the case. I found him intelligent, sensitive, humorous, even tempered, generous almost to a fault, always ready to be helpful, fun to be with, and to his fingertips a gentleman, that is, as in Cardinal Newman's famous definition, one who never inflicts pain. And, no small virtue in the context of September 1956, a capacity for serious and rigorous intellectual work.

Eugene Clark exerted a strong influence over me, not out of calculation on his part, but simply by being himself. And as time went by, I came to realize that his overall intellectual orientation represented a serious challenge to mine. I had always considered myself a liberal, proud to have cast my first vote in a national election for Adlai Stevenson. It was a mild tilt to the Left and — leaving aside strictly spiritual and creedal considerations — ran parallel to the judgments I routinely made about the Church. I was a "Commonweal Catholic" as the saying went, invoking the name of the distinguished lay journal notable for its "moderation." I frowned upon excessive clericalism, though I was never quite sure what "excessive" in this connection meant. Anyway, I prided myself on my acquaintance with contemporary European theologians —like Karl Adam, Louis Bouyer and Romano Guardini — who in their well-mannered way argued the compatibility of the traditional faith with modernity. I espoused the liturgical reforms and the related movements for social amelioration — labor unions, credit unions, Catholic Action organizations like Young Christian Students and Young Christian Workers — that had flourished in my Minnesota homeland.

To adopt such attitudes and values, it seemed to me and to the like-minded — all people of good will it went without saying — was necessary if the Church were to free itself from the siege mentality that had prevailed since the Protestant Reformation. Conservative Catholics, by contrast, preferred to live in a self-imposed ghetto. Thus they depended for news of the world on the narrow, sometimes bigoted, columns of the *Boston Pilot* or *The Wanderer*. For doctrinal instruction the more sophisticated among them turned to the likes of the reactionary theologian, Francis Connell, a Redemptorist who never encountered a question he could not answer apodictically. I suspected that many of them got their political insights from the radical John Birch Society. They spied a scheming Mason under every bush, and Communists playing a decisive role along the corridors of the United Nations, which institution, they fretted, was prelude to a totalitarian world government. They admired General Franco as much as they disliked and disdained the shade of Franklin Roosevelt. Not to put too fine a point on it, but with the brazen self-confidence of the young, I assumed that conservatives were stupid.

This rather sweeping negative judgment became awkward to maintain when I discovered that Gene Clark was a conservative.

The community of history graduate students at Notre Dame Gene and I joined was small but amiable. To us rookies of 1956 the veterans of the group — notably Philip Gleason, Walter Gray, James Sullivan — were friendly enough though somewhat remote; after all, they had already accomplished much of what we hoped eventually to accomplish. At this date Notre Dame was still a strongly masculine redoubt, and so it is no surprise that the colleagues I remember had names like Bob Jones, Peter Ford, Ed Gibbons and Tom Moriarty. They had graduated largely from eastern Catholic colleges like LaSalle and Fordham. I was a few years older than they, but this did not seem to inhibit my happy relations with them, nor, so far as I could tell, did the fact that I was a priest. Which makes the telling all the sadder that now their names are about all I can bring to mind about them. During the years immediately after Notre Dame I looked forward to meeting them at the annual convention of the American Historical Association — held in those days the week between Christmas and New Year's — but inevitably, as each of us settled into our life's work, our shared experience as graduate students faded in importance.

Thinking about these bright, genial young laymen of fifty years ago does, however, stir up one minor then-and-now observation. Whenever they attended class or any other formal university function, their garb included a jacket and tie. A far cry, I need hardly say, from the casual norms that have come to prevail since. On the same principle I dressed in clerical attire, black suit and Roman collar. Similarly the Holy Cross priests regularly appeared in the traditional habit, a black soutane buttoned up and down in the front, a short cape of the same color over the shoulders, and often with a good-sized crucifix, the foot of which thrust inward between the fourth and fifth buttons over the heart. In 1956 members of the Congregation of Holy Cross — C. S. C., *Congregatio a Sancta Cruce* — still played a dominant role across the whole spectrum of university life, as their predecessors had done since the founding of Notre Dame more than a century earlier. They occupied all the major administrative and academic offices, many of them served as classroom teachers in a variety of departments, and still others, as dormitory rectors, exercised control over the routine daily activities on the campus. This clerical ascendancy was destined shortly to diminish drastically, a victim of the cultural revolution of the 1960s, though nobody guessed so at the time.

The first Holy Cross priest I met was, appropriately, Thomas T. McAvoy — appropriately I say, because Father McAvoy was chairman of Notre Dame's Department of History. It was he therefore who had hired Philip

Hughes and who had persuaded the officials of the university to fund the Lingard Fellowship. Fifty-three years old, a short, wiry man with a mop of thick silverish hair, the first impression he made on me was that of pent-up energy. Born in Tipton, Indiana — "Terrible Tom from Tipton," as Hughes dubbed him in a moment of vexation — he appeared to have few interests aside from his work, and, for that matter, few friends either among his religious brethren or his fellow historians. Appointed university archivist shortly after his ordination in 1929, he applied himself relentlessly to putting into order the heaps of documents and memorabilia already accumulated relevant to the history of the Catholic Church in the United States and to broadening that collection. He continued in this position till his death forty years later, and so laid the professional foundation for the superb teaching and scholarly facility the Notre Dame Archives are today. By 1938 he had also earned a doctorate at Columbia University, and so that year he took charge of the history department as well.

Father McAvoy ruled his double fief from the archivist's office in the campus library — the building, much refurbished, that now houses the School of Architecture. He did so without feeling the need to consult with anybody. His was, I believe, a benign enough regime, and of course authoritarianism at this academic level was by no means rare fifty years ago. He often bragged about the victories he had won against the odds in disputes with the university administration — the "Main Building" — which, he maintained, had become the creature of anti- history philosophers. I seldom had occasion to meet with him privately, but when I did, I found the experience awkward. This was largely because he was so difficult to understand, even in a one-on-one conversation. He did not suffer from a speech impediment, like a stammer or a stutter; rather he seemed simply to swallow half the word as it emerged out of his mouth. This condition greatly reduced his effectiveness in the classroom. Not that he wasn't talkative, which in the event could itself prove embarrassing. I remember once he told me at some length about a faculty wife from New England who so despised the Midwest that she did her best to thwart her husband's Notre Dame career. As I struggled to discern just what he was saying, it struck me how inappropriate was this behavior, this telling of tales by the chief to one of the least of the Indians. I have wondered since whether McAvoy's intent was to share this intimate information with me in order to induce me to respond with some juicy in-house gossip of my own. If so, it didn't work; I didn't know anything along those lines.

Trained in a quality university like Columbia and working as he did daily among the primary sources under his care in the archives, Thomas McAvoy may not have been a particularly likable man, but he was a first-rate historian. The books and articles he published over his career testify to the breadth and soundness of his scholarship. He came to consider himself the historian of the Catholic minority in America, and not unjustly. The only competitor for such a title would have been his contemporary, Monsignor John Tracy Ellis of Catholic University, and I think an unbiased observer might well call the contest a draw. To be sure, McAvoy could not match the elegance of Ellis's prose and personality, nor the esteem Ellis enjoyed among the liberal elite, particularly after his 1955 article which sharply criticized American Catholics' anti-intellectualism and their "ghetto mentality." But in terms of sheer quantity and quality of historical work McAvoy needed to take a back seat to no one.

And as for Monsignor Ellis's reasonable but rather sweeping complaint about the state of the intellectual life among American Catholics — why are there no Catholic Rhodes scholars? —Father McAvoy addressed it in his own practical Hoosier fashion, within the context of his job at Notre Dame. As chairman of the Department of History he assembled a remarkably able faculty, people capable of and devoted to high caliber research and teaching. To mention some of their names rings bells in my memory. Aaron Abell, the courtly Kentuckian, chronicler of social justice movements in the United States; Marshall Smelser who knew everything about revolutionary America and about baseball; Matthew Fitzsimons, the sage of Columbia and Oxford, for whom all the secrets of the past and the means to unravel them were grist for his mill; Vincent DeSantis who made the American gilded age come to life; Leon Bernard, infinitely patient in the face of crippling polio, whose soft drawling Louisiana accent I can still hear as he puts flesh upon the bones of Robespierre and Napoleon; Fredrick Pike, still young in 1956 but McAvoy, even so, recognized the talent that destined him to be his generation's finest historian of Latin America, who became, incidentally, my very close friend; James Corbett, fresh from the Ecole des Chartes in Paris, an always courteous gentleman but also a lively medievalist aware of how to make the Middle Ages relevant to a later, more jaded time.

All these men, save Professor Abell, were my colleagues later, as were Philip Gleason and Bernard Norling who had received their Notre Dame doctorates toward the end of Father McAvoy's administration. They formed a most honorable company.

These people were, of course, strangers to me in 1956. But I did have an old friend on campus. And literally on campus: Ralph McInerny, who had joined the Notre Dame philosophy faculty the year before, was living with his wife and (so far) three children in Vetville, a thirteen- acre site directly north of what is now the Hesburgh Library. The university had spent $36,000 to clear the area on the east side of Juniper Road at Bulla, where thirty-nine military barracks were converted into 117 apartments, at a federal expenditure of about $400,000. Between 1946 and 1962 Vetville was Notre Dame's partial solution to a problem that afflicted every university in the country: what to do with the massive influx of students at the end of World War II, many of them married men, veterans armed not with rifles now but with the G. I. Bill of Rights. The swarms of small children made it clear that even if it had been available, conventional collegiate housing was not suitable. As intended the residents of Vetville were with few exceptions students; for example, the McInernys' next door neighbor was the captain of the football team, Jim Morse with his family. "Our living there as the family of a faculty member was a concession," Ralph recalled, "though it was difficult to think of it as a prize." Their apartment, 115A, like all the others was composed of a small parlor, a kitchen and bath and two tiny bedrooms. The ventilation system left much to be desired; I remember sitting in the living room on winter nights when the cold wind swept in under the front door. The rent was $27 a month. During the early years the Vetville chaplain was a young Holy Cross priest, just returned to Notre Dame with a doctorate in theology from Catholic University in Washington, Father Theodore Hesburgh.

In 1951, finally convinced that the celibate life-style was not for him — it is not hard to imagine how vexed he was when later so many priests ran off with Sister Mary Ann or her equivalent — McInerny departed the St. Paul Seminary after two years there. That proved, however, to have been time enough for him to undergo a conversion experience. Not of the religious variety — he remained as ever a good Commonweal Catholic. But intellectually a whole new world opened up for him. Through the courses

29

and tutoring of Father William Baumgaertner he was introduced into the Laval University school of philosophic thought, with its emphasis upon studying directly the texts of Aristotle and Thomas Aquinas. "I could not get enough of Aquinas," he wrote later. So impressed was he that in June of 1950 he rode the train to Quebec and enrolled in the Laval summer school. Ultimately, he received his doctorate from that institution, under the direction of the great Charles de Konnick himself.

This sudden turn to philosophy rather startled me at first. Our friendship, at Nazareth Hall and renewed at the Seminary, was based to a large degree on our common interest in literature. And not just in reading great authors, classic and contemporary. Somehow it appeared to us natural that in a local production of T. S. Eliot's *Murder in the Cathedral* I should play Becket and he the Chorus. Ralph had made no secret then that he intended to be a writer someday, a poet like Eliot maybe, a novelist certainly. My own aspirations were not so precise and I dare say much more adolescent than Ralph's. The two of us dabbled in compositions of one sort or another, even at one time determined to write alternate chapters for a joint novel; mercifully nothing came of this idea. No one will be surprised to hear that Ralph's efforts in these matters met with far more success than did mine. Indeed, I blush to recall that among the literary projects I took on was the composition of a play about the fabled Mary Queen of Scots, to be written, I loftily explained, in free verse. The basic difficulty soon surfaced, that all I knew about "free verse" was that the first word in each line was capitalized. Ah, the pretentiousness of the young.

Looking back now over all those years of double accomplishment, it is abundantly clear that Ralph McInerny was that rarity, a person who could flourish simultaneously in two quite distinct areas of creativity. He became the leading Thomist philosopher of his generation and, at the same time, both in quality and quantity a celebrated writer of fiction, literary criticism, *journalisme haute,* and, toward the end of his life, poetry. For him it was a matter not of inspiration but of persistent dedication. Every day without fail, as he put it, "I did my pages," whether an inquiry into the intricacies of analogical knowledge as Boethius perceived it, or descriptions of the mysteries solved by his fictional sleuth Father Dowling, or his analysis of the novels of Waugh and Greene. And when what he discerned to be a dangerous challenge to the integrity of Catholic orthodoxy rising out of the cultural chaos of the 1960s, he was not slow to take up the cudgels in defense of the old Church. As a controversialist he was always well-mannered and often very funny; but woe to those who proposed to redefine Catholicism not by accordance with the substance of the Second Vatican Council (1962-1965) but by way of that council's ill-defined "spirit."

So Ralph found consolation in philosophy, as Boethius had promised in the sixth century, and fulfillment at the same time as a literary man. But much more importantly, before he arrived at Notre Dame, he had found Connie. I had kept in touch with him after his departure from the Seminary, at least during my summers when I had a menial job — a stevedore once, a gandy dancer another time — and lived at home with my parents. Ralph meanwhile was working for a master's degree in philosophy at the University of Minnesota and getting reacquainted with the real world. On an evening now and then he and I would do some innocent carousing in various watering holes around Minneapolis. On one such occasion he said, "There is someone I want you to meet." In the rattle trap of my ancient Chevrolet, we drove out to a house on Xerxes Avenue South, where he introduced me to a petite pretty girl with coal black hair cut short in a page boy style, and a stunning smile.

Five months later Ralph McInerny and Constance Kunert were married in her parish church, St. Thomas the Apostle on West 44th Street, January 3, 1953. The courtship had moved so quickly that one might in describing it invoke the old cliché about love-at-first-sight. The marriage at any rate brought together not just two distinct personalities but two people so different from each other that their union proved greater than the sum of its parts. I observed it for nearly half a century, until Connie was struck down by cancer in the spring of 2002, and it always seemed to me to have worked to provide each of them a deep sense of completion; what strength one lacked the other possessed.

They left immediately after the wedding for Quebec, where they lived a life of genteel — or should I say scholarly — poverty, until Ralph completed his doctoral dissertation. Michael was born in December. In the autumn of 1954 they moved on to Omaha where Ralph secured an appointment as instructor in philosophy at Creighton University. The salary was $3700 for nine months. But Charles de Konnick had other plans for his protégé. He contacted another of his former students, Father Herman

Reith, C. S. C., who at the time was chairman of Notre Dame philosophy department. In December a letter duly arrived in Omaha announcing that a position at Notre Dame would be available the following academic year. So in the late summer of 1955 the three McInernys — soon to be four: Cathy was born in September — came down Notre Dame Avenue toward the fabled Golden Dome. Ralph remembered the moment poignantly: "I was coming home to a place where I had never been."

Chapter Four
Orientation

At dusk of my first Friday as a resident of Howard Hall Annex, I suddenly heard outside my window the rustle of many feet, then members of an apparently pick-up band blaring out as they passed the strains familiar even to me of the Notre Dame fight song. (Correction: It was forcefully pointed out to me early on that Notre Dame had no fight song, only a Victory March.) I went outside and was immediately caught up in the rush of the hundreds, swelling ultimately to thousands, of students sweeping across the campus from every direction toward the old Navy Drill Hall. Thus was I introduced to the Notre Dame pep-rally, held before every home football game. I don't remember just what transpired in detail — lots of cheering and boasting and back- slapping — nor do I, curiously, recall whether I ever attended another such bash. If I did, maybe each occasion was so much like another that the memories congealed into one.

I do recall the Drill Hall in another athletic connection, for this bleak unadorned building was the site of the Notre Dame home basketball games. It was not a spacious venue for this purpose; not a few of the several thousand spectators had to sit on the floor within inches, it seemed, of the out-of-bounds lines. Still, I don't believe I missed a game. And the team did well, compiling under Coach John Jordan a twenty and eight record as well as a victory in the first round of the post season tournament. Moreover, most of us in the Annex cheered on the captain of the team with special zest, because we knew John Smyth as an assistant rector of Howard Hall; none of us could have guessed then the remarkable educational record Smyth would carve out for himself in later years as a priest of the Archdiocese of Chicago. Jordan's team did even better the following year, going 24 and 5 during the regular season and winning twice in the NCAA tournament. But the most significant thing about the 1957 team was the presence on it of Tom Hawkins, the first African American to play varsity basketball for Notre Dame. By the end of his collegiate career he achieved all-American status and was the third pick in the National Basketball Association draft in the spring of 1959, after which he enjoyed a decade of success in the NBA. Over succeeding years Hawkins was followed under the Golden Dome by many other talented basketball players of color, including John Shumate, Dwight Clay, Adrian Dantley, and the incomparable Austin Carr. And many years later, in a nice touch of Notre Dame nostalgia, Tom Hawkins' son came to play as a walk-on on one of Digger Phelps' teams.

The 1956 football season ushered in by that pep rally had, however, little to recommend it. The 2 and 8 record was the worst in the history of Notre Dame, before or since. All the more remarkable was it then that Paul Hornung won the Heisman Trophy, the only member of a losing team ever to do so. He was popularly dubbed the Golden Boy, and his prodigious accomplishments on the field, on both sides of the ball, clearly justified the nickname. He contributed to it in his own flamboyant style too: when he ran back to the sideline for a brief rest, always to much cheering from the crowd, he took off his helmet so that the sunshine could brighten his yellow hair. But with my Minnesota roots I especially remember another individual player cheered during the course of many games that dismal season: "Nagurski, Nagurski, he's a Notre Dame man!" This was Bronko Nagurski Junior, whose burly father had defined University of Minnesota football during the late 1920s and the professional Chicago Bears after that. The story was that Mrs. Nagurski, convinced that her son would be hopelessly overshadowed by her husband's local fame if he stayed at home, determined that the boy should ply his athletic skills elsewhere, and Notre Dame proved an acceptable alternative. And the plan turned out well for him: Junior after college had a successful career in the Canadian Football League.

Aside from Hornung's heroics, the sport during the 1956 season pretty much managed to depress the ardent Irish fan. Perhaps it could be summed up by this wispy memory. We students sat in the northeast corner of the stadium. Late in the loss to Purdue, the Notre Dame team had driven almost to the Boilermakers' goal line at the south end. At the distance we could barely see the bodies banging against each other, but we could hear the sepulchral voice of the public address announcer. "Pietrosante fails to gain," he intoned solemnly. More banging down south, and then he said it again. And finally a third time. So it was that even tough fullback Nick

Pietrosante could not breach the Boilermakers' defensive line. The young Irish coach, Terry Brennan, himself a Notre Dame gridiron hero of a few years before, walked the sideline glumly, hands in pockets.

But the ambience was a different matter. For me, whose education up to this time had been confined to seminaries, the very color and excitement of Notre Dame home football games was a new and exhilarating experience. And over all the years that followed, through all the home games I attended — a hundred, probably more — it always remained so, always raised the goose bumps on the back of my neck as it had on that September day in 1956. The vast crowd, first of all, 60,000 loud and boisterous and mostly good-natured folks. The marching band, with the Irish Guard, delightful in sight and sound. Just before the kickoff the raising of the flag and the singing of "America the Beautiful." Then lots of other songs, to be sure more parochial ones, like Hike Notre Dame: "The march is on, no brain or brawn, can stop the charge of fighting men." Followed by the rousing chorus of the inimitable Victory March. In those days the students of St. Mary's College sat as a separate group to our left. During the halftime entertainment the band always concluded its program by assembling in front of the girls and playing, at an adagio pace, "The Bells of St. Mary's." (At that remote and unenlightened era it was not yet considered impertinent to refer to the collegiate women as "girls.")

At the end of October the University of Oklahoma came to town. Led by legendary coach Bud Wilkinson, the undefeated Sooners arrived ranked number one in the nation, and they proceeded with great efficiency to demonstrate why. Their dominance was total. Their last touchdown, in the middle of the fourth quarter, brought the score to 40 to 0. In the student section we graduates sat in the upper rows, behind the undergraduates with the band at the lowest level, next to the field. And all of us could see as our team lined up to receive the Oklahoma kickoff how dispirited and weary they appeared. The cheerleaders meanwhile seemed stunned. A momentary hush fell over the crowd, and then, twenty or thirty rows below where I was sitting, a single student began to shout, "Here come the Irish!" Then ten more undergraduates joined him, and then a hundred and then thousands, "Here come the Irish! Here come the Irish!" Finally, as though by some long determined and fateful schedule, the band broke into the Victory March.

The effect of this traditional challenge to the opposing team, no more this day than a hopeless gesture, nonetheless had a striking effect on the players; we could see their sagging shoulders straightened, their no longer bowed heads thrust forward, their arms swinging impatiently at their sides. "Here come the Irish!" No magical result emerged out of this rhapsodic moment; the humiliating defeat was sealed a few minutes later. But for me the boldness of the cheering for our players when they had no chance to win, and its effect on them, proved to be a rite of passage. I finally admitted to myself that there must be something to this Notre Dame mystique. Indeed, on that October day I became a Notre Dame man.

There was a sense in which the ordinary tenor of my life did not change essentially by this experience of graduate school. After all, the last four years of the seminary — the so-called theologate — had been graduate school too, had been an intense study of a particular subject. The bulk of my waking hours in both instances was devoted to the honing of my intellect. Of course the big difference was the freedom with which I did so now at Notre Dame. For the preceding twelve years I had lived under a horarium which dictated my every movement from the time I arose in the morning to the moment I retired at night, or, to say it another way, provided me with the bed I slept in and all the other necessities as well. Given my wayward temperament, that long period of detailed discipline, that imposition of dependency, was probably in many respects a good thing. Still, I was exhilarated to walk free of it, to assume the stance, really for the first time, of a full-fledged adult.

Nonetheless, despite such a heady realization, I still remained a school boy. By the terms of the Lingard Fellowship, my basic obligation was to follow the direction of Philip Hughes to a doctoral degree, but besides his lectures and tutorials I had other courses to take as well, some of them more memorable than others. Father McAvoy taught one in historiography and bibliography, required of every incoming graduate student. It was a mind-numbing experience, due partly to the material treated — as I recall it, endless lists, and then lists of lists, which seemed unrelated to each other — and partly to McAvoy's speech impediment. He used the course in his capacity as department chairman to assess the qualities of each crop of new students and to weed out those who he judged would not pass muster.

I enjoyed very much and profited from a survey of sixteenth century

European history, mostly political, taught by young Bernard Norling. A native of eastern Washington and an alumnus of Gonzaga University in Spokane, Norling came to Notre Dame from service in the army at the end of World War II and earned a doctorate in history, after which Father McAvoy, always with a good instinct for talent, recruited him for the faculty. He served on it with distinction for fifty years. When I returned to Notre Dame in 1972, Colleague Bernie and I became close golfing friends. He was a man utterly without guile, generous, industrious and conscientious almost to a fault. From that course in 1956 I recall to my chagrin that in a paper I wrote called "Some Mad Monarchs" I consistently misspelled the word "sovereign" (leaving out the first "e"). Professor Norling patiently corrected it each time.

McAvoy also demonstrated his administrative acumen by bringing to campus distinguished extern historians. In 1956 it was forty-four-year-old Guillaume de Bertier de Sauvigny, a Eudist priest who in later years was the jewel of the Institut Catholique in Paris. He specialized in the history of the Bourbon Restoration in France (1814-1830), which was featured in the course he taught us. He spoke a heavily accented but perfectly intelligible English in a kind of heavy voice, as though he were about to clear his throat; I don't remember that he ever did. He was courteous but remote. Without doubt the teacher I remember with the greatest fondness was Leon Bernard, whose course on the French Revolution and Napoleon still stands as my ideal of what a graduate inquiry in history ought to be. Text and lecture and, above all, seeking out and studying primary sources all blended together under Professor Bernard's gently guiding hand. With my northern, not to say Philistine, background I found it hard to discern whether my teacher's soft drawl was Louisiana or North Carolina, but in either case the words were suffused with charm, intensified by the gorgeous timber of the thirty-nine-year-old Bernard's voice. Moreover, the upbeat demeanor on constant display by this darkly handsome man, despite the fact that due to a bout with the dreaded poliomyelitis his legs didn't work anymore, testified to his deep conviction that teaching was a species of the Christian vocation.

The university library was located then in a modest building, now housing the architecture department, just behind Howard Hall Annex. The size of the collection was modest too, an enduring Notre Dame problem only partially solved by the erection during the middle 1960s of the magnificent Hesburgh Library. I spent a good deal of time in the former facility, roaming through the stacks in search of the source material required for the courses of Professor Bernard and Father Bertier; I found most of them and, aside from their immediate usefulness, reading them carefully helped to cultivate my use of French materials, which would be a boon throughout my career. The library staff — the one group on campus markedly female — was very able and helpful. One of its younger members was Maureen Lacey, lately of Pittsburgh. It was noted by many that senior history graduate student Philip Gleason was increasingly spied in the vicinity of the South Bend YWCA, where Maureen Lacey had taken up residence.

One of the happier features of residence in a university is the opportunity to imbibe other intellectual activities and impressions outside the traditional classroom. Thus we historians met with some regularity usually in one of the large discussion rooms on the main floor of the Rockne Memorial. Father McAvoy made it clear that graduate students' attendance at these evening sessions was not optional. Sometimes these gatherings dealt with technical and professional matters. I remember for instance one occasion when Aaron Abell debated Philip Hughes on the use of the footnote in historical narrative. Professor Abell took the position that citations should be brief and restricted to the identification of a source or sources; Father Hughes on the other hand argued that footnotes in addition should provide for a legitimate expansion or elaboration of the text. Now this event in the telling sounds deadly dull, but in fact the playful charm of the two participants is why I remember it.

Other times we were caught up in discussions of admittedly weightier subjects. I recall a meeting in that same Rockne venue which dealt with the Suez Canal crisis of October 1956. Several of the senior faculty took turns explaining various aspects of the tripartite invasion of Egypt. They necessarily touched upon the Cold War and post-colonial circumstances of the case and upon the rationale of President Gamel Abdel Nasser's nationalization of the Canal. They pretty much agreed that Nasser was a wicked fellow and a provocateur and that the Israeli, British, and French assault calculated to remove him from power was clearly justified. At the beginning of the question period that followed my fellow Lingard Fellow was on his feet. Is it not morally questionable, Eugene Clark said, for one nation to launch a surprise attack upon its neighbor as the Israelis did on October 30. And is it not at least possible that Britain and France supported Israel for selfish economic interests bound up with memories of colonial domination. The savants on the dais appeared a bit startled by this assertion, which they courteously dismissed. Of course we know now how much prior collusion there had been among the three invaders. What struck me at the time was Gene's willingness to assume an unpopular stance; it was unheard of in those days to be critical of Israel — a circumstance which moves one sixty years later to observe *plus ca change* . . . .

As I was to learn as the weeks and months passed, Clark assumed a lot of positions outside the mainstream. He was in fact a conservative. He was a friend of William F. Buckley, Jr., whose *God and Man at Yale* (1951) had been a spectacular indictment of academic liberalism. Buckley had followed this coup by founding in 1955 *National Review*, a journal destined to be the articulate and often irreverent voice most listened to by American conservatives. It was not lost on me that Buckley was a Catholic, a very devout one, Gene assured me. Moreover, he said, Buckley had assembled a talented group of editors for *National Review*, several of whom were converts to Catholicism. These people were not preaching theology, but when they approached the great political and economic issues of the time they did so, they claimed, imbued with Catholic ethical principles. For me, a Commonweal Catholic *par excellence*, this was all very puzzling.

Later in the semester Gene told me about a coming lecture on campus which I might easily have overlooked. It was sponsored by the government (political science) department and was held in a room on the first floor of the Main Building — I don't know which room, but there was a grand piano in one corner (another instance of the oddity of memory). The lecturer was Willmoore Kendall, an intellectual *wunderkind*, who had published his first book at the age of twenty. A Rhodes scholar who had gone to Spain during the civil war and had been disillusioned by the Republic's feckless socialism, he had spent fourteen tumultuous years on the faculty at Yale, where he had been William Buckley's mentor. His conservatism had so roiled his colleagues that they persuaded the university officials to offer to buy back Kendall's tenure, and he accepted. About the same time he became a Catholic. What I recall most about his lecture is his tall, rangy figure, with its bushy mound of hair, striding resolutely from one end of the room to the other. But I do remember one assertion of substance. In answer to a question he said (I paraphrase): If you look in the American founding documents you will not find the word equality. You can have liberty or equality. You cannot have both.

Not by such cerebral exercises alone doth the graduate student live and thrive. In the Fall of 1956 I saw my first opera. I had become a fan of classical music over the years but listened to it mostly on stereo machines which my cleverer friends put together. So, much as I had come to appreciate Mozart's genius, nothing prepared me for the dazzling splendor of *The Marriage of Figaro*. There is no way that I know of to pay adequate tribute to Figaro's mocking farewell to the love-sick page, Cherubino, banished at the end of act 1 to service in the count's regiment. The occasion was the dedication of the new O'Laughlin Auditorium in St. Mary's College's Moreau Center for the Arts. The production, stunning to me, was that of the NBC Opera Company. A purist might have been put off by a libretto translated into English — as I might have been myself in my later, stuffier years — but at the time it only added to my delight.

Another exhilarating immersion into the artistic high canon, this one on the Notre Dame campus, came by contrast from the work of an amateur company. Walter Kerr, later the Pulitzer Prize-winning drama critic for the *New York Herald Tribune* and the *New York Times* (1978), began his career as professor of speech and theater at Catholic University in Washington. There he organized a group of aspiring student-actors into a troupe which over the years established an enviable record for serious and sensitive dramatic performances, thanks not least to Kerr's direction. He took his players on tour regularly, and early in 1957 they came to Notre Dame. I saw them perform Shakespeare's *Henry IV, Part 1*. What a spectacle, the king darkly uneasy under the crown he had purloined, and all these noble dukes and princes conspiring with or against him for honors and power, while strutting among them the fat rogue Sir John Falstaff exuding a singular magic all his own. But what I remember best was the brawny masculinity of Sir Henry Percy, called Hotspur. I've been blessed to experience many grand Shakespeare productions since — among them *The Tempest* on Broadway, *Richard III* in Stratford Ontario, Derek Jacobi as *Macbeth* at the Barbican in London, *Coriolanus* in Stratford-upon-Avon. But unlikely as it may seem, none of the Bard's poetry stirs my memory more than that uttered by the brave, impetuous, impertinent, and somehow deeply vulnerable Hotspur on the relatively crude stage of Washington Hall, Notre Dame, in the winter of 1957. I wonder who that wonderfully talented actor was; I wonder what happened to him.

The provisions of the Lingard Fellowship, as Eugene Clark and I understood them, included university support for tuition and fees, supply of living space, and payment of a very modest stipend. Board and other necessities we had to supply on our own. This meant among other things many meals commonly eaten in the public cafeteria — the so-called "Pay Caf" — on the main floor of the south dining hall, located a few hundred feet from Howard Hall Annex. The food served there was edible without being particularly distinguished and was reasonably priced. A group of us Howard denizens often occupied a table and so made the meal a pleasant social occasion. Now and then at breakfast time I trod the serving line alone. I was too shy to seek out the company of faculty mandarins like the German-born polymath Anton-Hermann Chroust and the diffident Beowulf scholar Lewis Nicholson, who seemed to have made the cafeteria their special haven. So had Professor Bruno Schlesinger who that very year, 1956, founded the landmark Christian Humanism Program at St. Mary's; Bruno, destined in later years to be a treasured friend, found in the Pay Caf a masculine refuge from the world of women in which his profession had put him. I did break morning bread occasionally with Father Joseph Fichter, a Jesuit from New Orleans, who was on leave to research and write a book ultimately published with the title, *Parochial School: A Sociological Study* (1958). Fichter was a genial though quiet and self-possessed sort of man who stood on the cusp of a prolific writing career, and who, among other bits of professional advice, assured me that books got written "by perspiration, not inspiration." One morning in the spring of 1957, to my surprise I found myself pushing my breakfast tray alongside Paul Hornung. Apparently, he had decided to forgo that day seeking sustenance in the ordinary students' dining area. He proved to be perfectly charming and courteous. I remarked about the campus news that the senior class — his class — for their Lenten project had raised a goodly amount of money for poor relief. "Yes," he replied flashing the golden smile. "They've raised almost as much as I have." To this day I really don't know what he meant.

There were also occasional outings if the cost wasn't prohibitive. A favorite spot, especially for some reason on Sunday evenings, was a barbeque pit close to Niles, just across the state line into Michigan. A rather more formal and expensive excursion was a trip to Eddie's Steak House, then on Western Avenue in South Bend, which, as I mentioned above, was almost a second home for our housemate, Father Vinnie Lonergan. And for good reason: the steaks and chops — and for Vinnie the roast beef au jus — were always first rate, and the hors d'oeuvres for me especially memorable: the creamed herring, the liver pate, the garlic toast. To top off the experience, once the meal was finished invariably the hostess came to our table and said: "Mr. Eddie would like to send you an after-dinner drink." Ah yes, those were the days of the free drink and the ten percent clerical discount. That they have long since disappeared is no doubt a good thing, but I nonetheless look back with a certain happy nostalgia.

Sunny Italy, or Rosie's as we called it (I don't know why), on Niles Avenue in South Bend, was another eatery our Howard Annex people used. It was a standard spaghetti-and-meatball kind of Italian restaurant as it had been at the same location since 1926 and remains so to this day. I remember one occasion especially; we gathered at Rosie's on the evening of Tuesday, November 6, 1956, to celebrate or to bemoan, depending on one's political allegiances, the results of the general election, in which Dwight Eisenhower decisively defeated Adlai Stevenson for the presidency, as he had done four years earlier. I have no memory of any particular bitter or even strong partisan feelings expressed about the result, which we knew really before a fork was wrapped around a strand of spaghetti. Father Emmett O'Neil did give a sarcastic little speech in which he congratulated the victorious plutocrats in the name of those virtuous persons, like him and me, who had voted for Stevenson. Perhaps, he said, the most useful thing for people like us to do was to form a new religious order: the Little Brothers of the Rich.

But before that, in mid-October, came a shock. The Lingard checks arrived, and Clark and I discovered that the cost of our sumptuous accommodation in Howard Hall Annex had been subtracted from our stipend, leaving only a pitiful sum. My first reaction was despair; there was no way I could subsist on the amount thus provided. The Archdiocese of St. Paul would not support me; after all, I had been allowed to go on this intellectual excursion only because it was free. Which then brought to the fore my old resentment about my classmates who had enjoyed four years in Europe, all expenses paid. I have had in my lifetime — and not to my credit — various instances of negative thinking, but none, I think, so long lasting as this one.

At any rate, Gene and I naturally conferred and decided to seek an explanation from the Graduate School. The Dean at that time was a forty-five-year-old Holy Cross priest named Paul Beichner. He had earned a doctorate at Yale in English and medieval literature and had served the university in a variety of administrative positions. He enjoyed a reputation as something of a manual artist, specializing in woodcuts of wildlife scenes and in drawings of the facial features of some of his religious brethren (many of the latter now grace the corridors of Corby Hall). When Father Beichner granted us audience that morning in his office in the Main Building, he dismissed our queries with a shrug. You should have read the fine print in the Lingard proposal, he said. Then, turning to Clark, he added with a smirk: "You have to be the last person to complain about a lack of money. You have those fat New York Mass stipends to take care of you." He appeared serenely unaware of the utter tastelessness of this remark.

I left the meeting numbly turning over in my mind how I might most expeditiously pack my few belongings together for the trip back to Minnesota, to the unknown and not, alas, to Wanda. It solved nothing that I did not for a moment believe that the interpretation of "fine print" was a genuine issue. That afternoon I had my scheduled tutorial with Philip Hughes. At the end of it I told him in a few words what had happened. I don't recall whether he expressed any reaction. The next morning I received a message that Father Hesburgh wanted to see me. So I made my way back to the Main Building, this time climbing to the president's office on the second floor. Theodore Martin Hesburgh was then thirty-nine years old; he had been president of the university since 1952 and was destined to fill that office till 1987. His was a prodigious tenure, so much so that I came to consider him, as did many others, the second founder of Notre Dame. On this occasion, his trim figure dressed in the conventional Holy Cross habit of black soutane and short shoulder cape, he greeted me cordially and then went straight to the point. He had received last evening, he said, a telephone call from Father Hughes, who relayed to him the message that I and the other Lingard fellow had been surprised, disappointed, and distressed by the amount of money left in our stipends. Was this the case, he asked me. I answered haltingly in the affirmative, putting emphasis on the distress. All right, Hesburgh said, I'll take care of this, and then added in these exact words: "Downstairs they'll think me a bastard, but they already do, so that's no problem."

I hastened to share the good news with Gene Clark, and he responded in the generous manner which I learned over the years was characteristic of him and which helped to explain why he had so many friends and admirers. We must get the Old Man, he declared, a bottle of champagne, for a gesture of thanks and for a proper celebration. And so we did, Gene of course choosing the marque — French it need hardly be said. Father Hughes lived with his cousin Mrs. Margaret Laing, as he had for many years before in London, in a modest house hard by the St. Joseph River, on the edge of downtown South Bend. The only parking available was in the alley behind the house, and I remember drawing up there carrying our celebratory beverage in a plain brown bag. On the back porch was a touch of old England, a wheel of Stilton cheese, the smell of which was so strong that I was sure it must permeate the entire neighborhood. We then entered the house and Gene with a flourish handed Hughes the package. His eyes flashing with delight, he called out in a loud voice, "Margaret, look at this, Margaret. Eugene and Marvin have brought us a bottle of fizz."

Chapter Five
Magister

Father Thomas McAvoy habitually held court in his office amidst the dusty documents and old periodicals stored in the Notre Dame Archives. Shortly after my arrival at the university I received a summons to report there. The chairman, as was always the case, treated me kindly and courteously. Yet, as he leaned almost conspiratorially across his desk, his narrative was not easy to follow, even in this more or less intimate conversational setting. But if his physical speech was somewhat garbled, the sharply peering eyes left no doubt that he had in mind a definite purpose. On this occasion he was helping me to define my place within his bailiwick — an endowed fellowship put me a cut or two perhaps above the ordinary graduate student, but I remained reliant on the established framework of the history department. And then followed an expression of the McAvoy basic principle of administration: As you take on your work here as a Lingard Fellow, he said (I paraphrase), you must bear in mind that Father Hughes has already taken into account your youthfulness. Your associate, Eugene Clark, is several years your senior and comes from a much more sophisticated background. The implication was clear: your only true friend and support is here, in this office. So was I introduced to the Hoosier version of *divide et impera*.

A few days later, Philip Hughes delivered his inaugural lecture of the semester. As he walked toward the podium with a noticeable limp, he looked if anything older than his sixty-one years. He was dressed in a black cassock. His hair was white, thin, and unruly, his complexion ruddy. Once having sat down behind a small table he drew a sheaf of papers from the brief case he was carrying and placed it on the stand in front of him. There followed some fussing with spectacles, one horn-rimmed pair taken from his breast pocket replacing the pair he had worn when entering the room; it appeared he was uncomfortable with bifocals. He then began to speak about what he called the nature of the historical enterprise. "History," he said, "is the reconstruction of the past by the mind from sources." An abstract noun and three prepositional phrases provided a simple, straightforward definition, with no ideological baggage, no secret purpose, certainly no philosophical significance. Then, somewhat to my surprise, he cited Newman as an example of one who had skillfully employed history in this elemental sense and so fixed the intellectual ground upon which his soaring speculations could be rooted in hard reality.

The voice was at once high-pitched (as had been Newman's own, his Oxford contemporaries remembered) and yet strong and supple. Father Hughes seldom looked up from his text, but this mattered little as the graceful, elegant language came tripping off his tongue. It was the kind of pure Oxbridge eloquence that so fascinates and beguiles the American. His hearers numbered perhaps fifteen or twenty; the only woman among them was Maureen Lacey. They all paid him the compliment of total attention; the performance confirmed in me an appreciation of my good fortune.

But what if I were too young, as McAvoy had warned me, to take advantage of it? As the room began to empty, I could see Hughes looking sharply at me, clearly the youngest cleric *en scene.*

"Are you Father O'Connell?" he said. I took a few steps toward him and replied in the affirmative. "I understand you have only recently been ordained."

"Yes, Father," I answered, dry-mouthed. "In June."

"Well then, by all means, I must have your blessing." And grasping the table with both hands, he lowered himself awkwardly to his knees. I duly placed my hands on his bowed head and somehow got through the Latin formula. I then grasped his elbow and helped him to his feet. "Thank you," he said, short-breathed. *"Ad multos annos."*

In his own understated way Hughes had thus put to rest the uncertainty McAvoy had planted in me. You can imagine the rush of gratitude and affection I felt.

This was the second time I had seen and heard Philip Hughes in the flesh. In 1954 or 1955 he had given a lecture at the St. Paul Seminary. I don't remember anything about the occasion, though I suppose it's safe to say that we students recognized the notoriety of the author of the textbook used in Msgr. Busch's history course and that we were duly impressed by the speaker's "English" accent. What we did not know was why Hughes was then in our vicinity, a circumstance that was to come to affect me more or less directly. At that time a large percentage of the many thousands of students attending the University of Minnesota were Catholics, and for them the Newman Center, located on the edge of the Minneapolis campus, provided a unique set of services: social connections, to be sure, but liturgical and instructional ones as well. The liveliness of the place was due in large part to its director, Father Leonard Cowley, a man of immense charm and warmth, and his assistant, Father George Garrelts, who exhibited a charisma of his own and was endowed besides with somewhat more intellectual heft than Cowley. Both men were dedicated anglophiles, admirers specifically of the English Catholic literary revival that had boasted first of Belloc and Chesterton and then of the likes of Christopher Dawson and Alfred Noyes. With this mind-set Garrelts traveled to London in 1954 and persuaded Philip Hughes to accept appointment for a semester as scholar in residence at the Newman Center in Minneapolis. I never knew how aware Garrelts was at this time about Hughes' disaffection in England. I learned of it myself only in bits and pieces of anecdote over the thirty months of my close association with him. Hughes at any rate remained ever grateful to Garrelts for having ushered him into the American phase of his life, and in witness thereof dedicated a book to him. So it was there, at the Newman Center in 1955, that Thomas McAvoy found Philip Hughes and offered him a professorship at Notre Dame.

How many twists and turns there are in the human adventure. Leonard Cowley became a beloved auxiliary bishop, drank too much, and died young. George Garrelts ultimately left the priesthood and ended up a very successful city manager of a town in upstate New York. And, curiously, Philip Hughes in Minneapolis, as we shall see, was serving his second tour of duty in Minnesota.

Born in Manchester May 11, 1895, Philip attended the local parochial grammar school and St. Bede's College, and then in 1912 he entered St. Cuthbert's, Ushaw, near Durham, the principal seminary serving the six northernmost dioceses in England, among which was Salford encompassing the greater Manchester area. The bishop of Salford from 1902 till his death twenty-three years later was Louis Charles Casartelli, the son of Italian immigrants, who proved to all and sundry to be an extraordinarily gifted linguist. Armed with an earned doctorate in Oriental languages, the bishop enjoyed an enviable reputation for scholarship across the whole kingdom. This is the man who, in 1917, sent Philip Hughes to Louvain, his own alma mater, to complete his theological studies. He duly received his degree in 1921, a year after his ordination to the priesthood.

What followed remains something of a mystery. Instead of coming home and going to work in some diocesan assignment, young Father Hughes went off to Rome to engage in "historical research." I use that vague technical term, because no other is available. In all the conversations I had with him he never elaborated beyond the bare fact that he had spent a couple of years in Italy. I do see the fine hand of Casartelli here. The bishop had clearly made Hughes his protege, had discerned in the younger man the capacity for scholarship that he honored in himself. Perhaps he thought "research" in Rome might contribute to Hughes fashioning a doctoral program. If so, he was disappointed; Father Hughes never suggested such an intent, at least not to me, and in fact he never bothered to secure a Ph.D.

One more instance of the bishop's favoritism manifested itself about now, this one in a charming if rather bizarre fashion. While Hughes was resident at Louvain, he became close friends with a fellow student, an American called Coughlin (I forget his Christian name), a young priest from St. Paul in far off Minnesota. John Ireland, the great archbishop of St. Paul, had been recently succeeded by the diffident New Englander, Austin Dowling. Coughlin apparently — the details of the transaction remain for the most part obscure — told Dowling, a fervent student of history, that a young English priest, a product of Louvain, was somewhat at loose ends and might be available to teach history in Dowling's diocesan college, St. Thomas, and thus allow the release of one of the local priests for a year's study abroad. And so it worked out. Late in 1923 Philip Hughes, with Bishop Casartelli's permission, crossed the ocean on his way to the American Midwest, while young Father Nicholas Moelter passed him like a ship in the night going in the opposite direction and destined for matriculation at Louvain. Of course it is a matter of significance to me that Nick Moelter's home parish was St Mathias in Wanda, and that when I joined the history faculty at St. Thomas in 1958, Monsignor Moelter was my genial senior colleague. And significant too as I look back on these early days how often Louvain University figured in my affairs, even though it is a place I have seen only once, for ninety minutes or so, as a tourist in Belgium in the mid-1980s.

The memories Father Hughes shared with me of his first sojourn in Minnesota were episodic and to some degree whimsical. He recalled dining on a couple of occasions with Archbishop Dowling, whose knowledge of English ecclesiastical history much impressed him. He was impressed in a different way by what he witnessed of parish life, not just in the city but in far-flung villages, like Henderson and Shieldsville, to which he was dispatched on occasion to celebrate Mass. On a lighter note he remembered the jovial clerical culture, strongly Irish, that welcomed him, an Englishman, with no reservations; he paid special tribute to the pastor of St. Stephen's parish in Minneapolis who battled the dark forces of Prohibition by installing a still in his rectory.

Hughes had little to say about St. Thomas College, except to acknowledge the kindness of the Moynihan brothers, Humphrey and James, priests who dominated the academic scene as the stalwart guardians of John Ireland's legacy. Still, he could not have helped noticing during his year's residence that the college was in a pretty sorry condition; indeed, it was well on its way to a loss of accreditation. Its bad times were exacerbated by Dowling's foundation of the preparatory seminary, Nazareth Hall, in suburban Arden Hills, which institution undermined St. Thomas's financial base, created a rival clerical faculty, and limited the college's appeal to prospective students.

Young Father Hughes returned to Manchester from America at the beginning of 1925, just in time to learn of the death of Bishop Casartelli. Though I don't know that he ever did so, he might well have cited in his own case the line from the first chapter of Exodus: "Now there arose in Egypt a pharaoh who knew not Joseph." The allusion is apt only up to a point, but certainly the new bishop of Salford, Thomas Henshaw, had no obligation to treat his predecessor's protege with special deference. Nor did he. Hughes was first assigned as curate at St. John's Cathedral, then to several other parishes, culminating in appointment to St. Chad's, Cheetham Hill, the Catholic mother-church of Manchester, its roots deep in the eighteenth century. Hughes displayed prominently in his house in South Bend a greyish photograph of the austere facade and bell-tower of St. Chad's (which I inherited). He maintained a curiously high opinion of the lesser clergy; he once told me that he believed no man who had not served as a curate or assistant priest in a parish should be made a bishop; he would not pay the same compliment to pastors or professors.

I never heard Father Hughes criticize Bishop Henshaw by name, nor any other clerical potentate for that matter. But at the same time, when commenting on his life in England, he never tried to disguise the deep dissatisfaction he had felt. One need not go very far to discern the reason why. The English hierarchy, in his judgment, knew nothing and cared nothing about scholarship. The cultivation of a learned priesthood and elite laity did not figure much among bishops consumed by the brick-and-mortar demands of their people hardly delivered from the poverty and hardships of the largely Irish immigration. This conclusion was not altogether fair to Thomas Henshaw, who was himself a product of the Institut Catholique in Paris. But Hughes, strictly speaking a curate at St. Chad's, brought the matter into the open when in 1929 his first substantive piece of historical research was published in New York and London. *The Catholic Question, 1688–1829*, as its title suggests, was an expansive survey, 335 pages long, that traced the dramatic status of Catholics, first in England and then, as the polity evolved, in the United Kingdom, between the so-called Glorious Revolution with its imposition of the harshly discriminatory penal laws and Catholic Emancipation.

It was clearly not the work of an amateur. I wonder whether Bishop Henshaw read it. Two years later Philip Hughes departed Manchester. He never returned. The departure did not mean that he ceased being canonically a priest of the Diocese of Salford, always in perfectly good standing. He never told me about the details of his removal to London. Did he and Henshaw have an open quarrel? Did the bishop perhaps grant Hughes a temporary leave of absence to pursue work in another diocese, which leave due to unforeseen circumstances became permanent (as what happened in my case when I left St. Paul for Notre Dame in 1972)? Whatever the immediate causes, the result was that from 1931 London became Hughes' home for the next quarter of a century.

It was first the London of the Great Depression and then the London of the Battle of Britain and the Blitz. Till 1935 the socialist Ramsay Mac-Donald was prime minister of an all-party National Government which strove without much success to mitigate the hard economic times. King George V collected lots of stamps and shot lots of small animals and worried about his son and heir's propensity to pursue married women. Winston Churchill, out of office, worried about Gandhi's agitation for Indian independence and, increasingly, about German rearmament. MacDonald worried about the alleged condemnation of socialism in Pope Pius XI's social encyclical, *Quadragesimo anno,* until Francis Cardinal Bourne, the archbishop of Westminster, assured him that nothing said in that papal document would prevent a Catholic from voting for the Labour Party.

What I learned about Hughes' residence in London came in fits and starts of memory that he shared with me — anecdotal evidence, to be sure, but not without its value. He spoke, for instance, about the friends he cherished, men of his own generation, and thereby implicitly indicated to a degree in the direction of his own thinking. Closest to him probably was Douglas Woodruff, conservative and Oxford-educated, who as editor had turned a moribund Catholic periodical, *The Tablet,* into an esteemed journal of current events. Tom Burns also worked in publishing; while at Longmans he persuaded Graham Greene to write a novel set in the Mexican persecution of the 1920s, which became the compelling story of a whiskey-priest's struggle to keep the faith, *The Power and the Glory* (1940). Burns was both in manner and in overall attitude more liberal and less conscious of class than the staid Woodruff, whose wife, after all, was the daughter of Lord Acton. Perhaps the most distinguished among Hughes' London friends was Robert Speaight, a convert to Catholicism, a prolific author who had written biographies of Hilaire Belloc and Eric Gill, and who, besides, was an actor of renown; on June 15, 1935, he had played Becket in the first performance, in the Chapter House at Canterbury Cathedral, of T. S. Eliot's *Murder in the Cathedral.* Speaight was the only one of these gentlemen I ever met.

The immediate occasion for Father Hughes' move to the metropolis was an invitation from Frank Sheed. This brash Australia-born lawyer had come to England after the war and demonstrated from the first that he had brought with him a profound sense of a vocation to promote and defend the Catholic faith. Such dedication in time would produce a dozen books and perhaps a thousand speeches. Speeches, I say, not homilies or sermons; Sheed's growing erudition and his exposition of it served not a liturgical purpose but a more explicitly pedagogical one — apologetics in the best sense of the term. The title of the most famous among the books he wrote — *Theology and Sanity* — gives a hint as to the character of his personal apostolate. So once in London, he found at hand an institution perfectly in tune with his own aspirations. The Catholic Evidence Guild, a loose organization of chiefly lay volunteers, founded in the Archdiocese of Westminster — London north of the Thames — in 1918, aimed to bring cogent explanations of Catholic doctrine and practice to anyone who would care to listen.

And "listen" was the key word. Since the 1870s Londoners had gathered every Sunday at the northeast corner of Hyde Park where speakers of every possible persuasion set up their version of a soapbox and proceeded to harangue all those assembled out of interest or, more likely, out of simple curiosity. All shades of political opinion were heard — the Left perhaps rather more than the Right — and every possible program of social amelioration was explored.

Some speakers were half mad, others merely eccentric. Some of the great Eastern religions were represented, often exotically, and so was straightforward atheism. Speakers' Corner was an ideal *entrepot* for the men and women of the Catholic Evidence Guild. And no one performed more effectively in this oratorical environment than the young lawyer from Sydney.

On one such Sunday, Sheed met the woman destined to be his wife. Maisie Ward represented the third generation of a family most closely associated with the English Catholic revival of the nineteenth century — a daughter so to speak of the Oxford Movement. Like her father and her grandfather, she had remarkable literary ability — indeed, superior to theirs, at least in readability. Her biography of G. K. Chesterton has stood the test of time and remains a minor classic. Even more importantly, her dedication to a lively Catholicism was no less than that of her future husband. They were married in 1926, and the same year they embarked upon an equally hazardous venture: they founded a publishing house which, in a burst of optimism and self-confidence, they named after themselves.

Frank Sheed's nimble mind was never short of projects, not all of them successful. For example, a Catholic Centre for Higher Studies, in which he asked Philip Hughes to participate, never came to anything. The invitation was no doubt prompted by the impression Hughes' *The Catholic Question* had made on Sheed, who two years before had brought out the London edition of that book. Which provides me a convenient moment to assert that no single entity had more influence in shaping Catholic intellectual life in the English-speaking world for the next two generations than did Sheed & Ward, publishers. The firm at its most vibrant brought into the public square a host of writers representing the whole spectrum of Catholic thought, including individuals as disparate as the mystic Caryll House-lander and the polymath historian Christopher Dawson and the profound and, at the same time, playful Ronald Knox, very much a luminary of the British upper classes. Sadly, Maisie and Frank lived long enough to see the house fade into relative insignificance.

Besides *The Catholic Question,* Sheed & Ward published three of Philip Hughes' books. His rather pedestrian biography of Pope Pius XI appeared in 1938, as did *Meditations for Lent from St. Thomas Aquinas.* Father Hughes was an unabashed fan of Aquinas, an enthusiasm which, it would seem, he had brought with him from Louvain, since he regularly read the Angelic Doctor's works in a French translation. During the Blitz he happened one day by a London bookstore, bombed out the night before. Heaped on the sidewalk among other sad detritus was the magnificent multi-volume Leo-nine edition of the *Opera* of Aquinas, with its commentary by Cardinal Ca-jetan. He bought it for a song, and when he died, he left it to me.

One more debt I owe him.

The most significant work that Hughes wrote for Sheed & Ward was *A History of the Church,* the three volumes which I had read in the seminary as the text in Monsignor Busch's disappointing seminary course. The first volume of this sweeping survey came out in 1935, and over succeeding years, till 1952, the author continued to expand and refine it. But then came a disruption. The reader may remember that the third volume of this narrative *History* ended with the appearance on the scene of Martin Luther in the early sixteenth century; that is, the account stopped before the con-vulsions of the Protestant Reformation and so remained mute about all the facets of modernity that followed upon that revolutionary event. One might have assumed the publication of a fourth volume and, most likely, of a fifth. It never happened, because the relationship between the principals had soured into mutual antagonism. Not to put too fine a point on it, Hughes by the late 1940s believed Sheed had cheated him. I know none of the de-tails of the wrangle, none of the rights and wrongs, but I do remember clearly how tight-lipped Father Hughes was when he quoted for me his final verbal thrust at Sheed: "Frank, I take consolation in the sure knowledge that someday you must confront One who can neither deceive nor be deceived."

By no means was Sheed & Ward Philip Hughes' sole publisher during these creative years, and some of his books and articles, like the work on Aquinas mentioned above, reflected interests outside those he usually wrote about. *The Faith in Practice: Catholic Doctrine and Life* was published by Longmans in that notably productive year, 1938. Father Hughes always referred to it as "my doctrine book," and he was especially pleased at its reissue by a small American firm in 1965. In 1943 Burns and Oates published *The Popes' New Order: A Systematic Summary of the Social Encyclicals and Addresses from Leo XIII to Pius XII.* But the next year the same company brought out a book that marked Hughes' return, so to speak, to his usual institutional inquiries: *Rome and the Counter Reformation in England,* a powerful and ground-breaking study of the various currents of Catholic reform in the wake of the Council of Trent.

I suppose the variety of the material Hughes dealt with was at least partly due to the fact that he had never been an academic until he came to Notre Dame, and even then, as a kind of celebrity on campus, he felt little of the pressure ordinary professors experienced to be productive within the boundaries of their specialties. But the pressure he did feel during the 1930s and 1940s was financial. Not till he came to America did he receive adequate compensation. Scholarly books on whatever subject did not make much money. So to his relief in 1934 Father Hughes was appointed archivist of the Archdiocese of Westminster. This proved a double boon, because it put a cache of important primary documents at his ready disposal and it also provided a measure of income. But not enough; he also served as chaplain to several convents within greater London, pedaling his bicycle to one or another over several years. This experience did not appear to win from him much affection for nuns in general.

By the time the war began, in 1939, Father Hughes was living in a modest apartment in London with his cousin, Mrs. Margaret Laing, and her ten-year-old daughter, Audrey. Several times he mentioned to me its location, but I have long forgotten it. I was never told anything about Mr. Laing, nor did I ever ask about him. Nor did I ever call Mrs. Laing by her Christian name. She was a formidable lady to say the least, a truly *mulier fortis,* who invited friendliness but never familiarity. She was from

Manchester, and her brother, a diocesan priest, had been Hughes' fellow curate at St. Chad's. She was a deeply cultured woman and, at the same time, an eminently practical one — even to the point of skillfully and deliciously refuting the negative reputation of English cuisine.

This domestic arrangement, which lasted till Hughes died in 1967, apparently raised no eyebrows as unseemly in London, nor did it later at Notre Dame, except for one stuffy philosopher. The times then, I guess, were less jaded than they are now. In any case, one thing I must insist about it: This was an association of equals, not a master-servant relationship. And another: True enough, Audrey was grown and married by 1955 (and I am still, happily, in touch with her), but, even so, the sacrifice Margaret Laing made in leaving her family and coming 3000 miles to a country not her own cannot be overemphasized.

During the Blitz in the early autumn of 1940 the apartment was shredded by a German bomb, so that for a while the three of them had to make do in the relatively large bathroom. But for the most part Father Hughes did not talk to me much about the war. He did say that over those months of London's agony he so often administered the last sacraments that he came to know them by heart. And he did tell me about one intensely significant moment which, I believe, affected his personal spirituality as well as his work as an historian. One night during the bombing he had taken refuge, as so many Londoners habitually did, in an Underground (i.e., subway) station. With him was Father Vincent McNabb, the Irishman, now in his early seventies, who as a young man had joined the English Dominicans. Largely forgotten today, McNabb was enormously influential among Catholics during the first half of the twentieth century. His many publications, both popular and scholarly — the latter mostly devoted to the study of Aquinas — enjoyed a widespread readership. But it was the power of his personality, unique apparently and sometimes eccentric, that captivated the Bellocs and Chestertons, Frank Sheed and Maisie Ward, and their intellectual contemporaries. Hughes stood almost in awe of him. But ordinary people were no less drawn to McNabb. For many years he was a star performer at Speakers' Corner. This was the man who, in his white habit one good Friday, carried a cross on his shoulders the mile and a half down fashionable Oxford Street from Hyde Park to the junction with the Charing Cross Road.

As they huddled together in the Holborn or Picadilly station — these seem among the likely, but Father Hughes didn't tell me which one — Mc-Nabb said to his younger companion: "Philip, do you hear the explosions outside, do you know why this is happening, why these terrible events, this awful suffering has been imposed on us?" "Why, Father Vincent?" "Because of the sins of the Church. Notice, I don't say the sins of churchmen. That's the way apologists usually try to evade the real issue. No, the sins of the Church, the damaged Body of Christ. Of you and me."

Chapter Six
Past as Prologue

During my second year in graduate school, I was invited to review a book for *The Catholic Historical Review,* a biography of Charles Blount, Baron Mountjoy, Lord Deputy of Ireland during the last years of the reign of Elizabeth I. I was somewhat nonplussed since I still stood *in statu pupillari* and since I knew virtually nothing about Elizabethan Irish policy. Then it occurred to me that the invitation was meant by the editor of the *Review,* John Tracy Ellis, as a compliment — or maybe a challenge — to the mentor of the Lingard Fellows rather than to the young Fellow himself. It was widely alleged that Ellis often in his human relationships betrayed a feline streak, and I had heard the anonymous and somewhat snide observation — attributed by some to Father Hughes himself — that Ellis never judged a fellow historian positively — caressed him, so to speak — without leaving a trail of blood. So I asked said mentor what he would recommend I do. Immediately he brushed aside any consideration of Father Ellis' motives as undiscoverable; but Hughes added with a chuckle, if you do badly John won't be that much displeased. So write the review and write it well, as I'm confident you will. The point is, he insisted with great emphasis, that you should grasp any and every opportunity to publish. That is the ordinary way in which we demonstrate our professional proficiency. The result of this exchange you will find in the 1958 files of the *CHR,* a highly forgettable and mercifully short inquiry into the career of Baron Mountjoy, notable, I'm afraid, for lots of youthful pomposity.

The advice was sound, and over the succeeding years I have tried to abide by it, not without some success. Not that Hughes judged a page or two about a sixteenth-century Englishman imposing upon the unhappy Irish had itself any particular impetus for a young man's career. Toward the end of his life he put together a bibliography of his shorter published pieces. The resultant pile of three by five index cards — to be found today in the

Hughes papers in the Archives of the University of Notre Dame — was pretty slender. This is not to say that these essays were of small account; on the contrary, some of them were of genuine importance, like the pamphlet "Catholicism, Liberalism, and Italian Unity" written in 1935, or "The Continental Reformation: Luther, Calvin, Trent," a corrective commentary (1939) on a study just published that he considered a biased treatment of the Counter Reformation. But Father Hughes always made clear to me his conviction that whole books, monographs which required extensive research and analysis by a single author, were what defined the genuine historian. Indeed, fond as he became of his Notre Dame colleagues, he remained puzzled by their propensity to content themselves with writing articles limited in scope for the so-called learned journals rather than tackling a broader and more complex subject matter.

All that being said, there remained a harsh lesson Father Hughes had to learn during the productive days of the 1930s and 1940s: history books, whatever their quality, did not sell enough to reward their authors with much income. This was particularly the case with Catholic history, and particularly the case in Britain, where the Catholic population was small and largely working-class. So it proved for Hughes a significant financial breakthrough when Macmillan published his *A Popular History of the Catholic Church.* This survey boasted of many virtues; comprehensive and highly readable, it provided besides the text a set of helpful chronological tables, a brief bibliography ("recommendations for further reading"), and an unusually detailed (and therefore especially helpful) index. It sold relatively well from the beginning — six distinct printings between 1949 and 1953. And it received an enormous boost in 1954 when Doubleday, one of the biggest American publishing houses, included it among the first offerings of its new imprint, Image Books, which catered explicitly to American Catholic readers. Thus a huge new market was opened to the work of the sixty-year-old priest from Manchester. By 1957 *Popular History* had gone through seven more printings and had won selection by a nation-wide book club.

I was a seminarian at this time, reading for Msgr. Busch's class the three-volume *History of the Church,* which narrative Hughes had declined to carry past the end of the Middle Ages because (though I did not know this at the time) of a quarrel with publisher Frank Sheed. The second half of

Popular History provided something of a corrective, in that it treated in its final 150 pages relevant events during and since the Protestant Reformation, but of course this space was hardly sufficient to delve into details and nuances of so long and complicated an era. But even as *Popular History* was making its modest mark, Hughes had applied his mature talents to an inquiry into a discrete subject both broad and limited, and, in so doing, sealed his reputation as an historian of the first rank. Between 1950 and 1954, Hollis and Carter published the three volumes of *The Reformation in England.* I have no doubt that this project was one for which Father Hughes had been preparing all his life. Its fifteen hundred pages — divided by subtitle into "The King's Proceedings," "*Religio Depopulata,*" and "True Religion Now Established," each supported by a sophisticated scholarly apparatus and illuminated by contemporary illustrations — tells the richly dramatic story of how the religious changes in the England of the sixteenth century came about, so differently from what occurred on the European continent. Henry VIII was no Martin Luther. In its dismissal of so many myths and prejudices, in the immensity and variety of its sources, in its sensitive appreciation of the harsh internal struggles endured by the men and women of the time as they faced daunting questions about truth and error, about life and death — the book is a genuine *tour de force.*

It was well received across the ideological spectrum. Catholics delighted in it not least, they said, because it imposed balance on a subject long tangled in bias. Many Protestant and secularist scholars granted the point. Still, one of them — was it Conyers Read or Crane Brinton? — writing in the *American Historical Review* praised the book extensively but could not refrain from observing that the author showed "surprising objectivity" since he was, after all, a Catholic priest. Hughes deeply resented this remark, as well he should have; nevertheless he, like anyone who entered this intellectual minefield, had to realize the hostility of the traditional historiography, featuring as it did the black legend of popish conspirators and wicked Jesuits and cruel, swarthy Spaniards. Prejudices that had shaped England's religious self-consciousness for centuries could be summed up in the contrast commonly drawn between Bloody Mary and Good Queen Bess.

The Reformation in England enjoyed respectable commercial success, going into five editions; for the fifth Macmillan, in 1963, compressed the three volumes into one. Transatlantic recognition was widespread, but the specific form it took that ultimately changed my life occurred when Father George Garrelts came to London and invited Father Hughes to accept a semester's sinecure as Scholar-in-Residence at the Newman Center in Minneapolis. And a year after that, in 1954, Father Thomas McAvoy traveled to Minnesota from Notre Dame with an offer of fully compensated employment — something that had eluded Philip Hughes all his professional life. In his acceptance lay the germ of the Lingard Fellowship.

Meanwhile, during that warmly happy Wanda summer, Hughes' books stood heavily on my shelf and in my mind, as I wondered what being a Lingard Fellow would be like. Which, I'm content to say, made no difference at all to Hattie Hammerschmidt who went on her trek each evening at dusk up and down the hill to St. Mathias Church. Nor, I dare say, to the world at large.

By the time I came to know them Philip Hughes and Margaret Laing had settled into 701 Riverside Drive, a modest two-story house at the unfashionable end of that street, on the edge of downtown South Bend. Across the front was a rickety porch with an unimpeded view of the brownish waters of the St. Joseph, where Hughes always kept a bowl of nuts at hand: he took much pleasure in feeding the neighborhood squirrels. In the back of the house stood a kind of primitive lean-to where, as I mentioned before, the fragrant Stilton was kept. On the ground floor a narrow entrance area off the porch led into a moderately sized living room, furnished conventionally with a sofa, three or four comfortable chairs, lamps of various sizes, and small tables. This merged into the dining room, dominated by the large table in its center. Off the corner was a small indented space — it might have been at one time a pantry or a storeroom — where Father Hughes celebrated Mass, and beyond that Mrs. Laing's kitchen. Bedrooms were on the second floor, one of which served as Hughes' study, but I never saw them. Whether the furniture was, like the house, rented I never knew. Except for one piece: with the first Notre Dame check, Hughes told me with satisfaction, he had bought a "hi-fi player," and he pointed at the handsome cabinet that housed a stereo machine set at the bottom of the stairs and ready to play the vinyl thirty-three and a third rpm records of the day. The salary, not incidentally, was $15,000 per annum, a lot of money sixty years ago, equivalent perhaps in purchasing power to eight or ten times as much today.

It was to this house that I came one afternoon a week for my tutorial. Each session lasted about ninety minutes. Gene Clark did the same on a different day. Father Hughes made clear to both of us from the beginning that he had little sympathy with the American manner of evaluating senior students through tests and grades and other formalities. Indeed, at the end of the first semester he awarded Gene a grade of 98 and me a 96 — Notre Dame at the time used a numerical measure — on the grounds, he told us laughingly, that Gene was the elder. What did concern him was what he called the "paper" each of his Lingard fellows would write, by which he meant the doctoral dissertation. A certain irony exhibited itself in this regard, since he had never himself followed the formal doctoral route. But he realized, I think, that such was his obligation within the American context.

So early on he quizzed us as to what subjects we might have found appealing. Clark wanted to examine the quarrel between Catholic liberals and ultramontanes in the England of the mid-nineteenth century. And so he did, superbly, though he did not finish the work till 1964; a gifted young priest in the archdiocese of New York during the last years of Cardinal Spellman faced a host of distractions. In my initial interview I told Father Hughes that I would be interested in studying the work of Richard Hooker, the Anglican divine who at the end of the sixteenth century wrote the celebrated *Of the Laws of Ecclesiastical Polity*, reputed to be the founding document of what came to be called the Prayer Book or "High" tradition within the Church of England. Hooker, Hughes replied, is worthy of attention surely, the thinker who checkmated the aggressive Puritans. "But," he said with a certain warmth, "why not instead take a look into the career of one of our fellows who flourished during that same Elizabethan era." By "one of our fellows" he meant an English Catholic and he had a specific one in mind.

Thomas Stapleton (1535–1598), sometime fellow of New College, Oxford, and prebendary of Chichester Cathedral, theologian and controversialist, was a leading light among that extraordinarily talented band of exiles who gathered in the Low Countries to wage war with the printing press against the heretical regime in England until it should collapse — which of course it never did. Anyway, Father Hughes' proposal seemed more than agreeable. To be sure, I had never heard of Stapleton, but, beyond his name,

I knew hardly anything about Hooker either. I believe now, looking back, that I was attracted solely by Hooker's terse but astute summation of the causes of the religious controversies of his day: "Two things there are which trouble greatly these later times: one that the Church of Rome cannot, another that the Church of Geneva will not, err." Indeed, in a kind of accidental symmetry, it was this Genevan Church, self-confident under the leadership of John Calvin and Theodore Beza, against which Stapleton, Hooker's contemporary, strove hardest. At the end of his life he said that all he had written was intended as "antidotes" to the heretical poison that flooded westward out of the Swiss city, even so far as Britain: "[*Scribo*] *contra venenum Calvini Bezaque.*"

During that first conversation Hughes assured me that the originality required in a dissertation would be readily attainable, since virtually no scholarly work had been done on Stapleton. This was the case, he said, even though there had been left behind a large literary testament, written in both English and Latin. And so I found it to be, enormous in fact, millions of published words, a verbosity not unusual among the savants on both sides of the denominational divide. Stapleton first attracted attention by his translations from Latin into English, including that of the Venerable Bede's renowned *Historia ecclesiastica.* In three long literary duels with Anglican divines he proved himself quite able to hold his own substantively, and — here was a special boon — he wrote with an elegance of expression worthy of the century of Shakespeare and Spencer. But increasingly, as time passed, the theological treatises that issued from his pen on a vast variety of subjects were composed in the language of scholarship. After Stapleton died, all these works were collected into an *Omnia Opera* of four fat volumes (Paris, 1620). His Latin style I found convoluted and overly ornate, reflecting perhaps the artificial standards Renaissance intellectuals imposed upon themselves. The result at any rate made hard labor for me, but thanks to Father Hughes starting me out on the inquiry at the very beginning of my graduate experience, I had plenty of time to come to terms with the linguistic difficulties. It proved worth the effort. Three years later, under the patient and wonderfully erudite guidance of Philip Hughes, the dissertation emerged as "Thomas Stapleton and Nascent Protestantism," and five years after that it blossomed into *Thomas Stapleton and the Counter Reformation* (Yale University Press, 1964). The book, 221 pages long, cost six dollars.

I have described the one-on-one sessions I had with Philip Hughes at the small house on Riverside Drive as "tutorials." This was somewhat presumptuous of me, since I had no direct connection to the teaching methodology made famous by the traditional English universities. And it also touches upon a sensitivity felt by Hughes himself. He had not enjoyed the advantage of an education at Oxford or Cambridge, a fact which preyed to some extent on his mind. He always remained somewhat ambiguous in his attitude toward those institutions and the intellectual culture they had engendered. Indeed, as a born-Catholic, he felt also a measure of resentment at the fuss his co-religionists made over the literary Oxbridge converts, the likes of Christopher Dawson, Alfred Noyes, and Ronald Knox being treated as celebrities. Here as in so many social relationships in the Britain of those days class distinctions played a significant role. Hughes, a graduate of St. Bede's College in blue-collar Manchester, had little natural sympathy for the privileged denizens at Oxford during the 1920s. Nor, for that matter, they for him.

This ambivalence was reflected in an intriguing stylistic conundrum. When Philip Hughes spoke, whether in ordinary conversation or in a formal lecture mode, a hearer might assume he was listening to, say, an alumnus of Balliol College, Oxford, or of Magdalen, Cambridge. Word choice and sentence structure and points of emphasis all came together to sound like what one might have heard regularly on the BBC, before that institution was dumbed down some years ago. But read aloud a page or two of one of Hughes' books or articles and you will immediately discern the difference in its placement of adjectives and verbs, in the length of its sentences, in its overall cadence and rhythm. His published English prose sounds as though translated from the French, which I suspect in one sense it was. Upon reflection such is not really that surprising. Hughes' basic training took place at French-speaking Louvain, and the masters who formed his professional mind were the great French ecclesiastical historians of the early decades of the twentieth century: Louis Duchesne, Pierre Battifol, Marie-Joseph Lagrange. So the *viva voce* style was not the same as the written style; not more or less attractive, just different.

Not that Father Hughes in his capacity as my director ever tried to mold my literary style such as it was in those days — into his own image and likeness. He was far too liberal- minded, in the best sense of the term, to have done that. This was brought home to me some years later when I was asked to complete work he was engaged in when he died in 1967. William L. Langer, the distinguished chairman of the Harvard history department, had taken on the overall editorship of the prestigious twenty-volume "Rise of Modern Europe" series, published by Harper & Row. He had from the beginning determined to assign the composition of the book treating the Counter Reformation era to a Catholic scholar. I was back in St. Paul by this time, but I had remained in touch with Father Hughes, and I knew how pleased he was at Langer's invitation, which he thought would serve as a kind of secular imprimatur for his life's work. He had, to be sure, published two books since he had arrived at Notre Dame — *A Popular History of the Reformation* and *The Church in Crisis,* the latter a survey of past ecumenical councils, timed to take commercial advantage of the upcoming Vatican Council II (1962–1965) — but both of them were pretty pedestrian and certainly not likely to be accorded the same esteem as would have been a contribution to what came to be called simply the Langer Series.

Sometime early in 1968 I was contacted by Professor Langer. After expressing some conventional words of condolence, he went on to say that it would constitute a serious loss to the Series and to the profession generally if the work Monsignor Hughes had done on the Counter Reformation volume were abandoned. Would I therefore, as one who was well-acquainted with my director's mind and method, consider finishing the Hughes manuscript? I had no doubt of course that this proposal came from a recommendation by Mrs. Laing who was Father Hughes' literary executor. And out of my affection for her, as well as from a desire to memorialize this good and great man, I agreed to make the attempt. Langer sent me the bundle of materials, and I worked very hard with them over the next eighteen months. After which time, however, I had to admit, alas, that the task was quite beyond me. The typescript was uneven in quality, problematic from any point of view. The chronic illnesses that had dogged Father Hughes' last years had clearly compromised his powers and left him unable to deal adequately with, say, the complexities of the sixteenth-century French Religious Wars and the staggering inflation associated with the Price Revolution. And even the passages that rang with the clarity and vitality of former days were composed in what I called above his French style, which was impossible for me to simulate. So I told Professor Langer that in my judgment what Hughes had written was unworthy of him and not correctable. In addition, with an excess of boldness, I offered to start over and write the book myself — with which proposition, to my surprise and gratitude, he agreed.

I was very proud of *The Counter Reformation, 1559–1610* (1974), not least because it had such an intimate connection with Philip Hughes. None of my books earned a lot of money. But whatever amount this one made went directly to Margaret Laing, who in 1968 returned to England.

Chapter Seven
A Widening Field

When I was a young man, busy, busy about many things, I assumed that as I approached the end of this earthly adventure time would pass at a more leisurely pace. In fact, the contrary has proved to be the case. I find it shocking how quickly Easter now follows Christmas, how summer's greenery melds into the rich colors of autumn with hardly a sigh, and then, with a cosmic snap of the fingers, all is swallowed up by relentless banks of snow. And I believe that by and large my contemporaries agree with me. Indeed, they have reason to feel the swift passage of days even more sharply, because most of them, unlike me, have children whose diapers they changed in the long ago but who now rejoice in those babies with children and grandchildren of their own. It has always struck me — and it does so especially now that I live in a retirement community and mingle daily with the men and women of my own generation — that there is no human sorrow so piercing as when parents have to witness the burial of a child, whether that child is six or sixty. Circumstances of my vocation have, thank God, spared me that awful grief.

At the beginning of the fall semester of 1957, my physical lot as a graduate student at Notre Dame experienced a significant change, one which, as I shall explain shortly, came ultimately to remind me of the unforgiving nature of the march of time. St. Joseph's High School, located across the highway from the southwest corner of the Notre Dame campus, was a new co-instructional diocesan school staffed by Holy Cross Sisters charged with the girls and Holy Cross Brothers for the boys. Just off the north entrance to the large and handsome building of yellow stone was a modest apartment, enclosing a large sitting room, a bedroom and bath, and a kitchenette. This was intended to be a residence for the superintendent of the Fort Wayne Catholic schools. The officer holding this position at the time was Father John Vrabley, a youngish man and, as I remember him, a congenial fellow but clearly serious with regard to his job. It turned out that he preferred to reside at St. Bavo's parish in South Bend out of affection, as I understood it, for St. Bavo's aging pastor. So he canvassed the available priest-graduate students and, to my good fortune, settled on me.

I lived at St. Joseph's from September 1957 until late December 1958 when I returned to Minnesota. I was officially chaplain of the school, though the obligations of that office were minimal: sacramental confessions for the students on the first Thursday of every month and Mass the next day, celebrated in the gymnasium. I offered daily Mass in a small second floor room an hour before the first students arrived. Attending brightly every morning from the neighborhood was the dean of the Notre Dame Science College (whose name, I'm ashamed to admit, I don't remember) along with his wife, who regularly, once she had sat down, fell softly and quite beautifully asleep. Occasionally the Mass was served by the teen-aged Edward Krause, son of the renowned Moose Krause, and later a Holy Cross priest of distinction. I believe that in that small chapel — if one may call it so — the Blessed Sacrament was reserved, but I have no clear memory of it. Which is a depressing commentary on my piety.

After school hours and on weekends ordinarily I was the only person present at St. Joseph's. So I don't believe it is cynical to suggest that my position had as much to do with insurance rates as it did with chaplaining. Surely, to put it another way, it was good business practice to satisfy two needs with a single agent. Anyway, I settled happily into the apartment with all its amenities, not the least of which was privacy. I rented a microfilm reader and, thanks to the gathering of materials by the splendid staff of the university library — the mammoth Hesburgh Library was still some years off — I was able to spend day after day in relentless assault upon the *opera* of Thomas Stapleton, sometime Fellow of New College, Oxford.

As you might imagine, I harbor warm memories for the St. Joseph's of 1957. The school was sparkling new, boasting of all the latest pedagogical nostrums then in fashion, making it the pride of the Catholics of South Bend. And I, in a modest way, was part of it. But that was then, and this is now. Even as I write I can simply look down the road, and there, perhaps a two-iron shot away, stands St. Joseph's, empty and forlorn. The old St. Joseph's, that is, my St. Joseph's. It became so obsolete, you see, that a new St. Joseph's had to be set up a short distance away. It's the way of the world, no doubt, but I must say again, its clock runs too fast for me.

So it followed that I had to bid adieu to my colleagues and friends in Howard Hall Annex. Many of them, however, by the beginning of the 1957 fall semester, were already gone. Father Vinnie Lonergan went back to naval duty taking with him, in hand, a master's degree in philosophy; while Father Emmet O'Neil, the pride of Butte, Montana, similarly now a master of arts, returned west to continue his restless search for a just and compassionate polity. I often thought of his toast on election night; the "Little Brothers of the Rich" was a gentle rebuke to us all. The last time I heard from him came many years later, a telephone call from Brazil which had no purpose save greetings to a friend.

Also my fellow Lingard Fellow had left Howard Hall Annex and gone back to New York. Eugene Clark was too much a gentleman to have complained about his residence in the Midwest, but as I got to know him better, I realized he never ceased yearning to see again the majestic canyons of Manhattan and to experience all that they symbolized. His quick departure in the spring of 1957 suggested that Notre Dame in those days may have been more than a little careless about residence requirements for graduate students. But in any event Clark understood that he needed to present to the university a doctoral dissertation reflective of original research. Philip Hughes, with whom his relations remained as affectionate as before, was perfectly content to act as director *a longe*. Even so, the work took seven years to complete.

One reason was that at first Father Clark was given inappropriate or conflicting assignments. Thus he consumed more time and energy than was good for him intellectually when placed in the ever-hectic archdiocesan high school system. For a while he was stationed as chaplain-in-residence to a convent of Franciscan nuns up the Hudson, north of the city, and expected to commute several times a week to teach at a Catholic women's college on Staten Island. I learned later on that there were some clerical shenanigans behind this apparently official indifference to securing a free Ph.D., one closely associated with a famous historian, for service in the archdiocese. It seems that a personage of some importance in the chancery had a running feud with a professor in the minor seminary, Cathedral College, and as a result there was some attempt to thwart the career of a young man who was known to be the said professor's disciple. Petty as this sounds — and in fact was in many respects — the wrangle did touch upon some old rivalries that still stirred up political and cultural hostility. But the chief cleric in New York was originally from Boston and so cared little about hoary local quarrels. And the worth of the young priest was not lost on him. In 1959 Cardinal Spellman swept away any doubts by appointing Eugene Clark one of his secretaries. This was a high compliment indeed, but with the multitude of demands the job involved, it was not calculated to make it easier for the candidate to prepare a doctoral dissertation. All the more credit to him for having done it.

Graduate students, almost by definition, are short of money. This was true of me even after the partial restoration of the Lingard stipend, as described above. As a priest, however, I had opportunities to pick up a few extra dollars and, at the same time, to find a deeper fulfillment of my vocation to the sacramental ministry. The parishes round about Notre Dame often had need of temporary or even semi-permanent priestly assistance. Thus, while still living on campus, I was invited to celebrate Mass every weekday during the Lent of 1957 at St. Stanislaus church on the west side of South Bend. The monetary return was small but welcome; the sense of really being a priest — doing what priests do — was a far richer reward. And, incidentally, I got the chance to observe the liturgical vagaries of a pre-conciliar Polish parish, an eye-opener if ever there was one.

About the time I took up residence at St. Joseph's, I heard from one of my colleagues who, his graduate degree work finished, was returning to his diocese. He had for some time served as a weekend assistant in the parish in New Buffalo, Michigan, some thirty miles from South Bend. He would recommend me, he said, to be his successor, if I were interested. I was, and he did, and so began a very pleasant parochial experience.

New Buffalo was, and is, a lively little town whose claim to attention was its fine beaches along the shore of Lake Michigan. At the time perhaps 2000 people lived there and in the environs, a goodly number of whom were Catholics. St Mary of the Lake church was a handsome building located on the main street to the south of the town's modest business district. The rectory stood next door. Father Charles Smith, the pastor, was a man in his late thirties, congenial and good-natured if somewhat coarse in his manners. St. Mary's was his first pastorate, and so far as I could judge he proved himself an able administrator.

The regular drill had me drive to New Buffalo in time for dinner each Saturday evening. I remember some exquisite T-bone steaks on more than one occasion, prepared just right (medium rare) by the resident house-keeper, an amiable woman of advanced years (of an *aetas superadulta*, as the prudent canonical maxim had it). After dinner Smith and I went to the church to hear confessions, usually till about nine o'clock. I slept in the guest bedroom. On Sunday morning I said two Masses either at St. Mary's or, much more likely, at the mission in Bridgman, another lake town a few miles north of New Buffalo, for which Father Smith was also responsible. I say more likely me to the charming little church in Bridgman, which, in-cidentally involved hearing confessions there before the first Mass, because the pastor understandably preferred to spend the bulk of his energy in the home parish.

All this is changed now, gone like the Latin liturgy and the slate of pop-ular devotions developed over centuries. Since 1964 St. Mary of the Lake has a school which, as it always does, pretty much redefined its parochial priorities. Moreover Bridgman now has its own parish with a resident pas-tor, Our Lady Queen of Peace. With the collapse, since the Second Vatican Council, of the old rectory-centered clerical culture the kind of in-house domestic service that Father Smith enjoyed is now almost unthinkable. And speaking of culture, the institution dominating the economy of New Buf-falo today is not without cultural overtones: the Four Winds Casino, oper-ated by the Pokagon Band of the Potawatomi Indians, with whom there is a venerable connection to Notre Dame. Their ancestors in the 1840s figured large in the missionary program of Father Edward Sorin, even as he was going about the business of founding a university.

How much good my work may have done for the parishioners in New Buffalo and Bridgman I cannot say; I know it did a great deal for me. It was a lively reminder to me that the parish and its ministry remains forever the center of Catholic life. The academic activity I was legitimately engaged in was a kind of luxurious add-on as far as the larger Church was concerned. The good people I served for eighteen months in southern Michigan had little reason to wonder about Thomas Stapleton. Nor did they.

I found the routine of a weekend assistant predictable and prosaic. Even so, once in a while there came a moment of diversion. On Good Friday 1958 I chatted amiably with Mayor Richard J. Daley who had accompanied his wife and daughter to the service at St. Mary of the Lake. The Daley family maintained a vacation compound along the shore of Lake Michigan, south of New Buffalo, as did other prominent Chicagoans, like Father Andrew Greeley. Among the regular congregation I met at Bridgman was a stately-looking woman, tall and with jet black hair and heavy makeup, who turned out to be a White Russian countess who had fled the Bolsheviks east across Siberia to Vladivostok and thence to San Francisco. It was intriguing to observe how she was of two minds about the launching of the first Artificial Earth Satellite — the "Sputnik" — in October 1957: whether to take pride in her countrymen's great achievement or to despise it as the work of the wicked Communists.

On one Sunday in late May 1958 my two extra-academic activities merged and gave rise to a memorable moment. When I returned to St. Joseph's from New Buffalo shortly after noon, there in the apartment were John Vrabley and Leo Pursley, the bishop of Fort Wayne. It was commencement day for the high school seniors, and the bishop had come to preside at the ceremony. Father Vrabley introduced us, and then said to me, *sotto voce,* keep him occupied, I must see to the final arrangements. I kissed the episcopal ring, which, as I have noted before, was the custom in those days. The bishop showed himself a kindly man, with no pretensions to speak of, but when he learned I was associated in some way with Notre Dame his manner suddenly darkened.

Do you know, Father, he said (I paraphrase), how much negative mail I receive about Notre Dame. I confessed I did not. A lot, I assure you. And much of it concentrates on two objections. First, that the prices in the bookstore are doubled on football weekends; and second, that the girls depicted in the yearbook display far too much cleavage. Puzzled as I was as to how to reply, it didn't really matter, for the bishop intended no dialogue. Now, he went on, what am I to do? If I complain, will Hesburgh pay any attention to me? Of course not. What if I then appeal to Pacelli? Well, here's what Pacelli would say: Who is Leo Pursley? I never heard of him. But what about Ted Hesburgh? He'd say: I love Ted Hesburgh. Ted Hesburgh can do no wrong.

Pacelli, of course, was Pius XII, the pope who had made Pursley a bishop. To speak of the pontiff in this off-hand fashion suggests that his pique on this day arose from some discrete annoying incident. After all, he served honorably as bishop of Fort Wayne for twenty more years, during which time he coexisted successfully with Notre Dame and its president,

Father Theodore Hesburgh. Not that it is ever easy for a bishop to have flourishing within his diocese a semi-independent ecclesiastical institution boasting of a national, even an international, constituency of its own.

George Andrew Beck became bishop of Salford in 1955. Two years later Philip Hughes received word from England that he now had the right to refer to himself as "Monsignor." At that time there were various ranks among the worldwide class of *monsignori* — domestic prelates and chamberlains, some right reverend, others very reverend, distinctions reduced in recent years to a single category. All of them were, and as simplified continue to be, based on the fiction that a particular diocesan priest had been promoted to an office in the household of the pope. Purely honorary, they were traceable to the sixteenth century when the papacy, in imitation of the secular governments of the era, sold honors and offices as a means of raising desperately needed cash. In modern times such prelacies have commonly been in the gift of the honoree's bishop.

These appointments, if handled judiciously — if restricted to individuals genuinely worthy by reason of accomplishment or as the holder of an important office — can be a means of elevating the overall tone of a presbyterate. True, they can also be the source of jealousy among the local clergy, or of cynicism — it is said that Cardinal Spellman once at a clerical banquet created a new monsignor in order to have a balanced number on each side of the table. That George Beck had reached across the Atlantic to confer such an accolade upon this priest of the diocese of Salford — who had not actually served there for nearly thirty years — moved the recipient very deeply. The two had known one another casually when they were both young men, but not closely enough to have predicted this denouement. Bishop Beck made perfectly clear that his intention was to honor Monsignor Hughes — as we should now call him — as an historian who had rendered great service to the Church. And Hughes accepted it in that spirit. He was hugely pleased, because here was recognition of his labors for the first and only time from his own country. Even so, content with his internal satisfaction, he made no great show of this touch of the purple; seldom did he dress up in the full monsignorial regalia, though he did tend to favor pink socks with his sandals. He insisted that Clark and I continue to address him as "Father." Which we did.

Almost coincidental with his new title, Philip Hughes was stricken by his first heart attack. It proved severe enough to have required a lengthy hospitalization, followed at home by regular nurses' care in support of the indefatigable Margaret Laing. Never robust, his recovery was slow. Eventually, however, his doctors recommended that he gradually resume ordinary physical activity. One gentle way of easing his way into doing so was to put my two-door Chevrolet into service. Several afternoons a week over the next month or more I drove him in long rides across the singularly unlovely northern Indiana countryside. After a while it became clear even to my amateur eyes that this kind of therapy was freshening him, and for me the experience was one more instance of finding intellectual enrichment in this remarkable man. He talked about many things, about England, about the Church, about Douglas Woodruff and Vincent McNabb and other fascinating people. He fretted that "this Hanoverian woman," Queen Elizabeth II, "had given her children Stuart names," like Charles and Anne. He touched upon many a fascinating historical inquiry, but never about Thomas Stapleton — that was my business. Once, when we strayed to the outskirts of Gary, and were virtually enveloped in the smoke belching forth from the chimneys of the steel plants, he cried out, "Look, it's Lancashire! I'm home!"

But most memorable to me was what he had to say about John Henry Newman. His observations amounted almost to a lengthy and exhaustive elaboration of that first Notre Dame lecture I had heard him give. I knew something about Newman; I had read Wilfrid Ward's up to that time definitive two-volume biography, as well as Wilfrid's daughter Maisie's *Young Mr. Newman,* which covered thoroughly the Anglican years only outlined by her father. So I was prepared, I think, at least to a degree, to take in how deeply and sensitively Hughes grasped the essence of Newman's remarkable personality and how well he understood the context in which the drama of his life was played out. My Chevrolet Biscayne may have seemed an odd place for a literary genesis, but it was there that *The Oxford Conspirators,* my book on the Oxford Movement — the successor to *Stapleton* — had its beginning. The marks of Father Hughes are all over it.

Chapter Eight
Gotham

"W-N-E-W, New York, New York, New York!" I had just driven off the New Jersey Turnpike and onto the George Washington Bridge to take me across the Hudson River to the Washington Heights section of Manhattan. I was a bit nervous over the certainty that I was about to enter one of the great cities of the world. But just how great struck with special force the moment I heard over the radio a local station identifying itself with a jingle sung by, of all people, Patti Page. Patti Page, the living legend, America's sweetheart, the most successful recording artist of the era, who thrilled us with the sweet tones of "Tennessee Waltz" and "Old Cape Cod." And Patti Page worked for this radio station, WNEW. New York must be a special place indeed, I almost said aloud to myself, as I carefully steered my Chevrolet Biscayne, with its Minnesota license plates ("Land of the 10,000 Lakes"), along the right-most of the four lanes leading east.

That was in late May of 1957. I spent that summer and the next one in New York City, or, more precisely, I spent them at 110 Riverside Drive, not far from where I had exited the bridge. At this West Side of Manhattan address stood a substantial brownstone mansion in what had once been a fashionable neighborhood, for WASPs first at the turn of the previous century, then for Jews, then Italians, but now extensively occupied by Haitians and other West Indians. This last circumstance aroused a measure of cynicism: I was advised that when outdoors I should regularly wear my Roman collar so that, presumed by the neighbors to be a witch doctor, my safety would be guaranteed. The house had been divided into separate small but comfortable apartments for the priests who comprised the faculty of the Cathedral College. I've mentioned this institution before, a day school preparatory seminary on West End Avenue not far away, attended, you may recall, by Eugene Clark. It is long gone now, since 1968, when the Archdiocese of New York, like so many jurisdictions across the country, abandoned the traditional six-and-six-year system of minor and major seminaries for the training of its clergy.

The residents at 110 numbered about fifteen, my seniors perhaps by a dozen years, except for the rector, Monsignor Lenihan, and the dean, Father Considine, who were somewhat older. They were all were very kind and welcoming to me. They were a company of well-educated men, most of them with master's degrees and one or two with a Ph.D. As a group they represented their institution with distinction; as individuals they displayed a predictable variety in personality which made for a lively and sometimes hilarious household, demonstrated especially at the common dinner table. One of them proved of particular interest to me. Father Fred Durkin, the college's bursar or financial officer had personal commitments outside New York City — in Florida I think, though I never knew what they were. Consequently, he needed a surrogate to cover obligations he had assumed in addition to his ordinary duties: a priest to say daily Mass for the three or four Carmelite nuns who did the domestic work at 110, and a priest who had an automobile at his disposal, to celebrate two Sunday Masses in the school gym at St. Rose of Lima — a parish typical of the 1950s with large crowds, a challenge to accommodate — located in far-off Rockaway, near the facility then called the Idlewild International Airport. Since I wanted to go to New York and since I appeared to meet both Durkin's requirements satisfactorily, he and I had a brief and friendly exchange, after which he went on his way and I took up residence in his apartment.

Yes, I wanted to go to New York. Ph.D. candidacy exams at Notre Dame loomed over me in the coming autumn, and one of the areas in which I would be questioned was the history of late Latin antiquity. Several graduate courses offered at Columbia University during the summer of 1957 I believed could help prepare me for that field, and Columbia was only an easy walk from 110 Riverside Drive. And in fact the course in fourth-century urban life that I did take there was a first-rate experience. I wish I could remember the professor's name so that I might pay him, over these nearly sixty years, due tribute. Lively and learned, he treated us six or eight graduate students like adults, and toward me, sweating away in my heavy, double breasted black suit and Roman collar, he seemed particularly solicitous. But of course the availability of some practical benefit of the kind just described was never the chief reason I wanted to go to New York.

I wanted to go because New York City by all accounts was uniquely wonderful, no place like it anywhere else in the world; because it stood at the center of the universe; indeed, it *was* that center. As I look back now over all the years since, I can attest that it was an experience which left not a shred of disappointment.

A host of memories crowds my mind. One Sunday morning driving through the heart of Harlem on 125th Street on my way to the Triborough Bridge and the Van Wyck Expressway and so across Queens to Fred Durkin's parish, I looked to my right saw a huge banner-like sign: "Daddy Grace Will Baptize with a Fire Hose on July 10 at Amsterdam Avenue and 110th Street."

On a summer evening aboard the Staten Island Ferry crossing the harbor I watched a middle aged, well-dressed black man, standing on the deck alone, gaze up thoughtfully at the Statue of Liberty as we slowly passed by it. I learned about the joy of genuine French cuisine when I was taken to dine at Charles a la Pomme Souffle on East 55th Street, which featured those double fried potatoes, hollow inside, crackling crisp outside, served along with other succulent fare, in a charming interior courtyard with sky scrapers towering all around. I swam in the ocean for the first time, off Jones Beach on the southwest corner of Long Island. Father Jim Lynch, who taught sociology at Cathedral College, took me to a game at the old Yankee Stadium — the House that Ruth built — and I saw Yogi Berra hit a home run over the short right-field fence. On another summer evening, this one starry and cool from a breeze off the harbor, I rejoiced to hear one of the city's fine orchestras performing in the open air, at the Central Park's Sheep Meadow. The final piece on the program was Mendelssohn's Fourth Symphony, the "Italian." With the lush chords that begin the lively first moment, *allegro vivace,* I could see that the elderly couple sitting on lawn chairs in front of me were already holding hands. I cannot prove it, of course, but I believe they may well have been born in Naples. Of all the museums and galleries I was fortunate enough to visit, my favorite was the Frick Collection, on 5th Avenue at East 70th Street, primarily because it was small and controlled enough that the untutored, like me, had a chance to move unhindered through its rooms with enough leisure and space really to appreciate the beauty of the paintings on view. I've never forgotten my first entry into the Frick drawing room. There on the wall, flanking the fireplace, hung two Holbein portraits: Thomas Cromwell on one side and Thomas More on the other. It was as though the rivalries of Tudor days had come alive again.

On July 16, I joined the celebrants at the Church of Our Lady of Mount Carmel in East Harlem, who in their observance of a traditional feast lit up the whole of the ethnic neighborhood, and who displayed deep devotion and, from my straight-laced Midwestern point of view, considerable vulgarity. My guide for this adventure was Father Florence Daniel Cohalan, professor of history at Cathedral College. No more capable one could be imagined; Father Cohalan, fifty years old at this time, with degrees from Harvard and Catholic University, remained a New Yorker to his fingertips and to the depths of his soul. His friends used to tease him that he would be the last white man to leave Manhattan Island. He showed me in fascinating detail many grand places, beginning with that Gothic jewel on Fifth Avenue, St. Patrick's Cathedral — a special joy for me because, like many American Catholics, I thought of St. Patrick's as somehow my cathedral too. He brought me to many other worthy sites, not so spectacular but with intriguing ecclesiastical connections, about which my escort almost always could share a droll anecdote or two, often with a wryly and mildly offensive anti-clerical twist at the end.

The decisive life-principle of Florence Cohalan was a commitment without question or reservation to a sternly unemotional Catholic faith without a trace of sentimentality. And without much speculation either; he was no theologian. But he was confident enough — and knowledgeable enough — to discern the warts on the Body of Christ without suffering a crisis of belief. For instance, later convinced that Paul VI was an administrative failure, Father Cohalan added an intention to his Mass each day that the pope would abdicate — something unheard of in those days. There was a strong tribal element in all this, a phenomenon peculiarly Irish at a moment in time when the Irish immigrants and their children still dominated the Church in New York City and, incidentally, the Democratic Party there as well. Cohalan's father, after all, a state supreme court justice, had also served as Grand Sachem of Tammany Hall, and was said to have run guns to the rebels of the Easter Rising in Dublin, 1916. Father Florence in any case did not consider his objections to the reigning pope's policies a challenge to either man's faith.

Father Cohalan was a frail, homely man, whose jutting Hapsburg-like jaw gave a strange twist to his face. He suffered from chronic hypoglycemia, an insufficiency of blood sugar which untreated or intensified by a careless diet could lead to severe loss of energy. It was startling to see him pour spoonful after heaping spoonful of sugar into his afternoon cup of tea. Despite his less than fetching appearance, he proved attractive to all sorts of people. His deep intelligence, his sly humor, his elegant speech with its faintly anachronistic overtones, and perhaps most of all his almost playful tolerance for everyone he met, foibles and all, won him wide admiration and affection. Among the students in the College, he played the role of a Pied Piper; many of them, intrigued by the breadth of his knowledge, which he wore with an easy grace, and by the candor with which he dismissed what he considered "humbug," took him as their special mentor. Gene Clark was one of them. Such relationships might well have sparked jealousy among his faculty colleagues, but I saw no evidence of this; on the contrary Florence Cohalan appeared to be everybody's favorite person at 110.

Father Cohalan took his conservative principles seriously, took them, one might say, as a matter of course, and felt no need to belabor them or defend them. No doubt he assumed that I, a clever young fellow, agreed with him, and as the months passed such increasingly became the case. At the same time the example of one of his disciples pointed me in the same ideological direction. This of course was my fellow Lingard Fellow, Eugene Clark, liberated now from the academic Midwest and returned to the glamor of New York City. Though I hardly sensed it then, a group of talented young conservative Catholics, clerical and lay, was beginning to take shape in New York, informal as yet but already attracting attention, the most notable of whom was William F. Buckley, Jr., author of the truly bold attack in 1951 on academic secularism, *God and Man at Yale,* and founder just four years later of what came to be the immensely influential journal, *National Review.* I do not mean to suggest the American conservative movement that took flight during the 1950s, especially in New York, was a kind of clericalist cabal, but at the same time I would argue that the Catholic element — in the traditional sense of the Latin liturgy and the *Baltimore Catechism* — played an important role in its development.

Permit me briefly to get ahead of my story. Back in Minneapolis several years later, I attended a William Buckley lecture in the ballroom of a local hotel. After its conclusion several people approached the podium to have a private word with the speaker. As did I, although such ordinarily was not (and is not) my style. When my turn came, I shyly gave him my name and asked whether he knew my friends Monsignor (as he was by then) Cohalan and Father Clark. "Do I know them," Buckley replied, flailing his long arms and indulging in those physical contortions, especially around his mouth made famous in later years on his long-standing television talk show, *Firing Line* (1966–1999). "Know them? I *revere* them. They are my inspiration and indeed the inspiration of my colleagues at the *Review*. They are in truth our chaplains." I was fortunate enough to come to know Bill Buckley fairly well in later years, and fortunate enough, too, to get the opportunity to pay public tribute to him for his immense services to his country and his faith.

I suppose Clark rather more consciously tried during those two summers to nudge me to the right; if so, there was nothing solemn about it; one might say he proceeded on a fun-and- games level. He introduced me to his family, to his delightful mother first of all, the long- widowed Kathryn Clark who in due time would welcome my long-widowed mother to her home in the Bronx. And to his brother Jack, a sometime soldier and criminologist, and his family. And then to a coterie of cousins of varying degrees, sturdily middle- and working-class, and strikingly genial and kindly and hard-working, very much my kind of people. Many a Sunday noontime during both my summers, having just finished my parochial duty at St. Rose of Lima in Queens, I drove directly over the Whitestone Bridge and joined the Clark family for a Bronx picnic.

Gene remained always close to his family, as they did to him, until the tragic ending of his life. Their intimate relationship is particularly worth stressing because, as the years rolled by, he had become increasingly the companion of the fashionable and the rich — not infrequently the very rich. I watched him function as local chaplain to the Knights of Malta, as the organizer of the powerhouse fund-raising Friends of the Vatican Museums, as the driving power behind the philanthropic Homeland Foundation — in all these capacities he established long-time contacts with the *crème de la crème* of New York society. Moreover, for many years, when he served as Director of the Office of Communications for the archdiocese, I witnessed — usually from a distance — how in one way or another he placed before his complex constituencies most of the great events and celebrities of the day. Sometimes humorously. Thus in 1979, when Pope John Paul II first visited the United States, Barbara Walters invited Gene and the pontiff to lunch with her at Club 21. (Alas, protocol determined that this interview never took place. What a cultural loss was it that *il Papa Polacco* and the queen of American daytime television never got a chance to indulge in canapés together.)

Once he had met such people Gene's charm and his deep desire to be of service to them priestly and humane — guaranteed that they would not forget him; many of them — not Barbara Walters, to be sure — would become his friends. Which however was never a put-down in any sense of his ordinary relatives, not of his mother or Uncle Bill or Cousin Ruth, and he never hesitated to mix them socially together with his prominent associates. And when he did, at a party, say, or an outing, they all got along very well indeed, an example perhaps of admirable American classlessness. Persons with different educational backgrounds, different vocations, different speech patterns, but lots of mutual regard. Kathryn once asked her son whether, if she had visited him "out west" — i.e., at Notre Dame — people there would have thought she "talked funny"; when she called him by his Christian name, she regularly put emphasis on the first syllable. Nobody was embarrassed.

And Eugene Clark introduced me to the Hamptons. Even simply to mention the word is to conjure up an image of a playground set aside for the very rich and famous. This cluster of settlements on the south fork of the far east end of Long Island traced itself back to the middle of the seventeenth century. Over the years since, a kind of imprecision in naming them had developed; for instance, one community called itself Bridge Hampton while another was known as Hampton Bays. But the significant administrative entities in the area were East Hampton and Southampton, because they were real towns and stood responsible for the various hamlets and villages within their respective limits. Thus East Hampton's jurisdiction extended from its center over the fourteen miles east to Montauk Point, beyond which lay only the Atlantic. And halfway between them was the unincorporated village of Amagansett.

Perhaps he told me, but if so, I have long since forgotten how Gene managed to finance construction of a house in this pricey corner of the world. Of course sixty years ago the Hamptons had not yet become defined as the weekend summer residence of financial moguls, of affluent patrons of the arts and, after Jackson Pollock's arrival in 1945, of well-heeled artists, all of them celebrities in one way or another in flight from the city. Indeed, the small farmers and fishermen, descendants of the original settlers, carried on a traditional unassuming lifestyle. They proved that though a poor person could hardly have expected to survive in the Hamptons one need not have been immensely wealthy to do so.

Clark's presence there provided further evidence of the same. The house he had built, for instance, was located in a relatively unfashionable place — some miles north of Amagansett's little business district, an elevated site we used to refer to laughingly as Louse Point, much closer to dull Gardiner's Bay than to the ocean. The house itself, moreover, was modest in size and by no means elaborate. A large and airy living room, a master bedroom with bath, two small bedrooms — one of which was permanently reserved for Kathryn Clark — and a kitchen that merged into a dining area. Over the years that followed many tasteful additions were made to the house, the first as I remember a screened-in porch and a lengthy deck, on which not a few toasts were raised to the genial host. And all the while the value of the property relentlessly increased; I speak as one less wise, but I'm sure that by the time the final amenity was added, the swimming pool, it was worth well into seven figures. It remained for Gene at any rate a wonderful *refugium* from his immensely busy life in the city.

Most summers from 1957, I spent at least a week or ten days at Amagansett. What attracted me there, besides the bond of friendship, was what attracted everybody else: the salubrious climate, the seemingly endless beaches of white sand, the ingenious, mouth-watering ways in which local chefs prepared all manners of fish. A cocktail and dinner hour seldom passed without the emergence of some exhilarating conversation and sometimes of a personality worth cultivating. Once during the early 1960s Gene and I arranged for Father Hughes and Mrs. Laing to take rooms briefly in one of the better resort hotels along the beach. Despite some relaxing days in the sun for them, this did not prove an altogether successful departure from their ordinary routine. I remember best the echoes of Hughes's voice after we had all sat through an amateur production of an eighteenth-century play by Brinsley Sheridan: "Margaret," he said with a puzzled air, "Margaret, they took out all the parts about the Jews."

.I have always been a fitful sleeper, often shaken awake by peculiar dreams. Not so at Louse Point, where I slept every night the full eight hours in utter serenity; perhaps it was the ocean air. Even so, I never assumed that I was anything more than a passing visitor to the Hamptons, a place as remote from my real life as the Riviera. Especially was this the case as the years passed and East Hampton became ever more a center of wealth and celebrity. By contrast it was clearly not possible for Gene Clark to elude the consequences of fixing a semi-permanent domicile in such a beguiling, even seductive environment, nor did he express any desire to do so. How much the glamor of the Hamptons affected him remains an intriguing question; I'm not sure I was ever in a position to answer it.

None of my conservative New York friends had much good to say about the United Nations. Indeed, they were much more likely to make bad jokes about the monstrous tall building along the East River and the wrong-headed if not downright evil policies they thought were promoted there. So I never told them that one evening during the summer of 1957, when most of the UN personnel were on holiday, I stood at the podium and looked out over the rows of seats slanting upwards in the General Assembly Hall — the very platform from which all the leading statesmen of the day delivered their annual *pronunciamentos* — and imagined myself for the moment anyway a person of some consequence. Four score and seven years ago, I intoned, and waited for the echo.

This was a simplistic daydream of course, but I considered it then, and still do, as no harm, no foul. So did my guide on the tour of the virtually empty UN facility; in fact he clearly rejoiced at my interest in the various departmental details he showed and explained to me. But then John Peter Grady was joyous man, whose seldom-fading grin testified to an abiding sense of wellbeing, a confidence that somehow all things work out in accord with God's plan. His entree to the building stemmed from his position as envoy to the UN of the Young Christian Workers and the Young Christian Students. These organizations were first-rank products of the Catholic Action movement of the 1920s and 1930s — "the participation of the laity in the apostolate of the hierarchy," as Pope Pius XI expressed it in 1927. There might well have been secular objections to such groups enjoying formal UN recognition. Even if so, nobody could doubt that the YCW and YCS stood in strong support of the principles and ambitions of the United

Nations. And anyway John Peter Grady could make the case for acceptability with cheerful panache.

A couple of years earlier John Peter had married Teresa Shaughnessy — whom he recognized as his soul-mate, as she did him — and Teresa was my cousin, second cousin to be precise. Our branches of the family had not mingled much until recent events: the death and expansive funeral of Grandma Shaughnessy Kelly (my mother's mother), Cousin Tessie's wedding, and my ordination and first Mass. Grady was a native of the Bronx, and there he settled with his bride in a small apartment, just off the Grand Concourse. I visited them there now and then, and spent an occasional Sunday afternoon with them at the beach. I wish I had seen more of them. If love is the genuine sign of the living Christian — and love particularly for life's losers, the morally and physically halt and lame — John Peter and Tessie were among the liveliest people I have ever known. They brought deep understanding of and commitment to Catholic social teaching, not as some abstract philosophical system but as a ministry to serve the least of Christ's brethren, and to do it gently and humanely. When I came to write my novel *McElroy* during the 1970s, my portrait of the neighborhood Samaritan House and the couple who directed it was closer to reality than any other section of the book. Grady became "Brady;" that was the only change. There is one line which I attributed to Teresa — and proud that I did — when it seemed as though Samaritan House might have to close. Teresa said simply: "There is always need for people like us." And how right she was.

Chapter Nine
Back Home Again

Father Thomas Wood — you may recall the name from the list of my colleagues in Howard Hall Annex in September 1956, a Sulpician priest from Seattle — had been assigned to Notre Dame to earn a graduate degree in American history. He was a short wiry, curly-haired man, whose herky-jerky gestures suggested taut nerves, a heavy smoker, given to almost embarrassingly pious platitudes as long as he was sober. As most of our evenings wore on, however, and the drinks multiplied, his piety gave way to a stinging wit, the chief target of which were his religious superiors in whom, he protested, could be found few redeeming qualities. But amid the general laughter at his sallies, we who listened to them gradually came to realize that Tom had forfeited a measure of control over himself. Ultimately, he bought a second-hand automobile without permission, and one night he waited in the car park outside Eddie's Steak House until closing and tried to pick up one of the waitresses. After this fairly ludicrous adventure my friend Tom had run out of options.

I don't remember how the Michigan Sulpicians got in touch with me. The Society of Saint-Sulpice, founded in seventeenth-century France, had taken on as its major ministry the training of prospective candidates for the diocesan priesthood. Its methodology and principles of formation ultimately became the universal norm. In 1948 St. John's Provincial Seminary opened its doors in Plymouth, a town twenty-five miles west of Detroit, where a Sulpician administration and faculty were established to prepare men for ordination in all seven dioceses in Michigan. Those immediate post-war years were a heady time for American Catholics, when the booming religious vocations were but one sign of the Church's physical and spiritual well-being. It seemed almost a golden age; even Henry Ford became a Catholic. Of course nobody knew then that a revolution was already beginning to take shape right around the corner.

My assignment (however it was conveyed to me) was to deliver Tom and his unauthorized automobile to the seminary staff in Plymouth. The two of us undertook the journey northward on a cold and dreary Saturday afternoon in late December 1958. I don't remember who drove; it might very well have been Tom — the car was, after all, still technically his and he was stone cold sober. We were both tense, and conversation lagged; small-talk proved quite beyond us. A half hour from our destination we stopped at a convenience store so that Tom could buy a bottle of beer. He drank it quickly and then made a bad joke about this being his last hurrah; neither of us laughed much.

The welcome at Plymouth was chilly. The rector, who was courteous enough, promptly whisked Tom away. He invited me to stay for supper, at which I found the assembled fathers cold and distant. Perhaps they suspected that I had been Tom's drinking buddy and had led their fellow Sulpician down the primrose path. (In fact, at this date I was still a teetotaler.) After the meal — the food incidentally was execrable: in my experience seminaries rank only with hospitals and airplanes in serving tasteless victuals — the rector, with Tom Wood in tow, drove me to downtown Plymouth where I boarded the Greyhound bus for the trip back to South Bend.

Before I did, I shook Tom's hand and mumbled some banal remark about hopes for the future. I never saw him again or heard from or about him.

Only a few days later I was scheduled to return home to Minnesota.

The sad saga of Tom Wood may strike you as an inappropriate way to begin a new chapter of this Memoir, and of course you may be right. One possible rebuttal would be that the story is not necessarily as sad as it might appear, that it might indeed have had a happy ending. Maybe once restored to his Sulpician brethren Tom received the help and support he needed to refresh the roots of his religious vocation. But I don't really require a lot of reflection to see that that is not much of an apologia. So let me suggest this. My memory of the trip to Plymouth is an eloquent reminder to me of how at that moment my life underwent a significant change that brought with it a measure of sadness and apprehension. After nearly twenty-five years, I was no longer a student, no longer able to define myself as a person for whom somebody else was responsible — a status Tom Wood had so deeply resented. A bit scary, to say the least. I was about to say goodbye to Notre

Dame and the rich personal and professional experience I had had in that unique institution, that "special place," and I assumed at the time that I would never see the Golden Dome again, except as a tourist. And finally, I had to bid adieu to my beloved mentor who had opened up for me so many intellectual vistas I had not dreamed of before. Shortly before my parting with Tom Wood I spent an evening at the house on Riverside Drive in South Bend — far different from the eponymous address on the west side of Manhattan — with Father Hughes and Mrs. Laing. I remember that we listened to a recording of Mozart's delightful *Die Entführung aus dem Serail.*

I returned home to Minnesota just before Christmas, 1958, and was glad to do so, though not altogether easy in my mind. Because now I had reached that estate by which adulthood is defined in our economic and political system, and how success is measured. From now on I would have a job.

The College of St. Thomas had been founded in the mid-1880s by John Ireland, the formidable archbishop of St. Paul. He called it originally the St. Thomas Aquinas Seminary, and in so doing revealed a strategy common among Catholic prelates during the late nineteenth century: the institution would prepare candidates for the priesthood, both intellectually and spiritually, but would also provide training for young Catholic laymen who wanted to enter the various secular professions. The fees paid by the latter would contribute to the support of the whole enterprise. Over the longer term the college would be able to count upon financial aid from its doggedly loyal clerical alumni. So at least went the theory.

But St. Thomas differed in one important respect from most other Catholic colleges established during the same era in that it remained a stoutly diocesan institution, unlike, for example, Notre Dame, the creation of the Congregation of Holy Cross with only a nod now and then to the bishops of Indiana. John Ireland harbored a deep suspicion of religious orders and what he judged to be their internationalist pretensions. The saying went that a Jesuit dared not even change trains in St. Paul during Ireland's tenure. There was at any rate a happy if unintended consequence to Ireland's exclusionist policy: the bonding of the local clergy with the lay elite through their common experience at St. Thomas invigorated the Catholic community in St. Paul and its environs and lent it a remarkable strength and coherence. Ten years later James J. Hill, the railroad magnate, provided money to build and endow a separate major seminary, the one I attended. The multiple buildings of "Mr. Hill's seminary," as it was popularly known, stood on a piece of property overlooking the Mississippi, just kitty-corner from the college, at the end of St. Paul's long and prosperous Summit Avenue.

From that time on, the college along with its high school department — the St. Thomas Military Academy (Ireland, proud to have been a Civil War veteran, insisted there be a soldierly presence on campus) — served an exclusively male lay clientele, but it remained, predictably, very much under local clerical control. The archbishop was *ex officio* chairman of a tame board of trustees. All the high offices of the institution were filled by diocesan priests. When I came back from Notre Dame, I was assigned to the history faculty in the college on the same principle whereby my seminary classmates were named assistant pastors. It was a canonical, not a pedagogical, act. Indeed, Archbishop William O. Brady (whom readers met briefly endorsing my acceptance of the Lingard Fellowship) was hardly less imperious than Ireland had been, and, like his great predecessor, was no believer in consultation. He was, however, a strong believer in keeping his clergy docile. The first time I met him after my return — at some parochial function or other — he made a point of remarking to me, "Glad to see you home, Father. We need you for weekend work in the parishes." So much for my brand new Ph.D., which had been earned in record time under highly prestigious auspices and which had cost the archdiocese nary a dime.

The College of St. Thomas over the years had endured many more downs than ups. At one especially dark moment it had lost its accreditation. Always short of money, the institution teetered more than once on the edge of dissolution and had to be rescued by appeals to ordinary Catholic parishioners, an unfailingly generous people who never dreamed of a higher education for themselves. But these dire days were over by the time I reported for duty. At the end of 1958 St. Thomas was experiencing a kind of renaissance. It had nothing to do with my arrival, of course. Rather the brighter prospects resulted primarily from economic changes that had emerged out of the Second World War. During the course of that conflict St. Thomas, like a lot of small colleges, had maintained itself and managed to keep most of its staff on salary by providing at the behest of the government centers for the training of prospective military officers. Then after the war came a rush of students who, as veterans and thanks to the GI Bill, could afford to pay full tuition for a college education.

And happily for all concerned, there appeared on the scene a man to match the moment. I never knew Vincent Flynn. But though he died young, his achievement in creating the modern St. Thomas spoke for itself and was also testified to by a legion of admirers and disciples. His narrowly provincial beginnings gave no hint of the sweep of his ambition or the strength of his resolve. He hailed from a tiny town in the southwest corner of Minnesota, graduated in turn from both St. Thomas institutions, then crossed Summit Avenue to enter Mr. Hill's seminary, and was ordained a priest in 1927. Seventeen years later, aged forty-three, he was named President of St. Thomas College and Academy. By then, through lessons learned in a series of ever more responsible positions, he had pretty much mastered the mechanics of academic governance and had besides earned prestigious graduate degrees from the universities of Minnesota and Chicago.

By then, 1944, the end of the war was in sight and relief from the Great Depression well on its way. A new world was opening itself, and Father Flynn recognized the need to adapt to it. The changes were subtle, but clearly the days of casual leadership at St. Thomas were over. Although Flynn's predecessors, all worthy men and well thought-of priests, had assumed office with nothing but the best intentions, none of them had been equipped to deal with the educational challenges of these latter times. Most of them were relatively well-read — they knew their Latin classics along with a smattering of Dante and the likes of Bossuet in translation — and, Irishmen all, they assumed that Celtic eloquence was part of their birthright. But they had had no intellectual training beyond their seminary days, not an encouraging prospect, and, most crucially, they thought themselves to be essentially parish pastors and felt uneasy and inadequate in any other setting. They were, in short, respectable clerical gentlemen of the old school, of an era now past.

Vincent Flynn's sudden death in July 1956, sent shock tremors through the St. Paul community, since the President of St. Thomas, fiercely active up to the end, was only fifty-five years old. I recall I drove in from Wanda and attended the funeral, though I have no memory of the ceremony — probably because Flynn and St. Thomas at this moment in my life meant nothing to me, and I was ready to use any excuse to come into the city to see friends and maybe play a round of golf at Highland Park or Como. Only later did I come to recognize that the College of St. Thomas to which I was assigned at the end of 1958 had been the creation of Vincent Flynn's twelve-year-long administration. But Flynn was gone now, and what would happen in the cloudy atmosphere of the succession?

By the time of Flynn's death, Archbishop Murray had entered into his final illness and had taken up residence in St. Joseph's Hospital in St. Paul, a place he never left till he died there the following October. Which meant that in effect Coadjutor William Brady had assumed charge of the arch-diocese. And he who, as observed above, had little interest in consultation did not indulge in any on this occasion. Shortly after Flynn's funeral he summoned to his presence a thirty-four-year-old assistant professor from the Department of History, a newly minted Yale Ph.D. You (I paraphrase) are now the president of St. Thomas, he told the young priest. Who responded with considerable diffidence: I am so green and inexperienced, would it not be wiser to seek out the opinions of some of the senior St. Thomas faculty or at least some of the older priests in the diocese? No need for further conversation, Brady replied with characteristic hauteur. I've made up my mind. The appointment takes effect immediately.

I first met James Patrick Shannon in September 1948, as did all the students at Nazareth Hall when we returned to school at the end of the summer holiday. Sweeping changes, we soon learned, had been made across the minor seminary's faculty and administration, and Shannon had been assigned to teach English literature and Greek to us in the college depart-ment. He made no particular impression in the classroom, though it would be wrong to suggest that as a teacher he was inept or indifferent to the task. One difficulty not of his making was that it had been pretty well agreed by all sides that we were not in fact going to master biblical Greek, so that les-sons in that subject were reduced largely to *pro forma* recitations. Father Shannon clearly liked the English romantic poets and wanted us to appre-ciate them too — I remember reciting for him, with flourishes he approved of, "My heart leaps up when I behold a rainbow in the sky." A desultory treatment of the fiction of Joseph Conrad did provide us with a nickname, though the very ordinariness of one novel's protagonist, to say nothing of his moral ambiguity, gave us pause. We nonetheless dubbed this tidy man of average weight and height with closely cropped sand-colored hair, always neatly trimmed, who smiled a great deal, Lord Jim.

But as a matter of fact, in doing so we were speaking more wisely than we knew. Shannon spent only two years on the faculty at the Hall, my two last years as a student there. I cannot pretend that during that short stretch I came to know him in any serious way or to realize that he did indeed possess extraordinary, even lordly, gifts. But clearly, he did not belong in the backwater of the little school on Lake Johanna. Over the next twelve years James Shannon and his mystique were to exert a powerful influence not just on the College of St. Thomas — which under his direction flourished as never before — but on the life of the archdiocese as a whole. His triumphs were many, though finally some species of disappointment caught hold of him and laid him low. To have been elevated to a college presidency at the age of thirty-five may have surprised some people; not those who had come into contact with him, even from his adolescence. From his earliest years Shannon showed extraordinary promise. Valedictorian of his class at St. Thomas Academy, he completed the four-year course at the college in three and graduated *summa cum laude* with a double major in classics and history. Ordained in 1946, he was assigned to the cathedral and so came into daily contact with Archbishop Murray. During his brief interlude at Nazareth Hall he earned a master's degree in English from the University of Minnesota. At Yale his prize-winning doctoral dissertation — a study of Archbishop Ireland's colonies in western Minnesota — was published to universal praise by Yale University Press.

One should not, however, conclude from these academic achievements that young Shannon was a bookish recluse. On the contrary, his outgoing personality, natural friendliness, and geniality won as much applause as his intellectual prowess. In high school he was commander of the crack drill squad of cadets. In college he was a superb debater on a team that competed successfully all over Minnesota and beyond. As a senior the St. Thomas student body elected him "Mr. Tommy," an award made annually to the man who best embodied the qualities held in special esteem at the college. And now, fifteen years later, he was leader of all the Tommies.

Thanks, that is, to William O. Brady's decisiveness. A man of some culture and of much pragmatic sense, the new archbishop saw clearly enough that Vincent Flynn had put together a viable institution of higher learning where only a glorified junior college had existed before. Therefore he had every reason to tap James Shannon, a person who appeared to have all the required credentials, to carry the work forward. Easier to do in those days, to be sure, when the clerical boss could act as he pleased without any interference. Yet there remained an element of risk-taking for which Brady perhaps does not receive all the credit he deserves. He knew nothing about the tertiary education of the laity, and so in this instance his reputation as a leader he placed in the hands of a charming youngster. Well, it could not have worked out better for him or for St. Thomas.

I considered it a great honor then, and I still do, to have been a member of the faculty of the College of St. Thomas from 1958 till 1972. I was blessed, first of all, by the fraternity of historians I joined. Father (later Monsignor) Nicholas Moelter — native, interestingly enough, of Wanda — who had grown old graciously probing the insights of Thucydides and Tacitus; suave and facile George Martin, who never faltered as he traced the intricate doings of the European Great Powers; and J. Hermann Shauinger, a small man with a large vision, sardonic sometimes, straightforward always, tireless chronicler of the pioneer days of American Catholicism. And Robert Fogerty, tall and lean and bow-tied, who knew everything there was to know about American politics, the ideal teacher and administrator, devoted to his students and his colleagues and totally committed to the well-being of the college, beautifully courteous, utterly selfless. They welcomed me with such warmth that it brings tears to my eyes just to look back upon it.

More broadly, almost from the moment I first set foot on the campus I realized I was joining a most distinguished company. What Father Flynn had nurtured into being and Father Shannon had endowed with his unique species of inspiration — yes, that is the correct word — was a group of dedicated teachers who manifested deep learning across the whole spectrum of the arts and sciences. Nor should the word "dedicated" used here be taken lightly. I worked with these men every day — and with the one woman among them, the delightful Ann Hoverson, Professor of English — drank coffee with them, shared jokes and bits of gossip, and exchanged ideas with them, some trivial, some substantial, and so witnessed how strong was their commitment to their profession and to the students whose intellectual needs they pledged to treat.

I have no doubt that many of my faculty colleagues believed they were responding to a call, a vocation — a semi-religious experience which prepared them to accept less compensation and fewer research opportunities than those offered elsewhere, freeing them to teach at an institution like St. Thomas. Certainly this was the case with Robert Fogerty. "Vocation" appears to have a Catholic ring to it, but not necessarily so. Martin Allen, the eminent chemist whom the most prestigious universities in the country would have recruited in a heartbeat, chose instead to take the noble task in hand at this little Midwestern Catholic college; Professor Allen was Jewish. Here was a group of genuine professionals, defined by the work they did. And it was of no small significance how well they got on with each other: hard scientists chatting with litterateurs, mathematicians with psychologists, each of them, whatever his discipline, treating his confrere with respect. This reality manifested itself in different ways, not least in a vibrant social life. Faculty parties, and there were plenty of them, besides being pleasurable occasions, served to strengthen collegial bonds. Incidentally, if there existed within the faculty tension between cleric and layman, I did not feel it.

Over the next decade an orgy of construction completely changed the aspect of the campus. The makeshift temporary structures which had served during the war were swept away, and a sparkling set of up-to-date academic facilities sprang up, most notably a magnificent new library. The library was the gift of St. Thomas's chief benefactor, the alumnus oilman I. A. O'Shaughnessy, whose generosity in support of various of the college's endeavors remained a constant feature of these and succeeding years. Other donors came forward too, increasingly so, all of them impressed by President Shannon's determination to render permanent the Flynn intellectual achievement by putting the college on a firm financial footing, something never yet achieved in its history. In 1962 — I remember it well — he mounted, in cooperation with the Ford Foundation, St. Thomas's first ever capital campaign. "A Program for Great Teaching" it was appropriately called, and its remarkable success was due in no small measure to Shannon's own personal charisma, which had a glamor all its own. The objectives of the campaign, as publicly stated, had been improvement of faculty salaries and expanded support of student scholarships. Little wonder glasses were raised around campus in affectionate salute to Lord Jim.

Chapter Ten
"A Little Wine at Christmas"

I don't believe anybody at the time could have commented helpfully on the impact the 'sixties had on our culture or, indeed, on our inner selves. It remains hard to do even now, fifty years after the fact. At the beginning of the decade my concerns were pretty narrowly focused: I wanted to establish myself as a worthwhile and productive member of the faculty of the College of St. Thomas. Before that could be done, however, one last bit of drama had to be played out on the Notre Dame stage. "Defense of Dissertation" was one of those academic formalities that possessed little intrinsic significance and yet was included as a requirement for the doctoral degree. So in the spring of 1959 I made my way to South Bend and in accord with the schedule given me by the graduate school took my seat along with several senior professors in one of the bland classrooms of O'Shaughnessy Hall. Clearly, even spectacularly, present was my mentor, Philip Hughes, carefully garbed in all his monsignorial splendor, including purple socks peeking out between the sandal straps and a purple pompom fixed to the top of his biretta.

There was some desultory discussion of my work on Thomas Stapleton, a few questions directed at me about sources and methodology, none of them particularly searching and yet certainly not hostile. One official reader complained mildly at the large number of typos in the text of the dissertation. Then Father Hughes rose to his feet. I am the last person, he said (I paraphrase), who should have been chosen to direct Father O'Connell's thesis. Because, you see, and he looked down at his colleagues — I never received a "Ph.D." — P-h-D, these three letters he drew out at length, smilingly but also with a hint of mockery. When I finished my first book, he continued, I sent a copy to the authorities at Louvain, expecting to receive my "Ph.D." by return of post. But it didn't happen. So I sent off the next book as well. Once again, no result. By then I had come to realize that no matter what I wrote it was not my lot to have those three letters pasted after my name. I had no choice therefore — and he raised an index finger over the assembled professors, all of whom were of course Ph.D.s and all of whom had posted publication records far inferior to his — but to let my books speak for themselves. With that a wide grin lit up his face. He winked at me and sat down.

I remember nothing more of that somewhat bizarre performance or indeed any other detail of that strange day. It was quite uncharacteristic of Philip Hughes to embarrass his faculty colleagues, so I have to conclude that this disdainful if playful dismissal of the conventional academic rankings was a message not to them but to me on this our last formal engagement together. Put first things first, he was telling me, an admonition I have striven hard always to abide by, though with no more than limited success. At any rate in early June 1959, I was awarded my degree and became a genuine Ph.D. Over succeeding years I have directed the endeavors of others who as a result have been likewise endowed with that title. There is nothing essentially wrong with the system. But, even so, Philip was right: it's the quality of the work that in the last analysis really matters.

In my case there is a sad addendum to record. In a perverted sense of duty I did not go to Notre Dame for the graduation ceremony in 1959 and so received my degree *in absentia*. Instead, on that weekend I served as ordained helper in a parish assigned me by the chancery in St. Paul. I don't even remember which parish, an indication of how unimportant my participation really was. My father, only fifty-five years old, died of a heart attack a few months later, and I have ever since bitterly put these two events together. Richard Clarence O'Connell was the finest man I ever knew, one whom the Evangelist might have had in mind when he invoked "the just man." My admiration for him knew no bounds. No O'Connell of his generation had attended college, much less graduate school. He would have relished much the pomp and circumstance of a Notre Dame commencement and the accompanying elevation of his son to the higher realms of academe. I deprived him of that. Mea culpa.

I remember when mother and I learned that Dad had died we were standing on the front porch of our little house on 2nd Avenue South and 47th Street in Minneapolis. My prayer then was simple and direct: don't, dear Lord, let me predecease this wounded woman. That prayer was honored, but the widowhood for Anna Mae Kelly O'Connell lasted a daunting thirty-three years, as long a time indeed as Jesus lived among us. It was hard; she and my Dad had been all in all to each other, coworkers and lovers and pals. You should have seen them on the dance floor or at the bridge table. I did what I could to sustain her, but I know I should have done more — the dark dreams I have of her even now testify to that. But one memory stands out among all the others. Six months or so after Dad died an in-law, no doubt with the best of intentions, said to her, "Anna Mae, I'm sure you've adjusted to Dick's death or you soon will." I can still see my mother clench her little fists as she replied: *"I don't want to adjust."* And in some respects, I'm proud to say, she never did.

There is an oft-told story to the effect that a father who wanted his child to learn to swim simply tossed him into high water and told him to get himself out as best he could. Now I've never actually encountered a parent who employed this strategy, and I suspect you haven't either. Still, moralistic bromide as it may be, it has its metaphorical uses. I felt hefty waves pressing upon me as I began my teaching career at the College of St. Thomas, spring semester, 1959, and I learned quickly that the only way to escape their force was to do the job at hand day by day. I was assigned four courses (and three preparations) to be taught in three fifty-minute lecture classes per week, on a Monday-Wednesday-Friday or a Tuesday-Thursday-Saturday sequence. (Ah yes, Saturdays were not free in those antediluvian days.) Though some more or less cosmetic changes were introduced now and then — for instance, a lessening for one reason or another in the number of courses taught by an individual professor — this structure remained basically the same throughout my years at St. Thomas and, later, at Notre Dame. It followed the conventional description of courses as either lower or upper division, which allegedly reflected differences in the difficulty of the material to be studied and the maturity and sophistication of the student involved.

The fields for which I was made responsible included the ancient and medieval sections of the Western Civilization survey — the modern period was treated by Professor Martin. Back then "Western Civ" was the old war horse which undergirded every collegiate history program everywhere. Not so anymore, now that serious if often cynical questions are raised as to whether the West ever was really civilized. I was expected as well to ease myself into the courses on classical Greece and Rome taught by Father Moelter, who would retire in the not too distant future. Tudor and Stuart England were mine from the beginning, as was the Renaissance and Reformation. In later years I experimented with a course in seventeenth-century France — *le grand siècle* — and, just once, with a simple man's inquiry into Europe's economic past. My intention in this last, if memory serves, was to persuade the students that Marx was by no means unique in positing economic phenomena — getting and spending — as fundamental in understanding the structures of society.

"Methodology" is too fancy a term to describe my performance in the classroom. I simply gloried in constructing an attractive verbal framework for the material at hand to present to my bright young audience. I enjoyed lecturing, and indeed I have come to believe that there must be something of the vaudeville stand-up comic or else a secret desire to play Hamlet in every successful collegiate teacher. Except for maps, always important to me, I remained impatient of most visual aids. Nor did I much care for ordinary textbooks. In effect I made myself the textbook, assigning to the students in the Western Civ sections collateral readings from literary sources like *The Iliad, The Gallic Wars, The Prince,* and *The Canterbury Tales.* To make this system work in the days before lap-top computers I had to insist that the students take detailed written notes of what I said in class. This I justified by invoking a kind of pseudo-Aristotelian explanation: one learns by putting to use the physical senses, and in writing down lecture notes one employs hearing, sight, and touch, all combined to permit the mind to capture the essence of what one is investigating. So "Write it down!" was my constant directive, not always gently delivered. (Even long afterward, former students would greet me by using that phrase along with a meaningful sarcastic grin.)

Looking back now over so many years and so many courses taught, I believe that overall my approach worked. That there was a good deal of hubris in it I can't deny. I recall how one Notre Dame student's anonymous reaction, expressed in an evaluation form, probably spoke for others less articulate: "His Eminence O'Connell comes down from Mount Olympus several times a week to share his thoughts with us groundlings." And yet, despite such caviling, most students left my courses ready to acknowledge that they had learned a great deal from them. I believe this positive and, admittedly, self-serving conclusion had much to do with the fact that for the most part I did not bore them, that the lectures I gave were interesting and not unrelated to matters of perennial importance. I made a point of assuring them that I welcomed comment and questions, that indeed even for the shyest person there was no such thing as a foolish question. I never went into a class unprepared. If I insisted on the students taking notes, I had already put down notes of my own on the subject to be discussed. Yet I seldom consulted them because I never sat down; rather as I spoke, I nervously moved around the room, creating emphasis by grabbing one student's shoulder here and another's there — a practice that in these jaded times probably would have got me into serious trouble.

But in one area my method failed. Not only might I have made better use of relevant textbooks in my courses or have incorporated into them more skillfully the outside readings. In a more general sense I did not teach my students how to think. This was always stated as an objective — perhaps the chief objective — of a university education, and it was one to which in the abstract I heartily subscribed, and yet somehow, I never quite understood how to attain it in the real world. One problem was that my students, good kids as they were, nonetheless found it hard to accept that there was any meaningful reality across the universe prior to their own births. I never learned how to counter this self-centered prejudice, this profound ignorance. World War II was as remote to them as the Peloponnesian War. I guess I did my best by proposing some historical conundrums in hopes that they might ignite a flicker of interest in the world outside themselves. How did the populist Roman Republic evolve into the dictatorial Roman Empire? How did Muslim aggression in the Mediterranean lead to the European Dark Ages? How significant to the artistic Renaissance was the monetary success of the Medici Bank?

By and large these ploys seemed to work. I enjoyed going at length into the legal intricacies of Henry VIII's divorce from Catherine of Aragon, and the students appeared to enjoy it too. And even more fetching was a detailed inquiry into Martin Luther's description of the process of justification by faith alone. Human beings, proclaimed the Sage of Wittenberg, are utterly and hopelessly depraved because of original sin and all the sins that have followed. Because of this state they are incapable of performing any good work. Every breath they take is a mortal sin, as one extreme expression put it. They can escape perdition only by a solemn act of faith, which means, using contemporary parlance, the acceptance of Christ as their personal savior. There is as a result of this commitment no essential change in them; they remain just as deeply sunk in corruption as before. But God in his mercy now sees them wrapped, as it were, in the glorious merits of his Son, which have been "imputed" to them as the fruit of their belief. I had a student years ago — how many I don't remember, nor do I remember his name — who I have no reason to believe was particularly outstanding. Even so, I've never forgotten how in answering an exam question he tersely summed up in ten words the contradiction that lies at the heart of Lutheran salvation theology. "It amounts to this," he wrote. "I'm not okay. And you're not okay. But that's okay."

Junior priests on the St. Thomas faculty took it for granted that their contribution to the well-being of the college — its "living endowment" as President Shannon liked to call it — extended well beyond the classroom. Of particular importance was their contribution to the maintenance of order on the campus. A large proportion of the 2000 or so students came from the Twin Cities metropolitan area, and most of these men presumably continued to live in their family homes and commuted to school. But by 1959 recruitment from the rest of Minnesota and nearby Wisconsin, and even from sites as far away as Chicago and Detroit, had begun to swell that number significantly. The attractiveness of St. Thomas stemmed from its modest size, from its growing positive reputation under the Flynn/Shannon regime, and, for parents at least, from its Catholic character. Whatever their reason for coming to college in St. Paul, housing obviously had to be provided for these young people.

Ireland Hall, built in 1918, had long served as the primary student dormitory on campus, as well as providing rooms for some of the senior priests. Several temporary structures had gone up during the war; some of which survived to serve as dorms, like "A Barracks" and "B Barracks." These left much to be desired; I spent my first semester at St. Thomas presiding in B Barracks, whose fragile wooden walls could not keep out the cruel north wind nor provide any kind of privacy for the inhabitants. But shortly after my arrival on campus such inadequate facilities were swept away when the handsome new four-story dormitory, Dowling Hall, was opened for the fall semester, 1960. For the next six years it was my job, with the help of a student assistant, to maintain order among the ninety freshmen who lived on Dowling's fourth floor.

Looking back on it now, my experience as prefect, a short step from being an all-absorbing task, was a wearisome one, and the telling of it in any detail would be tedious in the extreme. Let me say only that living with and taking responsibility for a bunch of restless adolescent males twenty-four hours a day, seven days a week, created a burden heavier than one should have been asked to assume. Especially, it seems to me, when these boys, emotionally ambivalent in their struggle to find a safe passage to manhood, were not one's own. Of course, in those days we paid more than nominal attention to the principle that people in positions like mine were acting *in loco parentis.* I think that policy as it directly affected the boarding students under my charge worked out positively in most instances, though by no means in all.

This is not to say that I and the parents of my freshmen were always on the same wavelength. *Au contraire.* I recall one not untypical case. At the beginning of the school year I interviewed the parents of each student assigned to fourth floor Dowling in order to explain to them the rules under which their son would be living. Not particularly onerous rules for the most part, except one. Please, before you go home, I said to the couple from Cicero, Illinois, please make it clear to Johnny that while he is here, he must abstain from all alcoholic beverages; otherwise he will find himself in serious trouble with the college and with the state of Minnesota. As I spoke, I assumed as stern a demeanor as possible. Even so, I could see that only the courtesy a good Catholic accorded a priest kept Johnny's father from interrupting me. When I paused to take a breath, he said: "Father, this won't be a problem. There'll be no trouble with Johnny on this score. You see, he doesn't really have time for drinking. You know, sports and other stuff. And besides, he doesn't like the taste of alcohol. No, for Johnny drinking only means a little wine at Christmas."

All in all, they were good years. Exceedingly busy, to be sure, and made even more so by added duties outside the St. Thomas campus, the most absorbing of which were the parochial assignments to be discussed below. For the most part I found the students I taught and those I prefected bright and responsive. The best of them were on a par with the best at Notre Dame. Of course they suffered from the sexual uncertainties common to men of their age, and, despite the denials of Johnny's father, they had in fact come to college to learn, among other things, how to drink. It is hard to exaggerate the satisfaction I felt — like, I dare say, all professors do — in watching the callow freshmen evolve into self-confident adults by the day of their graduation.

John Ireland in his heyday liked to assert that he had founded St. Thomas for the clergy of the archdiocese of St. Paul. In 1960 the number of priests serving on the faculty or in the college's administration was still significant, though it would decline sharply over succeeding years. The powerful personality and leadership skills of James Shannon were pervasive, though they did not win over everybody. For instance, big and burly Father Robert Wittman, the tough-talking registrar, appeared to feel that friendliness toward Flynn's successor would somehow be a black mark against Flynn himself: he dismissed Shannon with the scornful tag line "the little man." A few others of the holdovers may have agreed with him, but if so, they expressed their views *sotto voce*. Wittman's dislike extended to the dean of the college, William O'Donnell ("Okie"), and to everybody in the philosophy department. But Bob Wittman was shortly shipped off to a parish, long before his resentments could attain deep roots within the college. From the beginning he was a first-rate pastor, and so the separation proved to be a positive development all-round.

Among the philosophers Wittman didn't like were Father (later Monsignor) Henri DuLac and Father James Stromberg. Both of them were, like Ralph McInerny, products of Laval University in Quebec and representative of the uncompromising Thomism of Charles DeKonnick. Professionally they assumed around St. Thomas an almost haughty air of intellectual self-satisfaction, which may explain why Father Wittman and not a few others found them uncongenial. I too sensed this lavaliere hubris in them, but since I mostly agreed with their conclusions — to the degree that I understood them — it didn't bother me particularly. Besides, they were my friends.

Henri was a tall, handsome man, ten years or so my senior, whose whole being exuded elegance. Elegant to be sure as a thinker, confident in its capacity to unravel most intellectual problems, and especially the nature of a liberal arts education. This subject he made his specialty, and so he smilingly told his St. Thomas colleagues, much to the annoyance of many, what and how they should be teaching their students. But the elegance manifested itself in lesser realms as well. I was fortunate indeed to have traveled with him in later years across Britain and France, where he appeared to have cultivated lasting relationships with Michelin-starred restaurants. He took me to my first opera *(Le Nozze di Figaro)*. In London he joined me one unforgettable evening at a stunning production of Euripides' *Medea,* starring Diana Rigg.

Jim Stromberg, a year older than me, was very different, and yet the same. The same as Henri DuLac in his dedication to and knowledge of the works of St. Thomas Aquinas and in his readiness to defend them. The combative Charles DeKonnick was more a working model to him than a hero on a pedestal. Indeed, if anything, Stromberg was I believe the smartest person I ever knew. Always courteous in debate, he nevertheless had the soul of an assassin. But he was different too, in that he assumed a quieter, friendlier manner. He was a sporting man in a way that Father DuLac never was; for years I played golf with him and regularly lost (a dime a hole in the old days, we were both poor), even though he stood hardly half my size.

Jim had a seriousness about his priestly vocation that truly put to shame superficial folks like me. On the eve of his ordination in 1955 he was struck by that cruelest of spiritual afflictions, scrupulosity. I am not worthy of the sacrament, he said in effect, not worthy to have the consecrating hands placed on me. So he stepped aside as his classmates gathered in the sanctuary of the cathedral. The eccentric Archbishop Murray, whom you have already met in these pages, made it clear that he would never ordain Stromberg, even if the young man's doubts receded. But Murray died (October 1956) and Brady, his successor, felt no such compunction. So James Stromberg, having fought off the dark shadows, became, better late than never, one of the great priests of his generation.

The other priests in residence at St. Thomas were a diverse and intriguing group. The academic dean, "Okie" O'Donnell, had not been blessed with eloquence, but he guarded the college's budget, and so its very existence, with the fury of Cerberus; he also beat both me and Stromberg on the golf course, even in his last days when his sight was so bad that before a shot he needed his companions to point him in the correct direction. Richard Schuler was the brilliant professor of music and, despite a singularly ugly singing voice, the consummate organizer of choirs and chorales. Robert

Vashro, the dean of discipline, when he presided at college dances, was famous for loudly directing couples "to keep sufficient space between them," though in real emergencies he was mostly bluster. The linguist Walter Peters, who years before had taught me Latin at Nazareth Hall, still nursed a sore psyche given to his many ups and downs; it was not unknown for him to mutter at the breakfast table, only half in jest, "I have suicidal tendencies today." And most notable of all, James Lavin, the spiritual director of the whole St. Thomas community, the students' friend whether in the confessional, or with supplying sandwiches each evening on the third floor of Ireland Hall, or with the provision of tanks of coffee at Union Depot to greet students returning to school probably the worse for wear because of holiday drinking. "Scooter" they nicknamed him, admiringly and lovingly. He was always on the go.

Chapter Eleven
"A Clap of Thunder from a Cloudless Sky"

I wish the phrase in the chapter title just entered were of my invention, but it is not, and so I have enclosed it in inverted commas. I wish it were mine, because it states so succinctly my wonderment as to what had happened to us American Catholic priests during the 1960s. I am a verbal sort of person, and I need to find the words that express satisfactorily what is pressing on my mind; thus it is always important for me to choose an adequate metaphor. My search for this term's source has not been very fruitful; it has been mysteriously put to a literary use by a New Zealand rock band called Knightshade, which appears to have been inspired by a semi-fictional account of Jesus and his relatives, *The Gospel of the Long Walk* (2012). Take my word for it, inquiry in these directions does not result in enlightenment about loud noises out of the blue. I certainly have no desire to quarrel with the rock 'n' roll-culture, nor with attempts to render the person of Jesus more sympathetic to today's young people. At the same time, however, I'm too old, I'm afraid, to jettison the categories of thought and judgment which I have employed all my life. Nor am I slow to make public my biases. So let me testify to my traditional way of looking at things, and, as an instance of said settled tradition, say it straight out, politically incorrect as it may be: Shakespeare is the greatest poet who ever lived, Mozart the greatest musician. Dead white guys who have never been bettered or even equaled.

"A Clap of Thunder" suggests, does it not, a sudden intrusion into the ordinary course of events, and not a positive one. And unexpected as well, since thunder ordinarily rolls out of visible banks of deeply dark clouds, punctuated by stabs of fierce lightning bolts. To find such phenomena issuing out of "a Cloudless Sky" smacks of self-contradiction, which may be why the phrase intrigued me as it did. What happened among the presbyterate (to use the rather fancy but technically accurate word) during the 1960s was for me a sudden and negative intrusion, totally unexpected, like thunder out of a cloudless sky. Naive I may have been, and maybe my basic problem was that I had emerged out of the 1950s, that bland era of Eisenhower and Pius XII, when all problems seemed to admit of commonsensical solution. Change may indeed occur, I thought to myself, but life, after all, always goes on pretty much the same, generation after generation, and one trims one's sails in accord with the velocity and direction of the winds. But one does not respond by immediately abandoning ship.

Why were so many priests so unhappy that they found it right and necessary to break ranks? Many friends of mine of long years' standing simply turned their backs on what they had painstakingly prepared for and had aspired to be since childhood. Had they expected a rose garden? Did the clerical culture fail them or they it? How was it they concluded so soon that they were not bound by a permanent commitment? This to me was the crucial question, because in fact I did believe in moral permanence. How often and how seriously I may have failed to honor my ordination commitment, I could never quite convince myself I was free to set it entirely aside.

Even so, "simply" as used above is clearly the wrong word. To reach decisions of such import had to have involved a wrenching of the soul and a prolonged, piercingly painful self- examination. A step of complexity in the severest sense of the word. So eighteen of us were ordained for the Archdiocese of St. Paul in June 1956; within a relatively brief time eight of us had repudiated that formal call to ecclesiastical service. Similar percentages prevailed in classes chronologically contiguous to ours. Moreover, the St. Paul Seminary in those days had offered training for students in dioceses across the Midwest, and so I soon learned, to my sorrow and confusion, that other men dear to me, like Jasper de Maria in Kansas City, Missouri, and Joe Browne in Covington, Kentucky, had also gone home and declared that in effect they really didn't really want to be priests. It is a long time since I tried to judge these cases as though they all followed the same pattern. I now understand that every instance of departure from the priesthood back then possessed its own profoundly mysterious texture. The rush from celibacy, for instance, can explain what happened only up to a point. Better perhaps to set aside the abstractions. There was only one case in which I was genuinely familiar and involved. In 1960 Helen fell in love with Jim McDonell, and he loved her back. At least for a while.

Let me try to tell you about it.

"Have Gun, Will Travel" was the title of a television western popular during the late 'fifties and early 'sixties. It starred Richard Boone as a sophisticated gunman who put those words on his business card, indicating his willingness to use his violent skills, at a price, in behalf of clients whoever and wherever they might be. We young St. Thomas priests joked among ourselves that we could reasonably assume a similar emblem of identification: "Have Chalice, Will Travel." As you may remember, Archbishop Brady welcomed me back home not for my academic credentials but for my availability to serve weekends in a parish. So each Friday I could expect a phone call from the chancery informing me where I would be expected to report the next evening.

The principle guiding this policy was that we weekenders should help the resident priests do what they could not do by themselves. So the normal schedule was pretty much what I had followed in New Buffalo, that we should hear confessions on Saturday night and celebrate two Masses on Sunday morning. (At that time there was as yet no anticipatory Mass on Saturday or any permitted after noon on Sunday.) The reasons advanced for this intervention were predictable; illness of the pastor or advanced age or unavoidable absence or simply the size of the parish. For the most part the relationship between residents and their weekend helpers was honorable and straightforward — we were, after all, spiritual brothers. Alas, however, there were exceptions. One parish to which I was assigned had a very old church equipped with only a single confessional box. The pastor put me there on Saturday evening and announced that he would hear penitents in the sacristy. If I finished after he did, he added smoothly, would I please turn out the lights. Well, after nearly two hours, when I did emerge stiffly from the box, he was gone. During the ensuing week a little research among the brethren revealed that this pastor regularly indulged in a high-stakes poker game on Saturday evenings. I went back to his parish the next weekend as assigned, but, a small gesture of vengeance, this time I did not turn out the lights when I left.

All bureaucracies, I suppose, tend to seek out simplicity of procedure. As the years passed, the chancery officials drew up a list of more or less permanent weekend assignments, so the older the priest-professor, the less likely he was to be shifted each Friday from pillar to post. No doubt this development was adopted primarily because it meant less trouble for the chancery staff, but also, I assure you, its regularity made it most welcome to us. So as a result of this policy I did Saturday/Sunday duty in two parishes over my twelve years at St. Thomas. They proved to be different in many respects, but they both played out within the unprecedented ecclesiastical tumult of the 'sixties.

St. Elizabeth's had been founded during the 1880s by German immigrants, but by the time I went there in 1960 it had long since lost its national character and had lost as well the aura of sober middle-class respectability that it had cultivated in its earlier days. The church at that date and the rectory next door, built of faded yellow brick, stood forlornly amid a jumble of small repair shops and cut-rate food stores, many of them now closed and boarded up, along a trail of weedy vacant lots that marked the eastern edge of downtown Minneapolis The parish school had been empty for many years, but the rather ragged neighborhood children of various ethnic backgrounds were often seen playing some game or other in the large, untidy parking lot. St. Elizabeth's was responsible for sacramental service at the Hennepin County General Hospital and the Juvenile Detention Center nearby. Less formally some Catholics could be discerned in the long queues before the confessionals on the days immediately before Christmas and Easter, apparently preferring to be shriven by priests different from those in their home parishes. I recall at any rate how busy we were during those pre-festive weeks.

The pastor of St. Elizabeth's was Father Joseph Schabert, whom I had never met. But I had learned he was a living legend among the old-timers at St. Thomas, because he had virtually single-handedly held the college together during the dark days of the 'twenties and 'thirties, when even basic accreditation was under constant threat. As professor of philosophy — nobody defined that discipline as broadly as did Schabert — and as simultaneously dean of the college, he kept the wolf from the door, so to speak, by the quite incredible workload and leadership role he imposed upon himself and upon the academic environment. As for this legendary status alluded to above, perhaps the poet should be more carefully invoked: "A legend living and partly living." Because increasingly as the pressures, the exhaustions, the uncertainties bore him down, he turned for relief to alcohol, until drink became for him an all-consuming necessity. So now he had been relegated to the pastorate of a slum parish and, at the college he had served so unstintingly, reduced to a half-remembered token of past hard times. Over the four years I spent weekends with Father Schabert I heard him refer to the unhappy past only once. They wouldn't let me be president of St. Thomas, he said, because I wasn't Irish.

The vigor that had marked him before was pretty much gone. He walked with a halting step and spent a good part of the day in his room on the second floor of the rectory. But he was a sweet man all the same, kindly and courteous to everyone. He took delight in small gestures on behalf of his mostly poor parishioners, like the dimes he distributed to their children when they came to the door for tricks or treats on Hallowe'en. I remember the sermon he preached at Mass for the feast of the Epiphany in which he described the mystery of the star of Bethlehem and the wise men following it in terms of the distinction between solar and sidereal time. The congregation, including a scattering of working girls spiritually spruced up for the Christmas season, listened with rapt attention; not because they could follow his explanation or really cared about it, but because this good old man, once a famous professor, deigned to talk to them so seriously.

One might like to think that the powers that were in the archdiocesan chancery sent Father Schabert an assistant because of the good work he had done at St. Thomas in his younger days. Alas, however, chancery officials seldom entertained sentiments of this kind or considered people outside their own ambit worthy of special regard. In this instance, looking over their lists of personnel, they judged correctly that St. Elizabeth's, though long past its prime, could not be left solely in the hands of a semi-alcoholic. So when I reported for weekend duty there in 1960 the direction of the parish for all practical purposes was in the hands of the assistant pastor, Father James McDonell.

Nothing could have suited me better. Mac — as we always called him — had been my classmate through twelve years of the minor and major seminaries, and over all that time one of my closest friends. From the midway district in St. Paul, he was a broad shouldered five feet ten, a tough and dedicated hockey player who dabbled in the other sports and who, though by no means inarticulate, was never one to hurry into controversy. He took on the ordinary obligations of parochial administration with ease. He accorded Father Schabert affection and due respect, and among his less than socially significant parishioners he was immensely popular. As a theological student Mac had been able but not brilliant, and he tended to find intellectual solace in a more or less amateur inquiry into the psychological sciences. For instance, once at St. Elizabeth's, in his ministry to the morally compromised youths at the local Detention Center, he tried to find solutions by employing admittedly controversial testing procedures, like the famous Minnesota Multiphasic Personality Inventory.

In many respects the St. Elizabeth rectory was an odd place. Nominally presided over by an elderly priest scarcely *compos mentis,* it attracted a variety of people who in one way or another wanted to give their help to the struggling parish and its people, and so, at the same time, to find a deeper meaning for their own lives. A noble intent indeed, but as I soon discovered, many members of this menagerie were also drawn to the place by the charisma of the assistant pastor. There was, for instance, Louise (whose surname I have long since forgotten), an unmarried lady of middle years, a volunteer in the sad little parish choir, who made a point of always wearing some piece of clothing colored purple. "Oh," she said to me once with a kind of eucharistic solemnity, "if only I could take him [McDonell] in my arms. I would smother him so that he became one with me and I with him." There were other groupies, perhaps not so extreme as Louise but who, I believe, indulged in similar fantasies. Most of them were women but a dour young man also became a permanent fixture within this collection of eccentrics; in my mind's eye I can still see his tall lanky frame stretched out on a chair set up near the rectory's front door. He died years later of AIDS.

Helen was the housekeeper at the St. Elizabeth rectory. Recently divorced, she was mother to two (or was it three?) young daughters. She looked to me to be in her middle thirties (and so five or six years older than Mac or me), a slender, dark haired, finely featured woman, somewhat faded now, it was easy to conclude, by the vicissitudes time had imposed upon her. She made no apparent effort to enhance her appearance; she wore little if any makeup, and her clothing was pretty much off-the-rack house dresses and slacks and blouses of no particular style. Her demeanor was reserved, her voice soft, her smile warm. Household responsibilities at St. Elizabeth's were not pressing, but what there were she took charge of with no fuss. Intuitively, it seemed, she came to understand Father Schabert's unique situation, and she treated the old man kindly. I never knew what level of education she had attained, but I noticed that she always had a book close at hand. She lived with her children in a rickety upstairs apartment a couple of blocks from the rectory.

Her conversion to Catholicism, Helen shyly but firmly protested, was the most important event in her life. Of course there are all kinds of conversions, one not necessarily superior to another. In this case on offer was an introduction to an entirely different and hence unfamiliar mode of living that held a promise of purification and renewal from the contentions that had led to the break-up of her little family. Helen embraced it, and as a result she became a deeply spiritual and prayerful person, to whom domestic service at a poor and unconventional parish like St. Elizabeth's seemed a special touch of Providence. And along the way she fell in love with James McDonell, and he with her.

They were both exceptionally attractive people. I guess it was toward the end of 1963 when I realized they had arrived at a permanent — or, as it turned out, a semi-permanent — resolution to their problem. I was privy to much of the struggle they went through, which included Helen twice taking her daughters off to settle in far-off places, Phoenix first and then the Monterey Peninsula (Steinbeck's novels were fashionable reading in those days). But each time after a brief stay, she came back. For his part Mac sought and received a transfer to a parish in deeply middle-class south Minneapolis. Changes of venue, however, did not result in changes of mind or heart, nor did I believe then, and I do not today, that there was a scintilla of dishonor in either of them. Perhaps it was significant that Helen came from a non-Catholic tradition; there was nothing nunnish about her, no fragrance of the convent. But maybe that characteristic would have been more a come-on for me than for Mac. At any rate I knew the die had been cast when amid the chills of December I received among other yuletide gifts a charming stone letter-opener sculpted in an Amerindian style: "Love and Merry Christmas, from Jim and Helen."

In the spring of 1964, Macmillan, the publishing house, awarded me a modest grant in advance of royalty on the book I proposed to write on the history of the Oxford Movement. So came to early fruition the lengthy conversations about Newman that I had had with a convalescing Philip

Hughes six or seven years earlier. My first task was to set up an orderly plan to examine the primary sources that could put some flesh on the bones of the ideas I had been nurturing. To find such sources meant going to England, the England I had long dreamed about. It proved a wondrous summer for me, an adventure really. From the British Library on Great Russell Street in London to Keble College and Pusey House in Oxford to the Oratory in Birmingham: my search among heaps of printed pamphlets turned orange by age and dusty archives filled with reams of correspondence written precisely by the people I was interested in — the Victorians loved writing letters and preserving those they received — had pretty much established the direction and the basic outlines of my study.

When I returned home in September 1964 and to my ordinary duties at St. Thomas College, the archdiocesan chancery appointed me weekend assistant at St. Therese Parish in St. Paul's Highland Park district. The small handsome church stood on a knoll overlooking the confluence of the Minnesota and Mississippi Rivers, with the collection of buildings that made up the historic Fort Snelling visible just across the water. Next to the church was an unpretentious house that served as a rectory, and behind it a relatively new convent which housed the five or six Sisters of St. Joseph who taught in the parochial school across the street. With its congregation of middle and upper-middle class professional people — many of whom had built homes in the area to make sure that their children would have a Catholic school to attend — the parish manifested, as I look back now, an almost perfect representation of the calm self-satisfaction of the 1950s. No more the gritty St. Elizabeth's for me.

And no more either for Mac McDonell and his vocational crisis. I never saw him again, never talked to him even. My memory is blank — and my conscience silent — as to how I could have set aside so readily this friend of my youth with whose prior troubles I had tried to sympathize, even to the point perhaps of imprudence. It may be because I was simply weary of the long imbroglio. Or it is possible that I did not renew contact because I never got a chance to do so; Mac died very young, shortly after my return from England, victim of some weirdly unfamiliar cancer. More likely, I was angry with him that while I was abroad, he had formally declared his "resignation" from the priesthood, a burning of boats that I deemed childishly arrogant. (It seemed that every morning in those days — I exaggerate of course — one or another of my brethren was baring his troubled soul and his need for solace in the larger world to a reporter for the *Minneapolis Tribune.*) But down deep, odd as it may appear, I believe an overriding reason for my detachment from him was a certain disappointment with Mac the romantic. I learned in due time that he had indeed married, but when I heard the name of the bride, I did not recognize it. She was a woman Mac had been counseling, I was told (counseling about what it would be intriguing to know), and Helen, presumably, was no longer the love of his life. I saw Helen only once more after that, a couple of years later at a sad little testimonial for Father Schabert. She and I shared a tearless hug, and then she was gone.

Chapter Twelve
"Quod Scripsi, Scripsi"

Sixty years ago, when I was corresponding with Yale University Press about the publication of my *Stapleton*, one of the parcels of mail from New Haven included a single-page cartoon drawn in starkly black charcoal. It depicted a large desk whose surface was bare save for a name plate labeled EDITOR and a thick stack of papers tucked neatly in a manila folder. On one side of the desk sits a little troll-like figure of undetermined age and gender, wrapped in a dark cloak. Positioned opposite is a youngish man who sports a mop of untidy hair and a scraggly Van Dyck. He looks with uneasy anticipation at the editor, who, with a hint of a smile playing on his thin lips, reaches over and with his right index finger pushes the folder and its contents gently toward him. "Sorry" says the editor to him tonelessly. "It's been done."

Here is the nightmare for anybody who has labored maybe for years over the research and composition of his Ph.D. dissertation, only to discover when he submits a literary form of it for publication—which he desperately needs if he is to have any hope of finding an academic job—that his subject is already old hat. "It's been done." This particular circumstance did not directly affect me, because however the significance of Thomas Stapleton's work might be judged, no one before me had bothered to do so. Besides, I had a *padrone* at Yale in the person of James Shannon, whose own research had resulted in a doctoral thesis turned into a prize- winning book the Press had published. And Shannon, once my teacher and now my boss as president of St. Thomas College, possessed the kind of persuasive charm much appreciated in Ivy League circles. I hasten to assure you that this is no more than a learned guess on my part; Father Shannon never said he had intervened with his friends in New Haven, nor did anyone else. Nevertheless, I remain convinced such was the case, because I believe that, to his credit, Shannon realized his first duty was not to me but to the building up of the prestige of his faculty. Don't forget the old saying: It ain't what you know, it's who you know.

So, though I was to spend a lifetime quarreling with editors, I had no need on this occasion to be troubled by that cynical caricature. *Thomas Stapleton and the Counter Reformation* was duly published by Yale in 1964, a small handsome volume with a scarlet dust jacket, 220 pages, costing six dollars. Nor was I quite finished with the sixteenth-century pride of New College, Oxford, even then. Later editions of *The Dictionary of the Christian Church* (1957) contained my brief notice of Stapleton, and to my delight I was invited to prepare a much expanded one for the prestigious 60-volume *Oxford Dictionary of National Biography* (2004). It was as though the forty-year circle had closed; one could hardly have hoped for a more satisfying *finis* to a professional career.

But that circle during my years at St. Thomas was in its alpha, not its omega, stage. I had so many things to learn: how best to teach college students, how best to discipline them without imposing on them requirements akin to those imposed upon me in the seminary. These young men were not candidates for the priesthood. It took me a while in practice to adjust to this obvious, though for me, elusive distinction. The cooperative character of the college faculty was new to me. Academic decisions were arrived at through the work of committees, which, while often tedious, was far more efficacious in the long run than ukases from above or individual initiative. Ready consultation, rooted in mutual respect, meant compromise and a willingness to accept at the end of negotiation less than one's own ideal objective. I must admit I found this methodology extremely difficult to accept; I knew I was a clever and articulate fellow, and so I expected my colleagues to agree with me on every matter of substance. And if they didn't my instinct was to throw up my hands in despair at their obtuseness. I recall stalking angrily out of one committee meeting, but my fellow members—a physicist and a mathematician—remained entirely unimpressed by my petulance, and, much abashed, I soon rejoined them round the conference table.

It would be wrong to conclude from this hasty description that all was sweetness and light at St. Thomas during my years there. But I do believe, looking back, that there were more ups than downs. One important factor was the college's modest size. Notre Dame when I went there in 1972 was markedly different, strictly committed to a larger agenda and so to a more complex series of human relationships. At St. Thomas we all knew one another. I have already noted the remarkably edifying dedication of the faculty to teaching, and this commitment extended across the disciplines. Combine this with relatively enlightened leadership and you have a recipe for genuine cooperation. Cooperation, I stress, in creating a liberal arts program. Teaching was what mattered. The first capital fund-drive launched by President Shannon had for its slogan "A Program for Great Teaching." Nobody at St. Thomas was pressured to publish.

Nobody except me.

Added to the need to accommodate my day-job, I had to figure out the proper way to be a part-time parish priest, as I tried to explain above. Another novel experience beyond the academic was the weekly sacrament of penance administered to women religious. I was not unaware of the cynical observation that hearing the confessions of nuns was like being nibbled to death by ducks. I don't remember whether I considered this *bon mot* particularly clever—I hope not. What I do know is that I had little chance to adopt a frivolous attitude, largely because of the successive assignments I was given. The first was to serve the retired Sisters of St. Joseph in their large convent in St. Paul, and the second brought me as confessor to the then-booming novitiate of the Josephites, a few doors down the same street. So for several years I encountered every seven days, in relationships both human and spiritual, either the ripe wisdom of the elderly or the enthusiasm and warm aspirations of the young. No ducks they! I came away from these moments of grace much wiser (and perhaps even better) than before.

But the chronology must be borne in mind. I am speaking here of the early and mid- 'sixties. The revolution was just around the corner, though nobody knew it then. What I described a moment ago as the "booming novitiate" of the Sisters of St. Joseph—by far the largest and most influential women's congregation in the Upper Midwest—with recruits falling over each other in their rush to gain admission, suddenly went in reverse; by the end of the decade the vast building that had housed them stood virtually empty. At the time nobody could explain the suddenness with which this and other challenges to the status quo occurred. Later many commentators pointed to the awakening within the Church occasioned by the Second

Vatican Council (1962–1965). But maybe, on a less grandiose level, it happened because the sisters had grown weary of bad jokes told at their expense. And maybe, more deeply, because their predecessors having ushered the immigrants into the American middle class, they decided that their potential as women and as religious could no longer be realized by simply instructing the immigrants' grandchildren on how to spell and on how to memorize the answers in the *Baltimore Catechism*. I recall that Archbishop Dowling, in his *ad limina* report to Rome during the middle 'twenties, observed that humanly speaking the Archdiocese of St. Paul could not survive without the work of women religious. Now here, the sisters began to say to one another thirty years later, here is a truth to ponder and a path to explore.

I must qualify a remark made above. St. Thomas, like every American four-year institution of higher learning, set down three criteria for its faculty to meet: meaningful publication, community service, and skilled teaching, which three served also as conditions for promotion. But like other small liberal arts colleges, St. Thomas was not particularly serious about the publication requirement. The large number and variety of courses taught—the normal load was four per semester—along with the preparation each of them needed, left limited time and energy for independent research. Sabbaticals were unheard of in those days, and the notion that the college should provide extra resources to support faculty research projects smacked of the fanciful. And it was taken for granted in this kind of institution that students should receive a full measure of a professor's direct attention. These circumstances did not mean that an original article, especially in the physical sciences, didn't turn up now and then in a learned journal. But such was not the faculty member's ordinary contribution to the common good. The only notable exception I recall was that of my friend and colleague J. Herman Schauinger, who wrote several excellent historical inquiries about Catholicism in early America. Most of these books, however, had been published years before he arrived at St. Thomas.

So, as I said above, no pressure on the members of the St. Thomas faculty to publish. "Except on me." I believe this to have been the case. The pressure, however, was not exerted on me from the outside; it issued from within myself. I find it very difficult to explain this phenomenon, mostly, I suppose, because I didn't understand it then and I don't now. I should say

115

from the first that the administration of the college did not discourage me, and that my colleagues by and large assumed a positive if somewhat bemused attitude toward what many of them considered to be my eccentricity. The members of my own department were especially accommodating; thus my chairman, the ever-gracious and generous Robert Fogerty, arranged the scheduling of my classes so that I should have several consecutive hours a day to devote to whatever subject I had taken on. The new I. A. O'Shaughnessy Library provided several small offices on the ground floor, and the librarian, Father Clyde Eddy—with whom I used to dine regularly at the old Criterion Restaurant, with its tank full of live lobsters in the lobby—set aside one carrel for my use. Here I settled in for a couple of hours most weekday mornings and turned my mind exclusively to the project of the moment.

Why did I do it? This pretty basic question has never really been answered. Certainly I did not make the mistake of considering my initiative a virtue. It was a compulsion, and I recognized it as such. And maybe as time went on, I discovered I could produce some reputable work, and it became second nature to do so. I did the research and the writing because I could. Which then suggests a further not unrelated question: how did I do it? That I can't answer either. All I can say is that Father Eddy, and later others similarly well-disposed, gave me the space and time. And the jobs got done, well more than a million words by the end of the long day. I recall the exhilaration I felt when I unpacked the box from Yale University Press containing the ten complimentary author's copies of *Stapleton*. Might I have thought then that, though as a committed celibate I would never have children, a host of books and articles and reviews issuing from my pen would guarantee that part of me would endure? In fact, no such romantic hokum ever crossed my mind.

Once settled into my routine at St. Thomas, Father Shannon put me to work doing some writing for him. Or should I say writing over his signature: pleading a shortage of time—quite legitimately, I'm sure—he asked me to cover several commitments he had made and prepare five or six statements appropriate as introductions to books or as oral presentations to be given to various groups, mostly civic. This was hardly a burdensome nor really a frequent request, and I was happy to take it on. And it does not mean to suggest that Shannon was a fluff-off who routinely passed along rhetorical obligations to subordinates. Quite to the contrary; if he received a common criticism it was that he talked too much, too often.

The president also gave me a more demanding assignment, and a more rewarding one, to prepare a booklet of fifty or so pages describing the interior decoration of the college chapel. Designed by the same distinguished French architect, Emanuel Masqueray, who had presided over the construction of the St. Paul Cathedral, the chapel had opened its doors in 1918. From that date, however, it remained relatively stark inside, provided with all the liturgical and sacramental necessities but with few embellishments, until 1943 when St. Thomas' ever munificent alumnus and benefactor, I. A. O'Shaughnessy, provided funding for its adornment.

The chapel, like the college as a whole, was dedicated to Saint Thomas Aquinas. And it was the genius of Aquinas that guided the task of beautification. A plan put together by the veteran theology professor, Father Walter LeBeau, called for linking together original stained-glass and murals and auxiliary accoutrements in order to tell students—after all, this was a students' church—the Christian story in all its color and brilliance. Here was an artistic manifestation of the marriage of scripture and tradition with integrating commentary from the works of that greatest of teachers, Thomas Aquinas. My job, working with the college's genial photographer, Harry Webb, was to give an account of the process and to present the fruit of it in the form of a large descriptive pamphlet. So I did. "Decoration of the Campus Chapel College of St. Thomas" appeared May 7, 1961.

There was a charming footnote, not printed in "Decoration." Even as he agreed to pay for an appropriate brightening of the chapel's interior, Mr. O'Shaughnessy was shyly asked if he would at the same time care to purchase padding for the rough wooden kneelers. St. Thomas of course was still an all-male school in those days, and so the philanthropist's reply was brisk and pointed: "Why? Are you afraid the students will tear their nylons?" Padding had to await a later day.

When I was in residence at Oxford during the summer of 1964, in one of her letters my mother asked me to send her a description of the university campus. By no means an unreasonable request. Like any mother she wanted to understand as best she could what her far-off child was up to. She knew that Oxford's fame derived entirely from the university located there. And like any American she assumed "university" connoted a certain physical place of discernible dimensions, whether small or large, with a set of buildings of which one housed the institution's governing officers.

Of course I had to tell mother that at Oxford there was no campus to describe. Or rather there were a dozen small campuses, each of them connected with a distinct corporate body called a "college" anxious to surround itself with a memorable and beautiful setting. Indeed, "university" was almost an abstraction, drawn out of the collection of colleges and halls all of them independent and self-governing. Self-perpetuating as well, since the governing board of each college—the fellows or dons—elected its own officers and its new members. Here is where the real Oxford education took place, carried out by tutors chosen from among the dons and designed to deal directly with the entity to which the students applied for a degree after three years of residency. The examiners, it need hardly be said, were chosen from among the fellows of the various colleges. There were a few university professorships, but the incumbents satisfied the requirements of office by delivering a few general lectures each term.

There were close bonds between Oxford (and Cambridge too) and the Church of England. Much of the collegiate finance had ecclesiastical roots; some endowments came from a founding bishop and went back to the thirteenth century. All the dons were Anglican clergymen, and all of them were single. This last condition testified to the precedence set during the Middle Ages when those holding these positions were Roman clerics, bound by the rule of celibacy. A common practice during the early 1800s—the period in which I was interested—was that a man elected fellow of a college served in that capacity for some years, and then took a parish as rector or vicar, a parish frequently part of his college's endowment. More often than not he got married at the same time.

It is difficult to appreciate how small an institution Oxford University was in those days. Today the student population stands at about 23,000, back then it was scarcely more than a thousand. Today there are more than thirty colleges, then about a dozen. When John Keble, destined to be Newman's major collaborator in the Oxford Movement, came up to Corpus Christi College in 1808 at the age of sixteen, only twenty students were in residence there. The university was entirely residential; every student belonged to and lodged in a college. And one must forget most of the programs that we Americans naturally associate with an institution of higher learning. There was no distinction between graduates and undergraduates, no divisions of inquiries along disciplinary lines—no sociology department, I'm happy to say. There were no elective courses either, or major and minor concentrations, or anything that smacked of vocational training. Graduates of Oxford were not looking for a job. They were educated to be gentlemen and so take their place in the established order. To achieve this end it sufficed to study the classical languages and mathematics. No exceptions.

I can't remember when I determined that I wanted to write a history of the Oxford Movement, what Newman in the *Apologia* called "the religious movement of 1833." I suppose the seed was sown in those long conversations I had with Philip Hughes about Newman, to which I've referred several times. And the decision, as I have also already noted, brought with it a *refugium* of sorts from the increasingly messy and depressing McDonell/Helen affair. I was greatly heartened when I received a modest grant from a local foundation, and even more so when I was assured by an officer at Macmillan that his company might be interested in publishing such a story. It did so in 1969. I was very pleased with *The Oxford Conspirators: A History of the Oxford Movement, 1833–1845*, and I have remained so ever since. Certainly researching and writing up the subject enlightened me about an important moment in the life of the Christian Church, and I like to believe that it has similarly enlightened others, especially Americans, about the intellectual milieu that produced Cardinal Newman. The book's republication in 1990 has tended to confirm that brassy presumption of mine.

I had scarcely finished Oxford when, as I have explained above, Professor William Langer asked me to complete the volume Monsignor Hughes, recently deceased, had been invited to contribute to Harper & Row's task myself *ab initio*, Langer agreed. So I found myself back in the sixteenth century again, trying to put into book form all the complexities associated with the Counter Reformation, 1559–1610.

By that time, however, I had become closely involved in a very different kind of literary endeavor. How it began I remember only vaguely. Diocesan weeklies, more often than not bland and boring, were notorious for serving the convenience and sometimes the vanity of the local bishops. They were easy to ignore. In the course of 1965, however, there appeared in the St. Paul version, *The Catholic Bulletin*, an unusually powerful and well-argued article, or possibly a series of articles, by the *Bulletin's* editor, which included sharp criticism of William F. Buckley. I cannot for the life of me recall what the disagreement was substantively about. But whatever, these were the tumultuous 'sixties, a time of social upheaval and sexual revolution, of a continuing bitter crisis in race relations, of an increasingly unpopular war in Southeast Asia, and, for thoughtful Catholics, the mysteries surrounding the Second Vatican Council (still in session till the December of that year). In other words, the dispute could have been about any of a multitude of issues. And by then, for reasons I've already explained, I had pretty much given up on the *Commonweal*-Catholicism of my youth, with its commitment to a broadly defined liberalism. Buckley's *National Review* was my favorite journal now, and in its way it seemed to me practically a Catholic publication. Indeed, it had published an ecclesiastical spoof of mine earlier in the year, titled "Gnostics on a Train," poking fun at Catholic progressives in their search for "relevance." Of course, this change in allegiance had its expressly political side as well; the year before I had voted for Barry Goldwater for president.

The editor in question was named Bernard Casserly. He was a veteran newsman who had worked for many years at the *Minneapolis Star*. He brought to the *Bulletin* a journalistic skill and gravity which the paper had sorely lacked before his appointment. I decided to reply to his piece, which resulted in the first and, I believe, the only time I directed my views to a "Letters to the Editor" department of a newspaper. A few days later I received a phone call from Mr. Casserly, inviting me to lunch. I had never met him before we sat down at table together; I found him charmingly straightforward, and without guile. Clearly, he upheld the typical Irish Catholic's sympathies for liberal causes and for the Democratic Party. But there was nothing fanatical or even ideological about the manner in which he held his positions. Anxious as he was to serve the Church, it never occurred to him to do so except within the higher norms of his profession. Bernard Casserly for twenty-five years demonstrated how productive a diocesan weekly could be.

As it turned out, over lunch he put to me an intriguing proposal. I would write a column with a conservative bias, which would share a kind of op-ed page in the *Bulletin* with another written by Andrew Greeley, presumably from a liberal point of view. Father Greeley's column was already syndicated and so readily available at a limited cost. I can't recall what kind of mental gyrations I went through in considering this offer; apparently out of self-serving hubris I ignored the danger that with all my projects I was dangerously close to that presumption which Andrew Greeley was later accused of, that he never had a thought he did not publish. At any rate the arrangement as Casserly conceived it, a lively debate between spokesmen for the two bodies of opinion within the Church, never worked out. Mostly because Greeley and I were not in contact, and so one was not aware what the other was writing about; no debate possible on those grounds alone. And also because Father Greeley was totally unpredictable, liberal one moment and conservative the next; simply Greeleyesqe, his contributions might fairly be described.

Then Casserly made, for me, a fateful decision. He invited me to write a weekly column without any designated rebuttal. (Perhaps he felt, as I did, there were plenty of liberals around to advocate their perspective.) And I agreed, and so began my seven-year career as a journalist (1966–1971, 1972–1973). I wrote forty-eight essays per year, taking two weeks off in the summer and again in the winter. Each column had to be roughly the same length, 850 words. The grand total ran to about 300,000 words. I quickly learned that "roughly" was not to be casually applied; space had to be carefully allotted throughout the paper, and it was a grave matter when one feature exceeded its limits. I insisted that nothing be changed in any copy I submitted without my explicit consent, and the ever-gracious editor concurred. Nor was there ever a crisis or even a moment of tension between us. There was never a contract or written agreement. Our whole relationship, which included Casserly arranging for the column's syndication in thirty diocesan weeklies from Honolulu to Atlanta to New York, was based on a handshake.

I called the column "Tracts for the Times," a title stolen from the series of ninety essays and patristic reprints edited by Newman and Keble that formed the heart of the Oxford Movement, that gallant and ill-starred attempt in the mid-nineteenth century to establish the essential catholicism––note the lower case "c" —of the Anglican communion. The audience for which I wrote, people largely like myself, determined to a considerable degree the subjects I broached, though Bernard Casserly stressed that mine was to be an "anything" column, that I was free to write about any events

I thought worthy of attention. So the mandate included first of all religious matters of interest to Catholics—in an age of increasing polemic and even of *odium theologicum*—but by no means restricted to such. So I wrote about the Vietnam War, generally supportive of the American administration's policy but deeply uneasy about it. The same might be said about my reaction to the civil rights agitation; disdainful of the demagoguery of Jesse Jackson and his ilk, yet nonetheless sickened by the bombings in Birmingham and outraged by the brutality of Bull Connor.

Reactions to the column were various. When I wrote negatively about the charismatic movement, I received a flood of protest; one letter, several pages of vitriol, was signed, "Respectfully yours." My single biggest disaster was what I came to call the "Hi Marv" column. In it I protested that a few laypeople whom I scarcely knew had begun to call me by my Christian name instead of by my title. I tried to point out that many of my lay friends did call me "Marv" rather than Father; they did so precisely because they were my friends, not because, as was the case with these others, they wanted to state an ideological position about equality among the baptized. Perhaps I wrote this piece badly; whatever the reason it was misunderstood and hence ill received by friend and critic alike. Another misfire was occasioned by the publicity accorded a young nun performing as the lead in a romantic comedy produced by a local secular company, which was treated by some as indicative of the new religious commitment to the humane. The counter-argument in my column stressed that the serious devotion of the religious sisters did not imply sourness on the one hand or invite frivolity on the other. My punch-line, however, was most unfortunate: Dear sisters, please don't giggle.

Not every column was concerned with cosmic issues affecting Church and state. I remember how joyous all we Minnesotans were when the Vikings in 1970 won their way to the Super Bowl under the leadership of their rough-hewn quarterback, Joe Kapp. My tract for the times in honor of that event was a tribute to Kapp, who, when elected the team's MVP, refused to accept the trophy. "There is no one most valuable Viking," he said. "There are 40 most valuable Vikings." (The story would have had a perfect ending had the Vikings won the game; alas, it was not to be.)

Conservative I certainly was (and am), and this temperamental dislike of change of any kind was apparent in my tracts. Still, I like to believe I avoided any automatic commitment to right-wing causes. Thus, I accepted cheerfully the pronouncements in the documents passed by the Fathers of Vatican II; though the so-called "spirit" of the council was a different matter. At one point I questioned severely the practice I called "creeping infallibility" —by which I meant a tendency by some conservatives to attach to lesser magisterial teaching something of the character of that unique charism, so rarely invoked, papal infallibility. If the pope is free from error on big things, why not on smaller ones too? And some of my most loyal readers were bemused by my argument that, in accord with tradition, bishops should be chosen by the clergy of the diocese speaking for all the people—as has been and continues to be the case in the selection of the Bishop of Rome.

As I mentioned above, Bernard Casserly had assured me at our first meeting that mine was to be an "anything" column—no serious subject was out of bounds. With one exception: the current archbishop of St. Paul — Leo Binz — did not want raised any discussion in the *Bulletin* of birth control. As I recall the conversation, Casserly stressed the archbishop's prohibition stemmed from the fact that he was the chairman of the committee Pope Paul VI had appointed to review this tortured question and as such he would be personally embarrassed if it were brought up in his paper — technically Binz was publisher of the *Bulletin*. Far from resenting this bit of prior censorship I rejoiced in it. I had never been comfortable with the Catholic Church's total condemnation of any form of artificial contraception. I do not believe I ever preached on the subject, and I recall clearly how troubled I was when the matter came up in the confessional.

In July 1968, Paul VI issued his encyclical *Humanae vitae* which confirmed the Church's traditional position "on the regulation of birth." This document caused an inevitable firestorm within the Catholic community — not only because, it was argued by some, the development of the contraceptive pill had altered the science involved, but also because it was leaked that the majority on the Binz committee had voted to oppose the pope's decision. It would be feckless of me to go over the controversies that ensued, except to say that *Humanae vitae* has long proved its value as a beautiful evocation of married love. But I didn't believe then, and I don't believe now, that it presents the only possible evocation. I determined to explain what I meant in one of my tracts, and so I broke the agreement I had made to ignore the subject of birth control. I said nothing *viva voce* about this to Mr. Casserly or to Archbishop Binz, and they said nothing to me.

I chose what I think you will agree was a very odd metaphorical approach. As a Civil War buff, I was aware of the campaign in northern Virginia during the spring and summer of 1864. This was the classic and, as things turned out, the ultimate contest between Grant and Lee. Some of the bloodiest battles of the war were fought here during these months — the Wilderness, Spotsylvania Courthouse, Cold Harbor, where the union forces suffered 7,000 killed and wounded in twenty minutes. Repulsed and rebuffed by Lee the wily tactician, Grant continued even so to press southeast toward Richmond. His casualties were enormous, and the northern papers began to refer to "Butcher Grant." The Confederates lost fewer men, but they had fewer to lose, and Grant knew he would in the end win a war of attrition. And so, in April 1865, he did.

In my tract I quoted Grant who, in the blood and heat of July, subjected to almost universal criticism of his strategy, said: "I intend to fight it out on this line if it takes all summer." A prosaic sentence if ever there was one, but U.S. Grant was a prosaic sort of man, until the poet burst out of him in his *Memoirs,* composed as he lay dying twenty years later. It took longer than the summer, actually, and that was a point I was awkwardly trying to convey. No single battle, no independent initiative, no brilliant maneuver could settle the war for Richmond. It took time and patience. And so would it be with the Catholic quarrel over contraception. No single document, even from the loftiest source, would settle so complex an issue. Pope Paul and his opponents had to be ready to fight it out over many summers to come. Losses were inevitable: Paul VI never wrote another encyclical, and Father Charles Curran eventually became a professor at Southern Methodist University.

On the afternoon of the first Good Friday several members of the Sanhedrin called upon the Roman governor in his official residence in Jerusalem. Their complaint was explicit. You have labeled the cross on which the interloper from Galilee was hanged, "Jesus of Nazareth, King of the Jews." It should be read, "He Claimed to be King of the Jews." Pontius Pilate looked at them stonily. He knew full well that earlier in the day he had committed what was for a Roman official a mortal sin; he had surrendered to a local mob. He had determined Jesus' innocence and had tried to release him, but in the end he succumbed to the pressure exercised by these men and others like them. He was not about to do so again. "*Quod scripsi, scripsi*" ("What I have written, I have written"), he said, and then summoned a squad of heavily armed soldiers to escort the Jewish gentlemen out of the praetorium.

Even though I too can write *Quod scripsi, scripsi*, my trouble is not the same as Pilate's. My trouble has to do with the sheer bulk of what I have written over a long career. I'm startled when I contemplate what I've asked readers to accept from me: books (some very long), articles (some serious, some trivial), columns, reviews, sermons (some became essays and vice versa), and now even memoirs. It takes more than a snifter of pride to thrust such a mass of one's own stuff upon an unsuspecting public. I plead guilty and ask for forbearance. Yet I must say that, like Pilate, I'm pretty satisfied with what I have written.

Part Two
Essays

O'Connell loved Newman, and his frequent engagements with the great English cardinal reveal much about both of them. In the following two essays, O'Connell captures the human and institutional context of Newman's journeys in faith and reason. Does Newman still matter? O'Connell's reply is an urgent call for educators and students alike to discern the answer.

In the first essay, he examines the constraints upon Newman's insights in the academy of recent times, with specific reference to the University of Notre Dame. He points out imperfections along with inspirations, asking if Newman's lofty ideal is a lost cause.

In the second essay, O'Connell does not hesitate to judge the Oxford Movement, one century earlier, a lost cause. His assessment displays his own perspectives on the enduring challenges of advocacy for faith-informed values in an academic setting. Those interested in the trajectory of university learning will benefit from this priest-teacher's astute reflections on the limits encircling the project of truth in education. – WGS

Newman and the Ideal of a University
A Notre Dame Professor Explores
its Pertinence to His Own Institution

When he was sixty-three years old, John Henry Newman published a memoir, the *Apologia pro Vita Sua* (1864), which very soon achieved the status of a classic of autobiography. In it he recalled with special poignancy his arrival at Oxford nearly a half-century before and the first residence to which he was assigned: "There used to be much snapdragon growing on the walls opposite my freshman's rooms there, and I had for years taken it as the emblem of my own perpetual residence even unto death in my University." The poignancy arose from the fact that when Newman's conscience directed him to depart the Church of England for the Church of Rome, he had to give up Oxford too, because the university was in those days an exclusively Anglican institution. "I have never seen Oxford since, excepting its spires, as they are seen from the railway."

So it was that during the second half of his long life (1801–1890) New-man remained divorced from the university he had loved so deeply, but, even so, he never ceased to be an Oxford man. His interests, his habits, his priorities had long been fixed, and the change of confessional allegiances did not affect him. Indeed, when he became a Catholic priest and the pastor of a large working-class parish in Birmingham, he and the other convert-priests associated with him patterned their lives as closely as possible upon the model provided by the colleges of Oxford — purified, to be sure, and elevated but nevertheless always reminiscent of Christ Church and Oriel and Trinity. They intended themselves to be English gentlemen and schol-ars, even as they performed the tasks of the parochial ministry.

The distinction which nineteenth-century Oxford drew between "col-lege" and "university," quite unfamiliar to us, is crucial to an understanding of Newman's educational ideal. True to its medieval origins, Oxford still bore the character of a guild of masters and apprentices, distinguished at its foun-dation early in the thirteenth century from other guilds — of tailors, for in-stance, or ironmongers — by its educational objective and, implicitly, by its clerical personnel, since education in the Middle Ages was virtually the preserve of the clergy. A bachelor's degree was a license to teach. It signified a proficiency in the liberal arts analogous to the skill, gained after long years of training, of a master craftsman in silver or leather. The teaching process, in the beginning, took place in rented rooms, and for solemn occasions, like the conferring of degrees, the whole university gathered in the Oxford parish church of St. Mary the Virgin. The university was not a place one could point to; it was not a campus. It was rather a corporation, a band of brothers almost, a group of people bound together by a common interest.

At first Oxford students found what board and lodging they could in the town. Then, toward the end of the thirteenth century, when the university was about fifty years old, the all-important collegiate system began to develop. Though the evolution of each college differed in detail, the basic characteristics of the process were shared by all. A benefactor provided an endowment in land which would support a certain number of men who would otherwise be unable to pursue their studies. These scholars, called fellows (and nicknamed "dons"), took up residence to-gether in a "college" — a word whose root meaning, from the Latin, was simply a company or assemblage. They governed themselves according to a set of specific statutes which to varying degrees reflected the wishes of their patron. They chose a presiding officer from among their ranks and set up a method whereby new fellows could be supplied to replace those who died or departed. To be elected fellow of any college a man had to be a bachelor; he had to have spent, in other words, seven years already in the university and to have gained his arts degree. All these arrangements were calculated to free the fellows from financial worry and to give them a congenial atmosphere for the research which was their fundamental obligation.

Originally, therefore, a college was a place for advanced scholarship in theology, medicine, or law, not for instruction. But little by little the character of the college underwent a momentous change. Undergraduates came to be accepted into the colleges where they took up residence while they followed courses in the university. And as an inevitable consequence the function of the fellows, or at least of some of them, also changed. They gradually took upon themselves the task of instruction of the undergraduates in their midst, and so a new set of officers emerged from among the fellows: a dean to supervise discipline and tutors to engage formally in teaching.

By the time Newman came up to Trinity College as an undergraduate, Oxford had developed into a group of independent corporations — the colleges, whose spires the Catholic Newman saw from the railway — within the larger framework of the university corporation. If a man were designated — as Newman was from his election in 1822 until his conversion to Catholicism in 1845 — Fellow of Oriel College, Oxford, it meant he belonged to two corporate structures. The university gave final examinations, granted degrees, and offered general lectures through spokesmen now called professors. Oriel College, along with its research functions, was also charged with the day-to-day job of drilling and instructing its undergraduates who would ultimately stand for their degrees. Nevertheless, the university and the college remained in another sense indistinguishable, because the same people — whether undergraduates or fellows or professors — made up both.

In 1851, six years after Newman had joined the Catholic Church, the bishops of Ireland invited him to participate in their plan to found a university in Dublin, and, soon after, they offered him the rectorship of the proposed institution. At first, he hesitated, not unaware of the difficulties involved in such a venture. But, as he observed later, "from first to last education, in [the] large sense of the word, has been my line," and the prospect of contributing on a grand scale to the well-being of his new co-religionists, in a field in which he was demonstrably an expert, filled him with exhilaration. "It will be the Catholic University of the English tongue for the whole world," he said exultantly. And of course, he realized from the start that the academic environment in which he had grown up and in which he had gained so lofty a reputation explained why he had been given the invitation in the first place. "Curious it will be," he told a friend, "if Oxford is imported into Ireland, not in its members only, but in its principles, methods, ways, and arguments."

The Catholic University of Ireland did not prosper. The contentiousness of the bishops, the poverty of a country so recently ravaged by the horrors of the massive famine, the reluctance of English Catholics, particularly the few of them who possessed some wealth and standing, to associate themselves with an Irish institution, all contributed to the want of success. Newman himself remained at the helm until 1858, by which time it had become clear that only a fragment of the dream he had cherished would survive on Dublin's St. Stephen's Green. This bitter disappointment proved to be only the first in a long list of frustrations and failures which afflicted Newman during his years as a Catholic, so much so that, as he confided to his private journal, "I fear. . .the iron has entered into my soul. . . As a Protestant I felt my religion dreary but not my life — but, as a Catholic, my life dreary, not my religion."

But "my campaign in Ireland," as Newman came to describe it, was not without permanent fruit. The bishops' original invitation to him had included a request "to give us a few lectures on education." He agreed to do so and found the task immensely difficult. Though the "discourses," as he called them, were well received, "they have oppressed me more," he said, "than anything else of the kind in my life. I am out on the ocean with them, out of sight of land, with nothing but the stars." Ultimately, he published them, together with other lectures and essays written while he was rector, in one of the most celebrated of all his forty books, *The Idea of a University*.

Celebrated the *Idea* well may be, for its gorgeous prose and its broad, yet subtly discriminating, treatment of the field of higher education. Yet one might legitimately ask whether it does not propose an ideal rather than a living idea. Is the book more than an historical curiosity? Does it have anything valuable to say, after all this time, about university education? More specifically, does the Newman of Dublin and Oxford have anything relevant to say to that Notre Dame of the late twentieth century? In some regards the answer is definitely in the negative. Newman, first of all, was talking about the education of an elite; the mega-universities of our day, with their commitment to provide utilitarian training to virtually everybody within commuting distance, would have been beyond his comprehension. In accord with the mores of his own time, he gave no thought to coeducation. He knew nothing of elective curricula or undergraduate majors or auxiliary enterprises: a university book store, he would have supposed, was a place to find books. The term social science would have been a mystery to him. He took for granted the primacy of classical studies and mathematics, the core of the Oxford curriculum, and, more generally, of the need for all students to be thoroughly versed in the liberal arts before embarking upon any specialization. In these and similar convictions and assumptions, Newman clearly lived in a different world from ours.

But in other respects, the *Idea* witnesses to timeless truths, worth pondering because, if for no better reason, educational reformers routinely bring them forward to correct the excesses of this or that bout of innovation. No one, for example, has expressed more eloquently than Newman the constantly recurring denunciation of "the error of distracting and enfeebling the mind by an unmeaning profusion of subjects; of implying that a smattering in a dozen branches of study is not shallowness, which it really is, but enlargement, which it is not, of considering an acquaintance with the learned names of things and persons, and the possession of clever duodecimos, and attendance on eloquent lectures, and membership with scientific institutions, and the sight of the experiments of a platform and the specimens of a museum, that all this was not dissipation of mind, but progress. All things now are to be learned at once, not first one thing, then another, not one well, but many badly."

To take another instance, perhaps closer to home: How often these days do we not hear the complaint that graduates even of prestigious universities lack fundamental verbal skills? Says Newman trenchantly: "Till a man begins to put down his thoughts about a subject on paper he will not ascertain what he knows and what he does not know; and still less will he be able to express what he does know." Drill is what is needed to develop the art of writing, and indeed "formation of mind" in whatever discipline depends not upon "that barren mockery of knowledge which comes of attending on great Lecturers, or of mere acquaintance with reviews, magazines, newspapers" but upon "that catechetical instruction, which consists in a sort of conversation between your lecturer and you." Thus speaks the sometime don and tutor of Oriel College, Oxford.

And thus might be underscored a problem of growing concern on the campus of the University of Notre Dame. Drill and "catechetical instruction" take time. Conversation between professor and student demands the ready availability of the former to the latter. To be a good teacher at the university level involves intense preparation and the willingness to expend much energy and imagination in presenting the required material. But what happens when the professor is convinced that his professional standing — indeed, his very employability — rests not upon his teaching but upon his productivity and visibility as a researcher? What if tenure and promotion are judged to flow chiefly from an accumulation of articles in specialized journals? Such a perception does not seem out of accord with Notre Dame's formal profession of its intention to become a great *research* institution. Nor has the recent administration of the university been behindhand in providing the incentives to the faculty to bring about this goal; sharply augmented remuneration over the past several years, together with considerable reduction in classroom obligations and enhanced opportunities for leave time and for research facilities, has led an increasingly talented body of professors to establish a commendable record of published scholarship.

But the results of this policy have, so far, been mixed. Undergraduate students at Notre Dame, themselves a highly talented group, do not read the learned journals in which appear their professors' articles. And more and more students are complaining about what they consider an undue emphasis upon graduate training and the consequent paucity of undergraduate courses, and about crowded classes, and about indifferent or ill-prepared teachers, and, most telling of all, about teachers never being available. The dilemma — for that is surely what it is — is often expressed in terms of the "new" Notre Dame versus the "old" Notre Dame, the up-to-date research institution on the cutting edge of discovery, in contrast to the traditional, perhaps anachronistic, center of a unique "experience" in a powerfully effective undergraduate program, carried on within the confines of the "Notre Dame Family."

It would be wrong of course to exaggerate this dichotomy, to label a crisis what is really a puzzle, a riddle. And maybe a challenge to all those who think of Notre Dame as a special place. One must take pains, to be sure, not to let nostalgia rule on the one hand, or academic trendiness on the other. Certainly, no natural or divine law has decreed that the astute researcher cannot be also inspiring and memorable teacher. For purpose of the present discussion, it may be significant that if the "old" Notre Dame had its "dons" — one thinks immediately of Joseph Evans, Paul Fenelon, Frank O'Malley — it also had its scholars. And among those faculty most identified with the ethos of the "new" Notre Dame are many brilliant classroom instructors.

There is at any rate no doubt upon which side of the debate Newman would have come down. A university, he wrote in the first sentences of the *Idea*, "is a place of *teaching* universal *knowledge*. This implies that its object is . . . the diffusion and extension of knowledge rather than the advancement. If its object were scientific and philosophical discovery, I do not see why a University should have students." He may have had in mind All Souls College, Oxford, a research center which supported a group of fellows but which in fact had no students and has none to this day. However that may be, Newman seems to have ruled himself out of court as a judge of higher education in the twentieth century by denying the university its fundamental obligation of "scientific and philosophical discovery." We can learn nothing from such a one.

Yet this might be too hasty a conclusion. For basic to Newman's definition lies a principle hard to challenge in any context and in any century: education is at heart a matter of personal influence. One might propose, as Newman implicitly did, the model of medieval Oxford where the university was simply a group of people — some learned, some eager to learn — bound together by their mutual interest in things of the mind. But whatever imagery one invokes to make the point, the person-to-person relationship between faculty and students remains a condition for genuine education, and, to the degree that this was a distinguishing feature of the "old" Notre Dame, it is far too valuable to lose. There need be no sentimentality in such a relationship, no pandering to the immature, no interference in the private lives of others. It need not involve the sacrifice of original scholarship. Nor can it be secured by administrative tinkering or press releases. What it needs to flourish is mutual respect and a rigorous dedication to bringing into reality the goal of a university education, the goal Newman described better than anyone else.

> *The intellect, which has been disciplined to the perfection of its powers, which knows, and thinks while it knows, which has learned to leaven the dense mass of facts and events with the elastic force of reason, such an intellect cannot be partial, cannot be exclusive, cannot be impetuous, cannot be at a loss, cannot but be patient, collected, and majestically calm, because it discerns the end in every beginning, the origin in every end, the law in every interruption, the limit in each delay; because it ever knows where it stands, and how its path lies from one point to another.*

Crisis, Volume 5, Issue 8, September 1987, Pages 22–25

Newman and the Oxford Movement

Oxford has sometimes been called the home of lost causes. Perhaps therein lies part of the mystique that undeniably envelops the city and the univer-sity. For there is enough of the romantic in most of us to harbor a measure of fascination with and even sympathy for lost causes. One reason may be that historical might-have-beens can be more intriguing than the actual, often humdrum events have proved to be. What if Barry Goldwater had defeated Lyndon Johnson in the presidential election of 1964? What if, more remotely, Prince Rupert and his dashing cavaliers had won out over the remorseless fire-power and grim ideology of Cromwell's Puritans? When a lost cause has brought to its banners individuals of particular attractive-ness, the game becomes still more engaging. What thoughtful American does not, even after all that has happened since, pay tribute to the nobility of Robert E. Lee, the almost mystical dedication of Stonewall Jackson, the gallantry of Jeb Stuart — the laughing chevalier with the ostrich plume in his hat — and to all those barefoot, ill-fed, ill-clothed, outnumbered, out-gunned, nameless Confederate soldiers who came within a whisker of vic-tory?

In fairness, however, the game of lost causes cannot be played without taking into account the consequences that might have been. If the royalists had won the English Civil War, what would have been the effect upon the principles of freedom of speech and assembly and upon the parliamentary tradition generally? If Lee and the Army of Northern Virginia had won the American Civil War — if Longstreet on July 3, 1863, had not waited six hours before sending Pickett forward against the federal lines at Gettysburg — what would that triumph of states' rights have involved? Would we be two nations now? or four? Or ten? And what would have been the impact upon our society of the prolongation of the "peculiar institution" — the euphemism employed a century and a half ago to disguise the vileness of black slavery?

If ever there was a movement without a chance of succeeding it was the one that began amidst the lush green lawns and clustered towers of Oxford in 1833. But if ever a lost cause could count among its adherents persons of transcendent charm and integrity and goodness, it was also the Oxford Movement. John Keble, the ideal of the Christian pastor — austere, playful, poetic, but with a will of steel; Edward Bouverie Pusey, the relentless scholar and ascetic whom no personal sorrow could divert from the seeking of God's will; Richard Hurrell Froude, the gadfly who hid his inner doubts beneath a mordant wit and the chronic cough of a consumptive; Charles Marriott who, in the midst of a plague of cholera, laid down his life for his friends; Frederic Rogers, a lawyer's lawyer, blunt and yet compassionate; Isaac Williams, gentle, self- effacing, and yet unswerving in his principles; Robert Isaac Wilberforce, scion of England's most distinguished house, whose father had freed the slaves and who himself sought through a score of arid years that freedom with which Christ has set us free. There were hundreds, even thousands, more — including many destined for greatness in the public arena, like William Ewart Gladstone and Henry Edward Manning — and, towering over all this "transfigured band" (in Matthew Arnold's phrase), was John Henry Newman, fellow of Oriel and vicar of St. Mary the Virgin.

But the significance of the Oxford Movement, and the significance of Newman's part in it, cannot fairly be judged by us children of the late twentieth century without considering what might have been had this lost cause actually succeeded. A great chasm separates our mindset from that of the thirty-two-year-old Newman who from its inception led and inspired the Movement. Values we and our culture have enshrined as absolutes were explicitly repudiated by him and his collaborators. Those prized achievements of modernity — democracy, toleration, "a free church in a free state," "different strokes for different folks" — were in the minds of the Oxford men evils to be avoided at all costs. And these evils stemmed, they thought, from the most radical evil of all: the privatization of religion. It was wrong, they argued, to consider religious adherence as a matter merely of taste or sentiment or opinion; wrong to define the Christian church as a private corporation to which an individual might or might not belong, according only to his choice in the matter; wrong to advance the view that error in religious doctrine was a matter of indifference to the state and to the larger society.

"The dictum was in force when I was young," Newman observed sadly in 1879, "that Christianity was the law of the land. Now everywhere that goodly framework of society, which is the creation of Christianity, is throwing off Christianity." The Oxford Movement was a last, gallant and, in the end, futile stand against the Western world's inexorable march into the post-Christian era.

The bare-bones facts about the Oxford Movement can be stated simply enough. In the summer of 1833 a group of young Anglican clergymen — most of them resident in Oxford or recently graduated from the university — began to publish a series of penny pamphlets called "Tracts for the Times." Each of these three- or four-page publications bore a title, but they were ordinarily designated simply by number. Their anonymous authors had been moved to undertake this project by their conviction that the Church of England stood at that moment in mortal peril. "Choose your side!" proclaimed the first of the tracts, written by Newman. "Fear to be of those whose line is decided for them by chance circumstances, and who may perchance find themselves with the enemies of Christ, while they think but to remove themselves from worldly politics." By 1841, when the series ended, ninety tracts had been published and in the later years they had tended to become long and often tedious treatises. But the short, pungent early tracts, with their emphasis on protest and on calls to action, set the tone of the Movement through the twelve stormy years of its existence.

The tracts testify to the largely literary character of the Movement — appropriate enough for a group of university men. But so do the pamphlets, sermons, learned books and editions, even poetry that tumbled from the presses. Eventually the Tractarians, as they soon came to be called, published their own magazine. This verbal avalanche was calculated to persuade the educated classes that the Church of England, their spiritual home, bases its claims on something more than and prior to its union with the state. Newman's reference, therefore, to "worldly politics" in Tract Number One was not at all incidental. The "danger" which so alarmed the Tractarians issued from a series of statutes recently passed by parliament that aimed to restructure and "reform" the church. But by what right, Newman demanded, did a group of politicians, many of them unbelievers, presume to interfere in the affairs of the "church catholic?"

By the phrase Newman did not of course mean, "Roman Catholic."

Rather he referred to the primitive "church catholic" of the first four centuries, confessed to in the ancient creeds and in other formularies found in the Book of Common Prayer. Indeed, he made the writers of that remote time — Athanasius, Basil, Gregory of Nyssa — his special study. In doing so, and in strongly endorsing their principles in everything he wrote, he represented one important part of the Anglican tradition, but by no means the only one.

Though in theory the Church of England enfolded within its wide embrace the whole nation, in fact a large and powerful minority of Protestants dissented from it, as did a tiny group of Roman Catholics. This failure of universal inclusion did not stem from want of effort, for in the area of doctrine the established church displayed to a remarkable degree the English genius for compromise and accommodation. Those with Protestant learning could point to the official norms of Anglican orthodoxy, the Thirty-nine Articles, drawn up during the time of the Reformation. The Anglo-Catholics, on the other hand, found their solace in the equally official Prayer Book, with its venerable chants and liturgies and its more than implicit assertion of a sacramental spirituality. Thus, room was provided for both "low" church and "high," a balance that seemed agreeable to most communicants.

Not to the Tractarians. "The Reformation was a limb badly set," said the outspoken Hurrell Froude. "It must be broken again in order to be righted." Oxford had long been the defender of "high" church principles, but by 1833 two new elements had altered that traditional stance into a crusade for at least some of the university's sons. First, the emergence of a powerful political liberalism seemed to signal an attempt to reduce the church to a docile department of the leviathan state. "National apostasy," an angry John Keble called it. "I have now made up my sage mind," Froude said, "that the country is too bad to deserve an established church." Secondly, the intense personal religiosity and zeal of the leaders of the Movement were in marked contrast to the detached, often agnostic attitudes prevalent among Oxford men of the previous generation. Newman was not untypical of his party in having undergone a personal conversion of such force that fifty years afterward he described it as a continuing reality "of which I am more certain than that I have hands and feet."

If only catholic truth could resist the incursions of the state and the wave of modern unbelief, then Anglicans, the Tractarians proclaimed, must assert beyond cavil the bedrock dogma of the apostolical succession of their bishops. "If we track back the power of ordination from hand to hand," Newman wrote in Tract Number One, "of course we shall come to the apostles at last. We know we do, as a plain historical fact." Orthodox doctrine and valid sacraments depended upon that sacred connection. Apostolicity and catholicity went majestically together, and under their aegis the Christian could steer safely between Protestant nihilism and Roman corruption. This is what Newman meant by his celebrated theory of the via media.

The bewigged bishops of the church, all political appointees, were much startled by the claims thus made for them. So too were the "low" church evangelicals, to say nothing of the dissenters and the liberals. And, out of habit perhaps as much as conviction, most ordinary Anglicans, pleased to consider themselves Protestants and with a hatred of Rome bred into their bones, had no quarrel with the Reformation. The catholic tradition had never enjoyed majority status within the Church of England, and so the aggressive new assertion of it at Oxford was bound to meet resistance, as it did, increasingly, over the years.

Inevitably the opponents of the Movement played the Roman card: "catholic" means Roman, they charged ever more stridently, and the ultimate objective of the Tractarians is to deliver the Church of England over to priest-craft and superstition. By 1841 the bishops themselves had come to agree. Isaac Williams saw the bitter irony as their lordships, one after another, condemned the Movement. "It is very trying to one's patience," he said. "We have bolstered up the bishops and made their words to be as weighty as gods, and all we get by it is their condemnation, which otherwise would have been as light as feathers." But by that time the Movement was bleeding to death anyway, because its peerless leader, Newman, had lost his faith in it. His confidence eroded by the mean accusations levelled against him, he came little by little to the conclusion that Anglo-Catholicism was a contradiction in terms, that the *via media* he had so painstakingly constructed was a mere "paper theory," that if St. Athanasius were suddenly to reappear on the earth and wend his way to Oxford, the great bishop of Alexandria would find himself at home, not in Newman's own parish, the university church of St. Mary the Virgin, but in the shabby little Roman Catholic chapel.

When Newman left the Church of England in 1845, he had perforce to leave Oxford too. He found, he said, "perfect peace and contentment" in his new communion, in which his genius was destined to come to full flower. But the separation was in human terms excruciatingly painful. The last sermon he preached as an Anglican was titled "The Parting of Friends." Many of the lesser figures in the Movement followed Newman's course and went to Rome, but not his oldest and dearest collaborators — not Keble or Pusey or Williams (Froude had died an Anglican in 1836). Thus the struggle for catholic and apostolical principles continued within the Church of England, and continues, though much straitened, to this day. But for Newman the cause had been lost beyond recovery, and vanished too, like a dream, were buoyant hopes of his youth. "There used to be much snap-dragon growing on the walls opposite my freshman's rooms," he wrote long after his departure, "and I had for years taken it as the emblem of my own perpetual residence even unto death in my University. I have never seen Oxford since, excepting its spires, as they are seen from the railway."

The Catholic World, Volume 233, Number 1393, Jan.–Feb. 1990, Pages 10–13

O'Connell presents in this essay his conviction that history and religion go to-gether. For him, the Catholic faith is deeply rooted in human history, from the events of Christ's life to the settling of moral debates and the cultivation of broad understanding as a groundwork for sound judgment in the present and future. Beliefs born only from present trends and private feelings may provide pragmatic justifications, but not potent judgments.

O'Connell draws on his own experience as a teacher of history to clarify the importance of knowing the past and using this context to choose a mature faith. Writing this piece as part of a special issue on "The Women Doctors of the Church," he notes his gratitude for the Church's recognition of Catherine of Siena, Teresa of Avila, and Therese of Lisieux as Doctors — a valuable, albeit tardy, unveiling of history that was kept all too private. These newly highlighted spiritual geniuses will inspire Christians "along the pilgrim way that lies ahead."
– WGS

Defenders of the Faith

My career as a university history teacher, now itself a tiny bit of history, was by and large happy and satisfying. Fortunately for me, it began before the fancies of the 'sixties took hold, and so I never had to pretend that my students knew as much as I did about the question at hand, never had to make believe that they and I were engaged in a joint investigation into the intricacies of the feudal system or of the English constitution. Needless to say, they knew much more than I did about a whole host of subjects, most of them, no doubt, far more pertinent to their lives than, say, the distinction between anarchists and syndicalists. But natively bright as most of them were, and accomplished in various ways, their ignorance of history — indeed, their indifference to anything that might have happened before their own precious appearance on the planet — was, well, dazzling.

This is not to say that youthful reluctance to inquire into the past cannot be overcome. Skillful and imaginative teaching can and does regularly succeed in doing so. The raw material is there for the asking. Mozart and Beethoven, after all, are at least as interesting as Elton John, and while the glamorous, shallow image of Princess Diana fades quickly from public consciousness, that of the bewitching Mary, Queen of Scots, or of the splendidly imperious Elizabeth I reasserts itself yet again. Would a conversation with Jacques Chirac be as fascinating as one with Napoleon? Would you prefer to go out to dinner with Martin Luther or Pat Robertson?

In short, nearly forty years in the classroom have convinced me that college students or indeed any person with a modicum of ordinary curiosity, if they are creatively engaged — if they can be persuaded that reality now passed can provide them with an enriching vicarious experience and thereby enlighten them to a degree about the human condition — will approach historical study with the same rigor they bring to other inquiries. Unless it be the history of religion. Now this is a problem of long standing, and an understandable one. Religion is a virtue, religion has to do with intensely personal belief, religion deals with deep moral and spiritual commitment in the here and now, for you, for me, for everybody. It is not readily apparent that the activities of some dead males — and a scattering of females — most of them white, have much to do with my practical religion or yours.

Yet for us Christians, and particularly for us Catholics, this attitude is a snare and a delusion. Christianity is nothing, humanly speaking, if it is not an historical phenomenon. Certain events occurred in a certain place and at a certain time, reaching a climax on the first Easter Sunday. If Christ has not risen from the dead, St. Paul asserts without qualification, then we who bear his name are the unhappiest, the most deceived of humankind. Moreover, for us religion is as much a corporate as an individual reality. We are members of one another, and when we confess to our belief in the Communion of Saints, we recognize the ties that bind us to everyone, past, present, or future, who has risen or will rise from the waters of baptism as a living sign of Christ's resurrection. There must be to all this an intellectual component; you must give reasons, the same St. Paul admonished us, for the faith that is in you.

The human mind, constituted as it is, cannot stand mute when it confronts Revelation. It must probe and piece, it must compare and analyze, and yes, argue about meaning and applicability. And Catholicism, constituted as it is, must carry out this task within the historical context where Providence has placed it. What Cardinal Newman called "the development of Christian doctrine" is a kind of organic growth through which the Church, Christ's Body — St. Paul again — mysteriously matures in time and space. The Church today is the same as, and yet different from, the assembly gathered in the upper room in Jerusalem on the first Pentecost.

There can be no dispute that anyone who wants to understand the beauty and coherence of Christianity must discern the essence of the Judaism from which Christianity sprang. All the more so must the believer be prepared to take into spiritual account the chronicle — with all its nuances, with all its crises, with all its human failures and triumphs — the historical record that describes how Jesus' good news spread out from the shores of the Sea of Galilee to Rome and Athens and to Moscow and Algiers and Saigon. We are what we are because of those who have gone before us.

But, alas, along with history's alleged superfluity for the religious person, referred to above, another difficulty faces us Catholics in these latter days. Let me suggest it by way of a professorial anecdote. During a class one day in the late 'seventies, I was attempting to explain the knotty intellectual problems in the controversies attendant upon the Protestant Reformation, specifically those connected to the key doctrine of justification — Thomists versus Scotists, nominalists versus realists, the Bible versus Tradition. A hand was raised tentatively in the air. As was my wont I acknowledged it, and the young person thus recognized said courteously albeit with unmistakable impatience: "I really wonder, you know, about the relevance of this discussion of these matters. I'm a Catholic, you know, but everybody knows that before Vatican II Catholicism was just, you know, a peasant religion. It didn't have any intellectual foundations until Vatican II."

You will be glad to learn that I repressed my initial visceral reaction, which was to point out that what we were engaged in was not a "discussion," since discussion requires the participation of more than one informed party, and the employment of the phrase "everybody knows" amounts, you know, to an admission of slothful ignorance. But I did invoke the shades of Pascal and Newman, of Moeller and Rosmini and Lacordaire, of Tertullian and Origen, of Justinian and Abelard and Marsiglio of Padua, of Lagrange and Balthasar and deLubac, even of John Courtney Murray and Edith Stein — until I realized that none of these names meant anything to the upturned, bland, sweetly innocent faces in front of me. These young Catholics, sprung from the school of religious "relevance," could not imagine that Luther or Luther's opponents had anything *intellectually* significant to say about the mysteries involved in justifying faith. The mental discipline required in the physical and social sciences seemed to them a necessity from which the "spirit of Vatican II" — that deceptive and most spiritually unhealthy of slogans — had delivered them.

Now it is certainly the case that not every theological tract, ecclesiastical treatise, papal decree, or even conciliar judgment fashioned over the last 2000 years bears equal importance to every other. Many a controversy has gone whistling down the wind and no longer needs or even deserves much examination — though the interplay between faith and good works in the process of justification surely is not one of them. Perhaps we may safely leave the altercations over the dating of Easter, or the duties of chantry-priests, or Pope Alexander VI's division of sovereignty in the Americas between Spain and Portugal (1494) to truly dedicated and somewhat eccentric antiquarians. Similar examples could of course be multiplied many times over. But it would cost us dearly to neglect Ignatius of Antioch's testimony, at the beginning of the second century, to the evolution of the Church's episcopal structure; to overlook Irenaeus' witness, a few decades later, to the Roman primacy; or Origen's formulation, some decades after that, of the Blessed Virgin's share in the economy of salvation as the *Theotokos*, the God-bearer; or Leo the Great's Tome (449) which proclaimed the unique personality of Christ, expressing itself in a duality of natures, at once human and divine.

These examples could be replicated over and over. My point is that they deserve examination and that if we disregard them we shall be, as believers, much impoverished and, as educated persons, we shall be left without the data we need to inform our religious commitments. Therefore, examination means exactly that, a careful and sustained scrutiny into the reasons why these thinkers came to the conclusions they did. Nor should such inquiry be restricted to the earliest centuries of the Church's pilgrimage as my examples have done. What, for instance, given the rather casual attitude toward the Eucharist often assumed these days, could be more *intellectually* useful than an investigation into the debates on this subject that raged during the sixteenth century? The ever-colorful Luther, once again, provides a dramatic scenario. Though he abominated the Mass and transubstantiation as a useless good work, he could not, as a devoté of the letter of the Bible, deny the Real Presence of Jesus in the Blessed Sacrament. When there occurred the celebrated meeting between him and Ulrich Zwingli, the Protestant leader from Switzerland, who considered the Eucharistic ceremony no more than a symbolic re-enactment of the Last Supper, an irreconcilable obstacle emerged to the hoped-for German-Swiss alliance against Roman superstition. Luther, we are told, regularly arrived a few minutes before Zwingli at the conference-room, where he would write upon the blackboard set up there the words, in upper case letters: "HOC EST CORPUS MEUM, NON SOLUM SYMBOLUM CORPORIS MEI." I have often imagined Luther standing there, next to his blackboard, his arms folded across his chest and his considerable jaw set out, looking rather like Mussolini on the balcony of the Palazzo Venezia, just after making some outrageous claim for Italian virility. Very early on the Church began to formalize its intellectual treasure, began to establish norms whereby doctrine could be distinguished from opinion, began as it were, to separate the wheat from the tares. This end was accomplished in a variety of ways, one of which was to single out those thinkers who had penetrated most deeply into the truths of Revelation and who had incorporated their insights into an intelligible literary testament. So, by the end of the fourth century, there came into common usage the term "Fathers of the Church," a designation restricted in the beginning to the bishops who had gathered at the first general council, that of Nicaea (325). Gradually however, the meaning evolved until it included those writers who provided in their works, taken together, a full picture of orthodox Christian teaching as it had emerged out of what we call antiquity.

Eventually a chronological line was drawn marking off these ancient defenders of the faith; the last Father of the Church was Pope St. Gregory the Great (d. 604) or perhaps — the line wavers a little depending on one's preferred geography — St. John of Damascus (d. 749). But if the age of the Fathers had passed, the *intellectual* challenge to Christian Revelation had only begun. So it was that a new designation was introduced to identify those savants who with special impact had built over succeeding centuries upon that learned patristic tradition. Indeed, the earliest "Doctors of the Church" overlapped with the most notable Fathers, like Saints Augustine, Jerome, and John Chrysostom, but from 1567 to 1959 twenty-two more Doctors were formally added to this list of singular honor.

Of course, they were all men. Now, in our time, that sorry imbalance has begun to be rectified. Saints Catherine of Siena and Teresa of Avila, in 1970, and, only months ago, St. Thérèse of Lisieux have joined the illustrious doctoral ranks and march in step with Thomas Aquinas, Francis de Sales, Robert Bellarmine, and the others. That the recognition of these great women-thinkers has come much later than it should have must make us blush, as must the insensitive, albeit perhaps unconscious, neglect paid in our liturgical texts to the noble women of the Old and New Testaments. But in any event the honor, tardy as it is, finally accorded to the heroic witness to the Catholic faith given by Catherine, Teresa, and Thérèse is more for our sake than for theirs. Their teaching will continue to enrich us, as it has long done, and it may well serve to inspire their sisters and brothers in Christ all along the pilgrim-way that lies ahead.

Catholic Dossier, **Volume 5, Number 2, March–April 1999, Pages 7–9**

While diligent in upholding objective principles of the history discipline in his own work, O'Connell admired the great English Catholic polemicist Hilaire Belloc's ventures into heroic story-telling. In this essay, O'Connell allows leeway when Belloc identifies himself as a "publicist" promoting hope based on the past.

Belloc's laxity when it comes to certain research details makes O'Connell skeptical of him as an historian, but not as a spokesman for faith. Belloc bears messages bigger than himself, teaching with more interest in timelessness and impact than in footnoted precision. The prolific demonstrations of Catholic imagination by this multi-dimensional Englishman reflect his exhilarating role as a prophet, O'Connell suggests. – WGS

Belloc and the Uses of History

I find it at once exhilarating and depressing to realize that more than a half-century has passed since I first encountered Hilaire Belloc. Exhilarating, because remembering it stirs up again those sentiments of excitement and awe I felt upon my initial contact with that expansive, passionate, singularly virile mind. Depressing, because so much of what Belloc stood for, so many of the causes to the service of which he devoted his great powers, seem to survive, in these bland and jaded times, only as neglected and crumbling monuments; and depressing also, I suppose, because I look back upon him through the prism of my own fifty years' experience of the tumultuous and morally ambivalent developments in the life of the Church and of the world.

It was the books I met, of course, not the man himself — the burly, barrel-chested man with the craggy features and brilliant eyes, garbed in his black cloak and black slouch hat — though it might be said that few thinkers have revealed as much of their inner selves as Belloc did on every page he wrote. I was a teen-age student in a preparatory seminary dedicated to the *Puer Nazarenus*, a place I still revere in memory, not so much for the priestly formation or religious commitment it fostered — a commentary not on the institution's but, alas, on my own spiritual inadequacies — as for the rich intellectual vistas it opened for me. I may well have belonged to the last generation of Americans to receive a classical education in the English public-school tradition: a solid basis of instruction in Latin and Greek, linked to a broad exposure to the best in English and American literature, and supported by an introduction to those talented enough — not me, I'm afraid — to the higher mathematics, to theoretical physics, and to laboratory chemistry.

(This preparatory seminary, incidentally, was housed in an imposingly large and remarkably beautiful building constructed in the Italian style, situated on the shores of a lake which embraced it on three sides. In "the spirit of Vatican II" — surely one of the slipperiest phrases in our contemporary lexicon — it was sold for a pittance by ecclesiastical bureaucrats to a well-meaning group of enthusiastic Protestants who, out of philistine ignorance rather than malice, managed to convert it into a temple of pedestrian ugliness. Thus, in one small corner of what was the Catholic world the vestiges of popery were stamped out. A desecration of beauty occurred — not so violently, to be sure, as that perpetrated during the seventeenth century by Oliver Cromwell's fanatical puritans who, as Hilaire Belloc disdainfully chronicled it, spent themselves systematically smashing the statuary and stained glass in the medieval English cathedrals and profaning the tombs of those buried there — but it was a desecration nonetheless.)

One of the wonderful venues of my prep-school was the wood-paneled library. As I reflect upon it now, it was in fact a rather small room containing only a modest collection of books. But to me, sprung from a blue-collar family barely subsisting during the Great Depression in a clutch of small, drab Minnesota towns, it displayed a peculiar magic and riches beyond dreaming. The library was organized according to the old-fashioned Dewey-Decimal system. As I passed dazzled from one stack of shelves to the next, I came finally to those books catalogued under the number 921. These were the biographies of eminent persons, some of whom I had heard of — Ward's *Life* of Newman was there and Freeman's magisterial study of General Lee and many others whose names were unknown to me. At random I picked a book from the shelf — it was called *Richelieu: A Study*. I flipped open the pages, and my adolescent eye fell upon this passage.

> Here was a man possessing beyond all other men of his time, and
> perhaps of centuries, three qualities — each rare, in combination

almost unknown: the gift of judging exactly the most complicated situation, in all its details and in right proportion; the gift of persuasion over individuals through a right choice of words and tones and a profound divination of the individual character; the gift of directing a whole policy in its largest outlines as well.

In the course of the half-century since I first read these lines, I have had occasion, as a professional historian, to examine the persona and the career of Cardinal Richelieu, the midwife of the modern centralized state, and never have I found a reason to challenge this judgment of Hilaire Belloc, rendered the year before I was born.

Richelieu was but the earliest of my excursions into the past under Belloc's guidance. I happily succumbed to the spell of that rhythmic prose, with its nobility of phrase, its grand sweep of description at once cosmic and intimate, its deep perception of human grandeur and human folly, and — perhaps most striking of all — its uncanny capacity to set out the linkages whereby one can see clearly both the forest and the trees. Thus, after recounting Louis XVI's tryst with the guillotine, Belloc wrote:

> So perished the French monarchy. Its dim origins stretched out and lost themselves in Rome; it had already learnt to speak and to recognize its own nature when the vaults of the Thermae echoed heavily to the slow footsteps of the Merovingian kings. Look up that valley of dead men crowned, and you may see the gigantic figure of Charlemagne, his brows level and his long white beard tangled like an undergrowth, having in his left hand the globe and in his right the hilt of his unconquerable sword.

But it was not just such poetic exuberance that made Belloc's histories so vibrant. No one had a better sense than he of how important physical place is in understanding human events or more skill in conveying it. He wrote a great deal of military history — "Battle-history," he once observed with pardonable exaggeration, "is the only true history in the world: men are then so alive" — and he never took up his pen until he had walked the battlefield himself. Indeed, he once traveled a sleepless forty-eight hours in third-class railway carriages to the Russian frontier, so that he could reconstruct the exact spot where Napoleon's *Grande Armée* had broken to pieces on its retreat from Moscow.

Yet for all Belloc's ability to conjure up places his readers had never seen, to draw them into the drama of past human adventure and travail, to delineate for them personalities as varied as Saladin and William III — history, he liked to say, "is the resurrection of the flesh" — there lay at the core of his historical work a vision as hard as a diamond and as unshakable as the mountains he loved to climb.

> I desire you to remember that we are Europe; we are a great people. The faith is not an accident among us, nor an imposition, nor a garment; it is bone of our bone and flesh of our flesh; it is a philosophy made by and making ourselves. We have adorned, explained, enlarged it; we have given it visible form. This is the service we Europeans have done to God. In return He has made us Christians.

It was only much later, after I had read a good portion of the Belloc *opera* — his account of English politics during the seventeenth and eighteenth centuries, his biographies of Danton and Robespierre and other fascinating figures who shared in the cataclysm of the French Revolution, his studies of the individual Stuart kings of England and Scotland — that I began to experience some doubts about his reliability as a chronicler of the past. It was not so much the furious assaults that were leveled against his work by persons who could be reasonably designated as his ideological rivals; he proved himself more than able to deal with such critics. Nor was it in itself an unease at the suspicion that no scholar could claim expertise in so varied an expanse of past events as Belloc confidently did — from the philosophical debates held in ancient Athens to the logistical arrangements adopted by Marshall Foch when he launched the great Allied offensive in the summer of 1918. Misgivings, to be sure, arose in my mind because of what seemed to be Belloc's studied carelessness about details; so many silly, easily correctable errors of fact tended to spoil the overall effect of the picture he drew, even if few of them were substantive.

But the most glaring difficulty stemmed from Belloc's stubborn refusal to include in his historical studies any reference to the sources he had employed in putting together his narrative, neither by way of conventional foot- or end-notes nor in a standard bibliography. There is no doubt that this disinclination left Belloc open to reproach not only from his declared enemies but from those who were basically his intellectual allies. Nor was this call for documentation a mere pedantic quibble. The reconstruction of the past can be legitimate only when it is founded upon testimony left behind by witnesses — what historians call "sources" — and one who reads a piece of history has a right to require that the author provide evidence of such testimony. Belloc cavalierly brushed aside such objections, with the simple and obviously inadequate claim that he had studied all the relevant material. When pressed on this conundrum during the 1930s by the young Father Philip Hughes — later the celebrated author of *The Reformation in England* and my own mentor — Belloc replied: "But then I am not an historian. I am a publicist."

This assertion should not be taken lightly, as though it were merely a way of putting off Hughes' (or by extension) my own complaint about this aspect of Belloc's work. He wrote his books, he said, not for the approval of academic historians or indeed for intellectuals generally, but for ordinary people. The validity of such a rejoinder depended, of course, on the definition of "ordinary people," which meant, for Belloc, the upper middle class from which he himself had come. And speaking of definitions, maybe "publicist," given its present pejorative connotation, is not quite the right word for us to employ; maybe simply "writer" serves better. For Hilaire Belloc was above all a literary man who flourished during a golden age of print. He produced hundreds of publications, millions of printed words. His earliest books were collections of verse for children, which still, after a hundred years, can charm and delight. As can rollicking lines composed later which showed that the poetic muse never deserted him: "Do you remember an Inn, Miranda,/ Do you remember an Inn? / And the spreading and the tedding / Of the straw for the bedding,/ And the fleas that tease/ In the high Pyrenees."

And his best books, the ones for which he will be longest remembered, were not his histories, admirable as these latter may be in many respects. Even *Danton* (1899), the first and best of his biographies, cannot be compared with *The Path to Rome* (1902), the splendid chronicle of the pilgrimage he made on foot to the Seat of the Apostles, a journey which began in Toul in northeast France (where he had served as a conscript in the French army); nor with *The Four Men* (1912), the somber, yet lyrical evocation of those southern English counties where the ever-restless Belloc found the only real home he ever had; nor with *The Cruise of the Nona* (1925), his tribute to the sea — "the common sacrament of the world," he called it — interspersed with autobiography and commentary on a vast range of subjects; nor, finally, with *Belinda* (1928), a novel which Belloc described as "a Tale of Affection in Youth and Age" and which summoned up the memory of his beloved wife who had died young and had taken with her a large measure of his *joie de vivre*.

What then of the histories, composed by the self-styled "publicist?" The word he chose itself points to a factor that cannot be overestimated. Belloc wrote for money to support himself and his family (he had five children). He lived well according to the standards of Edwardian England — there were always servants in his Sussex house, King's Land, as well as all the domestic amenities and especially fine wines aplenty; he traveled incessantly; he was prodigiously generous — but he was able to do so only by constant writing and lecturing. He adopted a work-schedule that would soon have killed a man of lesser stamina. In 1909, just short of his fortieth birthday, he expressed in a letter to a friend this unremitting necessity; if the tone was jocular, the substance was deadly serious.

> I received a telegram this morning from Glasgow saying, "Could you lecture on travel?" I will lecture on the Proper Method of Milking a Cow, which I have never done, or on Mowing a Field, which I can do jolly well. I will lecture on the Influence of the Jesuits on Europe, or on the Influence of Europe on the Jesuits. I will lecture in verse, like Milton, or in alternate verse, like Apuleius in the theater of Carthage. I will lecture on anything in any manner for money, and don't you forget it. I can lecture twice a day or three times. I can lecture on my hand, on my head, or between my legs, or with the dumb alphabet.

The bitterest and most abiding disappointment of Belloc's life was the refusal of any of the colleges at Oxford — he had been an undergraduate at Balliol, and he loved and revered the university — to offer him a position. He always maintained that had he enjoyed a secure and regular income, and the learned leisure to be found within the precincts of academe, the quality of his work would have been much enhanced. There seems little reason to doubt this avowal. As it was, Hilaire Belloc the historian dwelt in Grub Street, where little time or energy could be expended on checking details or citing sources.

But even more significantly, Belloc's histories must be judged within the context of two core principles. The first of these was that the breakdown of medieval Christendom at the time of the Protestant Reformation had inevitably led to a disintegration of European, and particularly of English, political institutions. The aristocracy that had emerged out of the spoliation of the Church by Henry VIII had evolved into a plutocracy which controlled capital and indeed all the means of production and so deprived the common man of his independence and dignity.

Representative democracy, as practiced in Britain and elsewhere, was a snare and a delusion, because the political parties — Belloc himself had been elected twice to the House of Commons as a Liberal — were merely the creatures of the monied interests. Only the reallocation of physical resources — hence the awkward term "Distributism" — could restore the craftsman, the small merchant, the self-reliant farmer to the autonomy without which there could not be a healthy society.

Allied to this distributist ideal, and indeed fundamental to all Belloc's thought, was his conviction that the Catholic religion had been the prime instrument in the formation of European culture. And as he traced in his books and pamphlets and lectures the step-by-step triumph of the vulgar and greedy plutocrats over the time-span since the Reformation, he invariably found this catastrophe to be rooted in the systematic destruction of Catholicism, especially in "England's green and pleasant land." His argument was remorseless and, though it may have been sometimes overstated, it nevertheless succeeded in forcing a salutary corrective upon reluctant academic historians, with all their Protestant, capitalist, and imperialist prejudices. For this notable intellectual achievement all persons of good will remain in Hilaire Belloc's debt.

"I am by all my nature skeptical," Belloc wrote Chesterton on the occasion of the latter's conversion. "But when religious doubt assails me," he continued, "I discover it to be false; a mood, not a conclusion. My conclusion is the Faith. Corporate, organized, a personality, teaching. A thing, not a theory. It." His religion was neither sentimental nor mystical. Indeed, when urged to read an essay on St. John of the Cross, "[I] found the whole thing repulsive." And, as his biographer records, "if a priest took more than

155

twenty minutes over his Mass, he suspected him of Modernism." Catholicism was "a thing, not a theory. It."

So Hilaire Belloc the Catholic lived, and so he died. Flawed historian he may have been, but he played the role of prophet — spokesman, that is, for a message greater than himself — to perfection. How appropriate, therefore, that Monsignor Ronald Knox chose the following text from Jeremiah for the sermon he preached at the memorial service for Belloc at Westminster Cathedral in August 1953: "Up then, gird thee like a man, and speak out all the message I give thee. Meet them undaunted, and they shall have no power to daunt thee. Strong I mean to make thee this day as fortified city, or pillar of iron, or wall of bronze, to meet king, prince, priest, and common fold all the country through."

Catholic Dossier, **Volume 4, Number 3, May–June 1999, Pages 7–10**

O'Connell the historian will not abide legends about the Spanish Inquisition which today would qualify as "fake news." In this essay on one of the most controversial periods in Catholic history, he counters purveyors of exaggeration by marshalling facts and context with depth and clarity.

His myth-busting insights include the crucially important fact that "Church and State" were one and the same during the Middle Ages, suggesting where both credit and discredit are due. The reader comes away not only better informed but encouraged by O'Connell's certitude that comprehensive understanding overcomes big lies. Truth is stronger than fiction. – WGS

The Spanish Inquisition:
Fact Versus Fiction

"Even while I breathed, there came to my nostrils the breath of the vapor of heated iron. A suffocating odor pervaded the prison. A deeper glow settled each moment in the eyes that glared at my agonies. A richer tint of crimson diffused itself over the pictured horrors of blood. There could be no doubt of the design of my tormentors. Oh, most unrelenting! Oh, most demoniac of men! 'Death,' I said, 'any death but that of the pit.'"

And so on for twenty pages reads the most familiar literary indictment of the wickedness of the Spanish Inquisition. Edgar Allen Poe's short story, "The Pit and the Pendulum," is, to be sure, a piece of fiction, its author a specialist in creating scenes of horror and dread, as the titles of some of his other works suggest: "The Murders in the Rue Morgue," "The Haunted Palace," "The Conqueror Worm." Yet Poe's hideous image of the red-hot poker being prepared as an instrument of torture by grinning Spanish sadists — the "most demoniac of men" — did not strain the credulity of his readers a century and a half ago, nor does it today. We may indeed express our abhorrence a little more light-heartedly — when Professor Higgins, in *My Fair Lady*, wishes to evoke the most frightful of possible alternatives, he sings, "I'd prefer a new edition/Of the Spanish Inquisition," and, with the shivers running up and down the spine, we know exactly what he means.

At a rather more sophisticated level was the picture drawn by Dostoyevsky who, in *The Brothers Karamazov*, imagines the Grand Inquisitor, with "his withered face and sunken eyes," in confrontation with Jesus on the streets of Seville, where the Savior has just restored life to a dead child. "The Inquisitor sees everything; he sees them set the coffin down at Jesus's feet, sees the child rise up, and his face darkens. He knits his thick grey brows, and his eyes gleam with a sinister light. He holds out his finger and bids the guards arrest Jesus. And such is his power, so completely are the people cowed into submission and trembling obedience to him, that the crowd immediately makes way for the guards, and in the midst of a death-like silence they lay hands on Jesus and take him to the Inquisitor who says: 'Tomorrow I shall condemn thee and burn thee at the stake as the worst of heretics'."

Once more, suspension of disbelief is not so difficult, because it is a given that the officers of the Spanish Inquisition were so glutted with pride and blood-lust that they would not have stopped at deicide to gain their ends. Does not the very name of Torquemada summon up visions of ruthlessness and cruelty?

And then of course there is the cinematic conception of the era of the Inquisition, brought to the silver screen in dozens of swashbuckling melodramas, in which the upright, truthful, intelligent, compassionate, handsome, brave Anglo, with his light complexion and buff-colored hair — this last constituent sends a strong ethnic message — crosses swords with the cruel, devious, lustful, foppish, superstitious, cowardly Spaniard with — please notice — his swarthy skin and greasy black hair and mustache. Needless to say, North Atlantic virtue always triumphs over Mediterranean depravity in these contests, Protestant blue-eyed heroism over intrinsically inferior Catholic dark-eyed perfidy, and the audience goes home contented, having seen the Spanish galleon, all afire, sink beneath the waves, while the gallant Errol Flynn (or someone like him) stands coolly self-possessed on the main deck of his ship, his protective arm around the waist of the beautiful blonde lady he has just rescued from the clutches of villainous Latins.

These pulp-fiction romances seldom advert directly to the Inquisition; movie moguls make it a rule to keep their plots uncomplicated. But they do trade in a deep-seated prejudice which has been so carefully cultivated over so long a time that it has become an integral part of our culture. It was not only Poe and Dostoyevsky and even Professor Higgins who assumed that the Spanish Inquisition was wicked because it was Spanish; the rest of us, the hoi polloi, concluded the same. To assert that conclusion was enough to establish its truth; no evidence was required and no rebuttal allowed. In one of the most enduring public relations victories ever accomplished, the history of the fifteenth and sixteenth centuries, Spain's Golden Age, was consciously and methodically distorted by what scholars now candidly call "the Black Legend." This collection of bitter fables, with their overtones of bigotry and racism, proves once more — if proof were necessary — that a lie told often enough and convincingly enough will in the end be accepted as gospel. "One of the great conditions of anger and hatred," the wryly cynical Thackeray observed, "is that you must tell and believe lies against the hated object in order to be consistent." The lies in this instance about the Spanish character and about the Catholicism practiced in the Spain of Queen Isabella, St. Teresa of Avila, and Cervantes were told in order to promote a Protestant and particularly an English Protestant ascendancy, which in due course crossed the Atlantic with the colonists who eventually founded the United States; the sad irony is that though any serious commitment to that cause has long since vanished from the old world and the new, the racist and bigoted distortions put on the record in its behalf by the concoctors of the Black Legend have proved to have a life of their own.

But perhaps the Spanish Inquisition was indeed a wicked institution. If so, that judgment should be made on the basis of those discernible facts an honest examination is able to reveal, and not upon the fevered testimony of self-interested politicians, biased preachers, witless pamphleteers, or — deriving from one or more of these — naive writers of fiction. And, as is the case with any historical reconstruction of a phenomenon now passed away, to understand the contextual framework is a condition for understanding the phenomenon itself. An organization as consequential as the Spanish Inquisition could not have taken shape in a vacuum, nor could its activities have been divorced from the circumstances of its time and place. The same principle therefore holds good in its regard as it does in analyzing other events contemporaneous with the early years of the Inquisition. Thus, for example, we need to know what political and social as well as theological concerns persuaded Queen Elizabeth I of England to treat her Catholic subjects with such barbarity; similarly, we need to recognize that the fanaticism that drove Dutch Calvinists to hang all the priests and vandalize all the churches that fell under their control was not unrelated to a primitive nationalism and even to a primitive capitalism.

As far as the Spanish Inquisition is concerned, one must look for context to chronology and geography. Chronology first. The Holy Office, as it was popularly called, was founded in 1478 on the strength of a papal rescript requested by the sovereigns of a newly united Spain, the wife and husband, Isabella of Castile and Ferdinand of Aragon. For precedent they cited the functioning of the Roman Inquisition during the thirteenth century when, under this rubric, the popes established special circuit courts to investigate and, when possible, to root up various heterodox movements, especially in southern France and northern Italy. These movements — lumped together under the rather sinister-sounding label "Cathari" — had alarmed the lords temporal of the time no less than the lords spiritual, because the Manichaean doctrines and life-style proposed by the Cathari were deemed as subversive of civil well-being as of ecclesiastical. Over the course of a hundred years or so the Cathari were pretty well stamped out or driven underground through the cooperative efforts of Church and State. The inquisitors' job had been to establish the juridical facts in each case, and if, as a result, an individual was judged to be an unyielding heretic, the government's job had been to exact punishment from that person, up to and including death.

Yet in many respects — and here is a truth extremely difficult for us at the end of the twentieth century to comprehend — to speak of "Church and State" during the Middle Ages, and indeed much later, is to draw a distinction without a difference. That the civil and ecclesiastical entities represented essentially separate spheres, that religion should be a strictly private matter left to the choice of each individual, that persons of conflicting religious views or with no religious views at all could live in fruitful harmony — these ideas were unknown during the time the Roman inquisitors were harassing the Albigensians in the south of France, and unknown also when, two centuries later, Ferdinand and Isabella asked for the establishment of an Inquisition unique to Spain. Pope Sixtus IV, in granting their request, explicitly testified to the principle that it was the first duty of kings to nurture and defend the faith of their people, and implicitly he professed what was for him and his contemporaries a truism, that no society could exist without religious uniformity, that — to appropriate a celebrated statement of another era — "a house divided against itself cannot stand." Here was a conviction fully appreciated, incidentally, by the likes of Elizabeth I and the Dutch Calvinists, who gave it full rein in their own persecution policies.

The organization of the Spanish Inquisition differed markedly from its Roman predecessor. The former, with its emphasis upon centralization and royal control, reflected the emergence of the nation-state and the responsibility the monarchy now assumed to guarantee religious orthodoxy. Thus the Grand Inquisitor was appointed by the king and answerable to him, with only the nominal approval of the pope. The Inquisitor in turn appointed the five members of the High Council over which he presided; this body, with its swarm of consultants and clerical staff, exercised ultimate power within the Inquisition's competence. It decided all disputed questions and heard all appeals from the lower inquisitorial courts, which by the middle of the sixteenth century numbered nineteen scattered across Spain and several more in Spanish-occupied territories in Italy and America. Without the permission of the High Council no priest or nobleman could be imprisoned. An *auto-da-fé*, the religious ceremony which included the punishment of convicted heretics and the reconciliation of those who recanted, could not be held anywhere without the sanction of the High Council. Control was also enhanced by the requirement that the lower courts submit to the Council yearly general reports and monthly financial ones.

As far as procedure was concerned, the Spanish Inquisition pretty much followed the precedent established in the thirteenth century and the models provided by secular tribunals. The legal machinery was put into motion by sworn denunciation of an individual or, on occasion, of a particular village or region. In the latter instance, prior to the formal inquiry a "term of grace" of thirty to forty days was routinely issued, during which period suspected dissidents could recant or prepare their defense. Once accused, a defendant was provided the services of a lawyer, and he could not be examined by the officers of the court without the presence of two disinterested priests. The identity of the witnesses of his alleged crime, however, was not revealed to him, and so he could not confront them. This was a severe disadvantage, even though harsh punishment was meted out to those revealed to have been false accusers.

Judges, not juries, decided questions of fact as well as of law, and in effect the Spanish Inquisition combined the functions of investigation, prosecution, and judgment. Indeed, anyone arrested by the Inquisition was presumed guilty until proven innocent, a circumstance very unsettling to us who have enjoyed the blessings of the English common law tradition. Torture, a commonplace with secular jurisdictions, had been forbidden at first in the old Roman Inquisition, but then it had gradually come into use, with the provisos that it be applied only once and that it not threaten life or limb. In Spain these rules were adopted from the start, but early on Sixtus IV, deluged with complaints, protested to the Spanish government that the Inquisition was employing torture too freely. Unhappily the pope's remonstrance fell on deaf ears.

But to return to the chronological consideration, with a bit of geography thrown in for good measure. In 1478, at the moment the Inquisition was set up, the Christians of the Iberian Peninsula had been engaged in a crusade for nearly seven hundred years. The fighting had not been constant, to be sure — it took our enlightened epoch to develop the fine art of total war — but ever since the eighth century, when the Arab Muslims had stormed across the straits of Gibraltar from Africa and with fire and sword had subjugated the peninsula as far north as the Ebro River, the native resistance to their occupation had been constant. And, by fits and starts, with frequent intervals of inactivity, resistance had gradually evolved into counterattack, into a growing determination to win back what had been lost to the alien invaders. Little by little this relentless process of reconquest — *la Reconquista* — drove the descendants of those invaders, the Moors, ever farther into the south until, in 1478, they had left to them only a small enclave around the city of Granada. The end of the crusade was in sight.

It would be difficult to exaggerate how profound an impact this extraordinarily long and all-consuming *cruzado* had upon the formation of Spanish public policy. Comparisons are impossible to draw, because no other Christian people had experienced anything even remotely similar. As suggested above, a Europe-wide consensus had indeed developed during the Middle Ages that religious dissidents could not be tolerated if true religion and harmonious society were to endure. Add to this the universal conviction that heretics adhered to their objectionable opinions not out of conscience but out of bad will, and it comes as no surprise that increasingly stringent laws were enacted throughout Christendom against those who refused to conform. Since such a refusal was judged the worst possible crime, the ultimate penalty for it everywhere was the worst form of capital punishment imaginable, burning at the stake. Though this ferocious sentence was carried out relatively rarely, the prospect of it did act as a deterrent and did induce all except the most stout-hearted to disavow their heterodoxies once brought to light by a judicial process. Still, the troublesome possibility remained that those who had formally recanted might have done so out of fear rather than conversion of mind, and that they continued to practice their subversive heresies in secret, waiting for a more propitious day.

In the Iberia of the *Reconquista* a scenario of this kind presented a danger profoundly more serious than elsewhere. As the Christians slowly reestablished their hegemony over the peninsula — expressed in the two distinct political entities, Portugal and Spain — the potential antagonists of religious uniformity they were determined to impose were not indigenous eccentrics, as was the case in other European countries (bear in mind that the Protestant Reformation was at this moment still forty years in the future), but a conquered population linked by ties of race and religion to the Muslims living in the principalities of North Africa, which at Gibraltar lay only sixteen watery miles away. Even more ominous from the Spanish point of view was the fact that these so-called barbary states — the modern nations of Morocco, Algeria, and Tunisia — formed part of a vast imperial system established by the Muslim Turks, a system as powerful and menacing to western Europe as the Soviet bloc was conceived to be in our day. As the *Reconquista* proceeded, therefore, and especially after Granada and the last remnant of Spanish Islam fell to the armies of Ferdinand and Isabella in 1492, policy-makers had to decide how to treat the Moors and the relatively small but influential Jewish community which, in marked contrast to what our century has witnessed, had flourished within a larger Islamic society. The Christian victors, fearful of Muslim sympathizers in their midst, offered no compromise: Moors and Jews had to accept baptism or face expulsion from the country now defined as entirely Catholic.

What this decision amounted to, of course, was a policy of forced conversion, something quite incompatible with traditional Catholic teaching. This fact was pointed out by several popes and numerous Spanish theologians over a long period, but the sentiment expressed by one of Ferdinand of Aragon's royal predecessors was the one that prevailed: "The enemies of the cross of Christ and violators of the Christian law are likewise our enemies and the enemies of our kingdom, and ought therefore to be dealt with as such."

Predictably, however, the stark choice between conformity and exile invited pretense and hypocrisy on the part of those dragooned into a faith not of their own choosing. The Jews and Moors who conformed rather than depart the land in which they and their ancestors had lived for hundreds of years did so with varying measures of reluctance, merging often into downright dissimulation. And this is precisely why the Inquisition was created by the Spanish monarchs: as the etymology of the word implies, the first task of this new judicial body was inquiry, specifically inquiry into the authenticity of the conversion of the Moors and Jews who had come under the sway of those monarchs.

But once again we must stress the chronological track, because the bloody reputation of the Spanish Inquisition — though it formally existed for more than three centuries — was earned during its first decade and a half, even before, that is, the capture of Granada. During this unhappy period perhaps as many as 2000 persons were burnt as heretics. Though this number is only a small fraction of what the Black Legend routinely alleged, it is nevertheless sobering enough. Almost all those executed were *conversos* or New Christians, converts, that is, from Judaism who were convicted of secretly practicing their former religion. It should be borne in mind that the Inquisition, as a church-court, had no jurisdiction over Moors and Jews as such. But, ironically, once such persons accepted baptism, they became capable of heresy in the technical sense of the word. Thus the early savagery of the Spanish Inquisition contributes another chapter to the sad history of anti-Semitism, motivated on this occasion, however, more by politico-religious expediency than by racial hatred. It was in any event an enormous and unforgivable miscalculation. Far from constituting a danger to the nation, the Jewish *conversos* of previous decades had already been admirably blended into the larger community. As Professor William Monter has pointed out, the New Christians "represent the first known large-scale and long-term assimilation of Jews into any Christian society. Although the process included many painful adaptations, some severe backlash and even a decade of brutal persecution under the Inquisition, it ended with their general integration into Spanish society. Their descendants quietly flouted racist codes and contributed to the vibrant Catholicism of Golden Age Spain; St. Teresa of Avila was the granddaughter of a New Christian penanced by the Inquisition."

It seems as though the violence with which the Spanish Inquisition began its tenure exhausted or perhaps shamed it into a moderation which the purveyors of the Black Legend stonily ignore. But the facts cannot be gainsaid. During the sixteenth and seventeenth centuries, when Spanish sovereignty extended from Italy to most of Latin America, on average less than three persons a year were executed by the Inquisition, which was formally constituted in all those places as well as at home. Or, to give the Spaniards the benefit of the doubt, perhaps as the bitter struggle of the *Reconquista* gradually faded from their collective memory, even as the Muslim threat itself receded, they exercised a restraint consistent with their principles. However that may be, for my part I am glad there is no longer in existence an Inquisition that might have me arrested on the basis of charges lodged by persons unknown to me, as happened to St. Ignatius Loyola. Yet as one who has lived through most of a century in which cruelty and atrocity and oppression have reached a pitch, quantitatively and qualitatively, inconceivable to our ancestors — inconceivable even to Torquemada — I think a measure of discretion would be appropriate when bemoaning the wickedness of the Spanish Inquisition, more discretion anyway than that exercised by Poe and Dostoyevsky.

Catholic Dossier, **Volume 2, Number 6, Nov.–Dec. 1996, Pages 6–10**

O'Connell's passionate defense of substantive, fruitful history pits him against outright disinformation — and also against what he sees as violations of sound scholarly practice. In the pair of essays presented here, O'Connell criticizes books by Richard McBrien, who was an influential professor of theology at the University of Notre Dame for many years.

Questionable traits cited include injections of opinion into texts, selection of sources without balance or objectivity, carelessness in checking details, and a paucity of serious, original research and writing. These reviews reveal O'Connell's combative demeanor when he believed the canons of serious history were ignored. His pugnacity is most in evidence in the second essay. The first essay is a dual review, in which his critique of an additional author includes vigorous scrutiny but does not rise to the same level of contention. – WGS

Not Infallible:
Two Histories of the Papacy

Featured Review
Saints and Sinners: A History of the Popes
by Eamon Duffy Yale University Press
Lives of the Popes
by Richard P. McBrien Harper San Francisco

The proudest royal houses are but of yesterday when compared with the line of Supreme Pontiffs. That line we trace back in an unbroken series, from the Pope who crowned Napoleon in the nineteenth century to the Pope who crowned Pepin in the eighth; and far beyond the time of Pepin the august dynasty extends, till it is lost in the twilight of fable. The republic of Venice came next in antiquity; but the republic of Venice is gone, and the Papacy remains. The Papacy remains, not in decay, not a mere antique, but full of life and vigor.

So wrote Macaulay more than 150 years ago. The occasion for the memorable essay, published in the *Edinburgh Review* in 1840, was the appearance of an English version of Leopold von Ranke's *The Ecclesiastical and Political History of the Popes of Rome During the Sixteenth and*

Seventeenth Centuries. Neither Ranke nor Macaulay entertained any intrinsic sympathy for the Church of Rome; both were Protestants, though it is probably safe to say that Ranke took his Lutheranism rather more seriously than Macaulay did the evangelical Anglicanism in which he had been reared. Macaulay at any rate tempered his appreciation of the papacy's "youthful vigor" with puzzlement: "The stronger our conviction that reason and scripture were decidedly on the side of Protestantism, the greater is the reluctant admiration with which we regard that system of tactics against which reason and scripture were employed in vain."

More to the point, perhaps, is the fact that both men, in quite different ways, stood at the cutting edge of the writing of history in their day; both represented the first generation of historians who consciously modeled their work on the inductive method of the physical sciences. Taking as their exemplar the physicist in his laboratory, this new breed of researchers into the past pulled away the straitjacket of moral uplift into which their discipline had been bound since Aristotle's time. They repudiated the traditional wisdom that history functioned as a barely respectable species of ethics, teaching virtue by examples. For Ranke, what mattered was to ransack the archives and to find the documentary sources that would make it possible to reconstruct the past "*wie es eigentlich gewesen* — as it had really happened"; for Macaulay, what mattered was a reconstruction of the past that would provide a literate and plausible explanation of the institutional realities of the present.

It cannot be surprising, therefore, that both of them, despite whatever confessional or intellectual distaste they may have felt, were fascinated by the papal phenomenon, by its antiquity, by its phoenix-like capacity to recover from calamity. Brought time and again to the brink of dissolution, most recently — indeed, within the living memory of them both — by the seemingly irresistible assault of Voltaire and Robespierre, of the Enlightenment and the Revolution, popery had emerged stronger than before. "It is not strange." Macaulay wrote, "that in the year 1799 even sagacious observers should have thought that, at length, the hour of the Church of Rome was come . . . But the end was not yet. Again doomed to death, the milk white hind was still fated not to die. Even before the funeral rites had been performed over the ashes of Pius VI, a great reaction had commenced, which, after the lapse of more than 40 years, appears still to be in progress." The "milk white hind" was, of course, Dryden's metaphor in *The Hind and the Panther*, which still rang with Catholic defiance of a Protestant culture: "In Pope and Council who denies the place, Assisted from above with God's unfailing grace."

If by some wizardry Macaulay were suddenly to reappear a century and a half after he had paid his reluctant tribute to the staying power of papal Rome, he would have had no difficulty expanding his original induction. All sorts of individuals and movements since 1840 have signaled the Roman church's impending demise. Freemasons and *libertins*, apostate intellectuals, radical traditionalists on the Right and liberation theologians on the Left, Nazis and Communists, blood-stained altars in the Mexico of the 1920s and the brutish cruelty of the gulag in the China of the 1990s — but none of them has succeeded any more than did Voltaire and Robespierre. "How many divisions has the pope?" Stalin asked contemptuously. But — to paraphrase Macaulay — the Soviet Union, like the Republic of Venice, is gone, and the papacy remains.

Why this should have happened involves an intriguing riddle, the solution to which may well depend on the eye of the beholder. Macaulay, for his part, had no doubts. "Tactics," he maintained, shrewd "human policy," a unique ability, for instance, to channel and control the passionate zeal of genius. "Place John Wesley at Rome [and] he is certain to be the first General of a new society devoted to the interests and honor of the Church. Place St. Teresa [of Avila] in London [and] her restless enthusiasm ferments into madness, not untinctured with craft." But this explanation, and any like it, sounds unpersuasive to a Catholic who wonders why "tactics" or "human policy" did not likewise save the Caesars, the Ming dynasty, the sultans of Constantinople, the British Empire, the first, second, third, and fourth French republics, and the Whig Party U.S.A. Indeed, any Christian who believes in Providence, however reserved he may be about this or that papal pretension, can hardly judge it absurd that Catholics should find in this, humanly speaking, incredible succession evidence of a moral miracle that betokens the continuation within the Church of the Petrine office. "Simon Peter," Jesus said, "do you love me more than these? Then feed my sheep."

Debate on this point will go on, no doubt, till the Second Coming. Meanwhile, the grand sweep of papal history continues to fascinate inquirers, as it does Eamon Duffy and Richard P. McBrien. In *Saints and Sinners: A History of the Popes*, Duffy, reader in Church History and fellow of Magdalen College, Cambridge, attempts, he tells us, "to provide an overview of the whole history of the papacy from the apostle Peter to Pope John Paul II." "This is a history of the popes," he adds sensibly; "it cannot claim to be the history of the popes. No one-volume survey of an institution so ancient and so embedded in human history and culture can be anything more than a sketch." Father McBrien, Crowley-O'Brien-Walter Professor of Theology at the University of Notre Dame, shows himself similarly diffident in tendering to the reading public his *Lives of the Popes*: "I cannot imagine any individual historian today writing a truly complete and comprehensive history of each of the more than 260 pontificates spread over the course of almost 2000 years."

With such disclaimers in hand, what have these books to offer us? Take Duffy's first. *Saints and Sinners*, it should be noted, is linked to a six-part television series shown in Britain, Australia, and the United States, and the book itself with its abundance of plates and photographs, most of them in color, furnishes a marvelous feast for the eye. In the midst of this visual elegance, Duffy carries his narrative forward through six chapters, each divided into four sections, presumably an arrangement conforming to the demands of the television series. Appended are a chronological list of popes, a glossary of terms, a bibliographical essay, and a few pro forma endnotes. Though there is nothing original in Duffy's text, it exhibits adequate acquaintance with the usual secondary sources. The prose reads smoothly for the most part, and surely no one can blame Duffy for emphasizing what he had chosen to emphasize. All in all, this is a useful volume, and certainly one that would grace any coffee table.

There are, however, problems, some of them related to careless editing. Thus, it is disconcerting to find a ludicrous numerical error in the opening sentence of the preface to *Saints and Sinners* — the very first sentence in the book. But more fundamental difficulties arise naturally from the genre itself. To write a survey of this kind requires the author to deal with subjects outside his demonstrated field of expertise — in Duffy's case, the Reformation in England — and yet to speak of them with enough confidence to earn the reader's trust. There is a fine line here between modesty and presumption, and Duffy does not always walk it nimbly. He would have done better had he displayed more reserve about his own capacity to discern the elements of thorny issues like the spread of Monophysitism (p. 41) or the character of Americanism (pp. 241–42) or the philosophical component of what Pius X condemned as "Modernism" (pp. 249–51).

Small errors of fact in a study of this scope — for instance, the date of

Constantine's death (p. 23), the identity of the tribe that sacked Rome in 410 (p. 36), the means by which Italy paid compensation to the Holy See in 1929 (p. 258) — are probably inevitable. Not so, however, the gossipy and condescending treatment of Pius XII's last days (p. 268) or the witless description of Sen. Joseph McCarthy as defender of a "right-wing" Catholicism (p. 266). Not so either the barrage of clichés that resounds especially through Duffy's early chapters: "If the fourth century papacy had not existed, it would have had to be invented" (p. 27); "For [Pope] Vigilius, however, chickens now began to come home to roost" (p. 43); "The relationship with Charlemagne was not all roses" (p. 73); "Unable to beat them, [Pope] Hadrian joined them" (p. 109). Perhaps these trite sayings as well as the frequent use of hyperbolic expressions — "nightmare complexities of eastern theological debates" (p. 25), "volcanic reaction" to a heretical proposition (p. 42), the "wildly extravagant" Avignon popes (p. 125) — are best explained by the connection of *Saints and Sinners* to its televised accompaniment. However that may be, Duffy, though a relatively young man, has already acquired the veteran academic's skill in composing a bibliographical essay that suggests an almost preternatural knowledge of the sources: If one wants to know the "best account of Constantine's religious beliefs," "the best treatment of the *Spirituali* of the sixteenth century," or the "best biography of Pius VI," one need only consult *Saints and Sinners*, pp. 308, 313, and 314.

Father McBrien, by contrast, virtually disdains critical bibliography or other conventional scholarly apparatus. His "Select Bibliography" takes up but three pages (and includes a mistitle for Pastor's celebrated *History of the Popes from the Close of the Middle Ages*), but in his own way he intimates that he, no less than Duffy, has pretty well mastered the "voluminous" literature. "The listing of titles," McBrien says, "is [meant] to provide a representative sample of scholarly, encyclopedic, and popular works" (p. 489). Whether it does so may be open to question, but more important is the assertion on the same page that expresses the *raison d'être* for *Lives of the Popes*: "If the author of this book could recommend another comprehensive, one-volume, historical, theological, canonical, and pastoral treatment of the popes and the papacy geared to the non- specialist reader, he would do so. But that is precisely the gap this book is intended to fill."

McBrien's book is not a history, like Duffy's — not, that is, a narrative concerned with context and transition. *Lives of the Popes* is rather a kind of catalogue or Who Was Who, supplemented by various lists, tables, and expanded explanations. Some of these latter are quite helpful, like the chronological rosters of popes and antipopes (pp. 443–50 and 466, respectively), a register of "key papal encyclicals" (458–65), and a description of the ways popes have been chosen over the centuries (403–16). Another appendix, "Rating the Popes" (429–42), can only be called — to put the kindest word on it — idiosyncratic. McBrien's own minimalist views about the papacy are clearly reflected in this section. Of the 262 pontiffs, he finds only two who were "outstanding": John XXIII (d. 1963) and Gregory I (d. 604). He adds another 12 who were "good or above average." The "worst of the worst" — an interestingly provocative phrase — number 24. It is intriguing that McBrien includes in this rogue's gallery Gregory XVI (d. 1846), who was pope at the time Macaulay thought the Roman church was "full of life and youthful vigor."

The bulk of Father McBrien's book (367 pages), however, is composed of sketches of the individual popes, and here there arises an extremely troubling problem. In his preface (p. 2), Father McBrien concedes that he has "relied on Kelly throughout" — the reference is to J. N. D. Kelly, *The Oxford Dictionary of the Popes* (Oxford University Press, 1986; 347 pages). "But this book," asserts McBrien, referring to his own, "differs from Kelly's in that it offers more than summaries of each pope's life and pontificate." This claim is legitimate only in the sense that the "more" on offer is McBrien's sometimes fatuous, usually debatable, and almost always unhistorical commentary. As far as quantity of *information* about the popes is concerned, Canon Kelly wins hands down. Moreover, the information McBrien *does* provide echoes almost to the word what Kelly published twelve years ago. In dealing with this admittedly delicate matter, only a comparison of texts will suffice.

"Profiting by the peaceful conditions ensured by Charlemagne, [Pope] Hadrian not only built, restored, or beautified an extraordinary number of Roman churches, but renewed the city's walls, strengthened the embankments of the Tiber, and completely reconstructed four great aqueducts" (Kelly, p. 97); "In Rome, the pope took advantage of the peaceful conditions made possible by Charlemagne and built and restored many churches, strengthened the walls of the city and the embankments of the Tiber River

. . . and completely reconstructed four great aqueducts" (McBrien, p. 126). "Although a harsh and divisive pontiff, [Pope Leo III] was included in the catalogue of saints in 1673 because of the presumed miracle of the restoration of his eyes and tongue" (Kelly, p. 99); "In spite of his severe, divisive, and morally dubious pontificate, [Leo III] was included in a catalogue of saints in 1673, because of the presumed 'miracle' of the restoration of his eyes and tongue" (McBrien, p. 131). "[Pope Martin V] showed unusual moderation towards the Jews, denouncing (1422 and 1429) violent anti-Jewish preaching and forbidding compulsory baptism of Jewish children under the age of twelve. In Rome he carried out a vast program of reconstruction of ruined churches and public buildings" (Kelly, p. 240); "[Martin V] displayed unusual sensitivity toward Jews. He denounced anti-Jewish preaching and forbade the compulsory baptism of Jewish children under the age of 12. In Rome he organized a vast program of reconstruction of ruined churches and public buildings." (McBrien, p. 255).

This sample could be replicated many times over. Which raises the question: why should Father McBrien's account be preferred to Canon Kelly's, when the former has clearly embraced the material in the latter — in a host of instances almost word-for-word — and when the latter has conscientiously identified its sources for each entry while the former has not? McBrien's answer (p. 2) is that Canon Kelly, an Anglican, "may have been under greater constraint than a tenured Catholic theologian, lest he [Kelly] cross the line of ecumenical propriety by raising awkward questions regarding papal claims or the implications of actions taken by individual popes."

One may doubt that the throne of Peter, after nearly 2,000 years, will tremble at the prospect of "awkward questions," even when raised by so formidable an authority as "a tenured Roman Catholic theologian." One may wonder too at this theologian's implicit charge that Kelly, a distinguished historian, has consciously repressed information found in his sources for the sake of "propriety." This is chutzpah at its least endearing. In short, if a reader wants to know what opinions Father McBrien holds about the papacy in 1998, this is the book for him; but if a reader wants to know about the lives of the popes, he should look elsewhere.

Macaulay concluded his colorful tribute to the longevity of the Roman church with an arresting image: "She may still exist in undiminished vigor when some traveler from New Zealand shall, in the midst of a vast solitude, take his stand on a broken arch of London Bridge to sketch the ruins of St. Paul's." One hundred and fifty years later, vibrant London belies this bit of whimsy, and Saint Paul's Cathedral still stands in all the splendor Christopher Wren gave it. But the London Bridge of Macaulay's day has indeed fallen down and has been erected again as a tourist attraction under the shadow of the Mojave Mountains, in far-western Arizona. Perhaps the whimsy contained a splinter of discernment after all.

Fellowship of Catholic Scholars Quarterly, Volume 21, Number 4, Fall 1998, Pages 61–64

A Bad Penny:
Richard McBrien Trivializes Politics and Religion

In the first sentence of *Caesar's Coin: Religion and Politics in America* (Macmillan, 294 pp., $19.95) Richard P. McBrien misquotes Lincoln. The error is only a trifling one; it alters neither the meaning of the president's words nor Father McBrien's application of them. But the resonances of the Gettysburg Address are so familiar to every American, from the age of ten onward, that even a slight distortion of that sacred text jars the ear and raises a tiny voice of doubt within the reader's mind. Will an author who begins a serious treatise with a thoughtless verbal slip prove equal to a complex subject such as "religion and politics in America"? The two hundred or so pages of *Caesar's Coin* which follow demonstrate that when a controversialist gets the bit in his teeth, small considerations such as complexity and accuracy hold no terrors for him.

Father McBrien describes himself as a "professionally active theologian" interested in politics since his days as a high school pupil. "This book," he says, "is simply a vehicle for sharing with others something of what I myself have had to struggle to learn." He intends to share, apparently, not all but at least a measure of what he has learned, for which, I suppose, we should be grateful. Father McBrien claims no particular training in political theory or history, nor, presumably, any experience of practical politics. As a *soi-disant* ecclesiologist, he is not unacquainted with questions of governance and of power-relationships which inevitably arise within religious institutions. Aside from the contribution to be expected from that sort of expertise, we may fairly assume that *Caesar's Coin* — a wonderful title — is the work of an auto-didact, who has built upon his adolescent insights.

Father McBrien divides his book into three parts, the first of which, in two chapters, is designed to establish the state of the question, to offer necessary definitions, and to draw proper distinctions. Here we are introduced to Father McBrien's method of discourse, which is a fascinating exercise in the arts of polemic. The principle applied is assault *en masse*, the piling up of references so varied and so numerous that the enthralled reader is borne away by their sheer quantity. This is apparently why Father McBrien loves lists, and why he hates to leave anybody or anything off his lists. He shares with us, for instance, the information that "the emergence of Islamic fundamentalism" has had a profound affect upon Iran, and, he adds gravely, "Islam generally has had a significant political impact upon such diverse countries as Pakistan, Saudi Arabia, Libya, Turkey, India, Malaysia, Indonesia, Afghanistan, Nigeria, the Sudan, Egypt, Syria, Iraq, Burma, Chad, Ethiopia, Cyprus, Lebanon, Thailand, and the Philippines."

This dedication to inclusivity possesses other rhetorical charms as well; thus, Father McBrien eschews the use of *Roman* Catholic as a denominational designation, because, he says, it excludes Catholics who are not of the Latin rite; and he refrains as much as possible from employing the term "American" for a citizen of the United States, "out of respect for our American neighbors in Canada and throughout Central and South America."

I am sure the glaring omission was not meant as a conscious slight to the Republic of Mexico, because Father McBrien clearly wants to leave no one out. This desire perhaps explains why he invokes so many authorities whose views really do not interest him very much. At any rate, as he leads us through the thickets of the terminology he has chosen for our enlightenment — church, sect, public religion, civil religion, community, society, nation, state, morality/moral values — he calls to duty a host of lesser guides whom he genially associates with himself. Plato and Aristotle of course are there, and so are Augustine of Hippo and the Apostle Paul. It is fascinating to learn that "with Cicero the field of [political] argument expanded beyond philosophy to theology." Father McBrien does not invite us to investigate the reasons for this arresting observation, but such diffidence appears in accord with his anxiety not to trouble us with distractions like evidence or coherent argument. He does not want us to have to struggle, as he did. Snippets of quotation are quite enough. Indeed, it suffices in most instances just to mention a lot of people, or, put more vulgarly, to drop a lot of names: Hobbes, Locke, Mill, Adam Smith, Machiavelli, Tocqueville, Thomas Paine. Father McBrien can tell us in a sentence what Calvin's political views were; Aquinas occupies him for two or three.

Nor does Father McBrien disdain the moderns. With the same serenity and self- confidence, he hovers over the surface of the thought of Robert Bellah, Martin Marty, and Walter Lippmann. George Will gets a friendly nod, as does Clifford Geertz and — an ecumenical touch — Milton Friedman. Ernst Troeltsch fulfills the requirement that an author must always, in this sort of inventory, bring forward a German Kantian of a couple of generations ago. For the most part Father McBrien is even-handed — what he calls "civil" — in that all the savants he refers to are treated with the same indifference. And even when he makes exceptions to this rule, he imitates the Lord who giveth even as He taketh away. Thus, as he sadly dismisses the thought of Jacques Maritain as derivative, he can recommend strongly the contributions to the science of politics of J. Bryan Hehir — the same Father Hehir, who is known by some among his many admirers as the Obadiah Slope of the National Conference of Catholic Bishops. And though the work of John Courtney Murray, excellent in its time, is now "dated," Father McBrien assures us that he himself will "update and move beyond" Murray's "extraordinary achievements."

But Father McBrien is at his best when he can combine his penchant for citing famous names with his predilection for drawing up lists. So, within a few pages, we are treated to Niebuhr's five Christ-and-Culture categories, Avery Dulles's "models of the Church" (also five), and David J. O'Brien's Catholic "options" (only four). Inclusion of such material has the incidental advantage of allowing the author to use words such as "schemata" and "problematic." And Father McBrien — surely as famous as the gentlemen just mentioned — tops them all by providing a list of eight (count them) "levels" on which the clergy participate in politics.

As I read this first section of *Caesar's Coin*, I sensed that I had encountered a similar methodology before, but, for the life of me, I could not remember where or when. It smacks of course of certain inferior varieties of social science, in which the guiding principle is a simple accumulation of instances, without analysis or synthesis, a rambling, unconnected catalogue — induction, as it were, run amok. Then it came to me: Father McBrien is only a year or two younger than I am, which means that his seminary education, like mine, took place in the 'fifties, the bad old days before the second Council of the Vatican. His procedure in *Caesar's Coin* is a mirror image of the theological manuals then in fashion. Those books, too, had the merit of assembling the great thinkers of the Western world, and, so to speak, putting them in their place. All nuance was readily dispensed with, as the wrong-headedness which lay at the core of the work of Rousseau or Kant or Loisy was presented to the reader on a half-page. No thought was required, no struggle, so that the seminarian, thus free from wrestling with the troublesome questions raised, say, by Hume's theory of natural religion, could spend his time more profitably learning the intricacies of parish finance.

The analogy, to be sure, limps in many respects, but there remains one essential characteristic common to Father McBrien and the manualists: he and they have already arrived at their conclusions before they trot out the texts they quote so summarily, the paraphrases they advance so confidently, the footnotes they append so pedantically. (*Caesar's Coin* has fifty-four pages of notes containing the usual citation of sources along with sustaining argument of one sort or another. Any graduate student preparing a seminar paper could well be proud of the apparatus. The book also includes two appendices [twenty-one pages] composed, predictably, of lists.) Father McBrien, for example, toward the end of the first section of *Caesar's Coin* boldly asserts that "the problems of church and state and of church and society are not the same as that [*sic*] of religion and politics." I am confident that he accepted this truism before he dipped into the works of Max Weber or Peter Berger, and one may legitimately doubt that Weber, Berger, and the others had much to do with the maturation of Father McBrien's own thought, such as it is. But certainly the old theological manualists, who sometimes put their conclusions into bold-face type so that the laziest seminarian could not miss them, would have nodded in approval at Father McBrien's decision to place a key definition in italics: "I should define *religion…as the whole* complexus *of attitudes, convictions, emotions, gestures, rituals, symbols, beliefs, and institutions by which persons come to terms with, and express, their personal and/or communal relationship with ultimate Reality (God and everything that pertains to God).*"

The mountain hath indeed been labor.

The pseudo-scholarship of the first section of *Caesar's Coin* invites — almost demands — ridicule. But one should take care not to be so distracted by the hilarity of it all that one misses Father McBrien's intent. He has written a highly partisan book, and he holds distinctly partisan positions. Speaking broadly, those positions represent the views of the bureaucracy of the

United States Catholic Conference, of Cardinal Joseph Bernardin, and of many other thoughtful persons. There is of course nothing wrong with choosing sides in a household dispute which turns for the most part on matters of opinion; there are many mansions in God's house, and Catholics have always argued zestfully among themselves. But Father McBrien wants to anoint his opinions on contemporary events with the oil of a scholarly tradition which he has invented for the purpose. How can one gainsay my arguments, he asks in effect, if I represent in this time and place the accumulated wisdom of the ages? This tactic might have succeeded had he been able at least to relate his present views to some respectable school of thought, but he has failed to do so and — the most curious feature of *Caesar's Coin* — he appears to have no interest in doing so. Plato, John Courtney Murray, and I, he seems content to say, have all contributed to political enlightenment. I suppose such a stance is part of the inevitable loneliness of the auto-didact.

The second section of *Caesar's Coin* (chapters three and four) proceeds pretty much along the lines of the first. Father McBrien's focus is narrower here, however, and so the narrative is relatively more intelligible. In chapter three he examines some of the background to the religion clause of the first amendment with special reference to the contrast between Jefferson's "wall" of separation dividing church and state and Madison's "line" of separation. Though some unnecessary confusion arises from a failure to delineate carefully enough Madison's use of "republic" and "democracy," the treatment otherwise is unexceptionable if pedestrian. But suddenly Father McBrien spies a chance to draw up a list, and, while he denies explicitly any "claim to constitutional expertise," he nevertheless provides thumbnail sketches of no less than fifty-eight decisions (by my rough count) of the U. S. Supreme Court in religion-related cases, all these in twenty pages.

In chapter four Father McBrien explores the response to the uniquely "American religious landscape" by the three major religious groupings in the United States. The Protestants receive eight pages in this discussion, the Jews three, and I feel no competence to comment on the author's observations about them, except to note his almost pathological distaste for Protestant fundamentalists. As for the Catholics (eighteen pages), Father McBrien begins with a startlingly muddled little historical survey; his description of the Americanist Crisis of the 1890s is wrong in almost every particular, and he flatly misstates — one hopes out of ignorance rather than malice — the thesis of the papal letter *Testem Benevolentiae* (1899). But I should hardly say "startlingly"; I am not alone among the practitioners of my humble craft to have noticed that the theologians who most loudly espouse an "historical" in preference to an "outmoded scholastic" perspective in their work often either refuse to learn any history, or, in the spirit of Father McBrien's mentors, the old theology manualists, pick and choose among the historical data to suit their preconceived notions.

Father McBrien at any rate is more comfortable talking about contemporary affairs, and, though he contends more than once that the thought of John Courtney Murray is "dated," his own book comes alive, at the end of chapter four, when he quotes extensively from Murray and summarizes the familiar story of the relationship between Murray's interventions and the genesis of the splendid decree of Vatican II on religious freedom. Father McBrien's intense desire to preempt Murray and the teachings of the council is quaintly transparent.

It is something of a relief to reach page 135 of *Caesar's Coin*, the beginning of chapter five (and of the third section), because there the point of Father McBrien's book — the purpose of all the flim-flam that has gone before — becomes clear. The chapter is entitled "Abortion: The Hardest Case," and it is the first of the two in which, Father McBrien says, he intends to move the discussion of religion and politics in America from the theoretical to the practical plane.

What it is in fact is an unabashed apologia for the views of Governor Mario Cuomo of New York. The vehicle Father McBrien uses is a lively and extremely biased account of how the abortion issue was played out during the presidential campaign of 1984.

There is no reason to enter once again into those quarrels of three years ago which seemed to pit Governor Cuomo against Archbishops O'Connor and Law (as they were then). Suffice it to say that Father McBrien here fits into place what I might call the last brick in the edifice of his methodology. He first defines what the middle ground is, then places Governor Cuomo (and himself) squarely upon it, and finally denounces those who disagree as extremists of the "left" or of the "right." Predictably, the extremists of the "right" are judged the worse: the quarrel was initiated by Archbishop O'Connor, complicated by the obtuseness of Archbishop Law, and exploited by the minions of the Republican administration. Representative Ferraro on the "left" does not, to be sure, escape altogether unscathed in this cautionary tale — even Homer sometimes nods — though her sins are venial compared to the "virulence" of "right-wing" Catholics and funda- mentalist Protestants. But why go on? The account is a classical example of propaganda.

The sixth and seventh chapters of *Caesar's Coin* contain a grab-bag of instructions on how to think properly about such disparate public questions as pornography, homosexuality, prayer in public schools and state financial aid to private schools, conscientious objection, and the sanctuary move- ment. There are a few pages — almost an afterthought — allotted to the Catholic bishops' recent pastoral letter on nuclear armaments. None of this commentary strays an inch from the party line, and at the end one grows weary of the pomposity, the jejune prose, the air of omniscience worthy of an anchor on the eleven o'clock news. And one grows almost angry at Fa- ther McBrien who identifies "civility" as agreement with himself and who has the chutzpah to demand that *Caesar's Coin* set the terms of the argu- ments presently raging among us Catholics about abortion and a host of other matters: "The public debate over abortion, even when conducted in a civil manner, can neither promote clarity nor facilitate the resolution of conflict unless the debate honors the basic definitions, distinctions, and principles that have been engaged throughout this book."

Father McBrien has not written a wicked book, only a trivial one. Un- less it could be argued that to trivialize such an important subject is itself a species of wickedness.

Crisis, Volume 5, Number 5, May 1987, Pages 6–9

O'Connell's mastery of facts and context allows for great stories to be told. But his revelations about a person's mind-frame or circumstances behind the scenes make the stories richer, explaining the "how" and the "why." His literary instincts and intuitions even led him to write a published novel.

The two essays presented here show O'Connell enjoyed pondering authors' fictionalized explorations of reason and faith, suffering and redemption. He proved a balanced observer of the work of two significant twentieth-century literary figures, novelist J. F. Powers and playwright Robert Bolt.

The first piece demonstrates a natural interest in the writing of Powers. His astute novels about Catholic culture in the Midwest sparked an assessment by an historian with first-hand knowledge of priests from Minnesota. – WGS

J. F. Powers: In Memoriam

"A big spider drowsy in his web, drugged with heat and sins, he waited for the next one to be hurled into his presence by guilt ruddy ripe, or, as with the old ladies who come early and try to stay late, by the spiritual famine of their lives or simply the desire to tell secrets in the dark."

Here is Father Ernest Burner, sitting in the confessional box, as depicted in J. F. Powers' most celebrated short story, "Prince of Darkness." And here on display is the author's ability to capture in a couple of metaphors the flavor of a religious era now gone. Not many Catholics, at least in the United States, go to confession anymore, not even old ladies anxious "to tell secrets in the dark," and priests are more likely to be attending a committee meeting than dispensing absolution. Many of us, who still remember that era fondly, regret that this should be so, but we should take care not to fall into a trap of sentiment and nostalgia; after all, Jesus made it perfectly plain that a permanent feature of His followers' pilgrimage will always be and has always been a mixture of the wheat and the tares. It would in any case be unfair to judge Powers' art by the hard edge in the sentence above, quoted as it is out of context, as though he were merely a sour chronicler of torpid priests and chattering women. On the contrary, the value of his work lies precisely in the skill he demonstrated in showing how, at a particular time and in a particular place, ordinary human beings coped with the awesome responsibility of a Christian calling. The time was the two decades or so after the Second World War, and the place was the American Midwest.

James Farr Powers died a few months ago. His passing could not be called astonishing: he was full of years, past eighty of them, and toward the end he had not enjoyed robust health. He left behind a slender literary testament: three collections of short stories and two novels, the total number of pages of which would scarcely equal one of Tom Wolfe's fiction effusions. He was a man of the Catholic Left, a disciple of Dorothy Day, a pacifist, and, during his most creative years, an intimate of the monks at St. John's Abbey in Minnesota and so on the cusp of the many reform movements that flourished there before Vatican II. He was, predictably, suspicious of capitalism. One of his bitterest stories, "The Forks," recounts how an idealistic young priest was rebuffed by a parishioner because, unlike the worldly pastor, he was incapable of providing stock-market tips: "'You're a nice young man,' Mrs. Klein said, 'but I got to say this — you ain't much of a priest.'" Also predictably, Powers was a strong advocate of racial justice; in "The Eye" — not one of his best efforts, partly because he employed in it an ersatz Louisiana dialect — he tells a horrific tale about a lynching.

J. F. Powers' justly lofty reputation as an artist, however, does not rest upon his social convictions, however firmly held. His genius lay in an uncanny faculty to see and describe the humdrum of everyday life within a spiritual context. Sometimes, to be sure, his method fell to the level of caricature; in "The Valiant Woman" the tyrannical rectory housekeeper, Mrs. Stoner, embodies every negative cliché imaginable about a regiment of women, usually underpaid and under-appreciated who, a generation ago, contributed more than their share to the well-being of parish life. But such extravagance was rare. Much more characteristic is "The Old Bird, a Love Story," about an elderly man who had lost his prestigious job and could find only temporary employment at Christmas time wrapping parcels in a wholesale house; when he returned home and, playing the actor, pretended to his wife that their fortunes had changed, "his only audience smiled and loved him." Indeed, as he matured as a writer, Powers grew mellower and more tolerant of quirks and foibles. Not that he ever lost sight of the peculiarities and distresses and small tragedies inherent in American life during the 'fifties. "Blue Island" tells of how Ralph, ne Raffaele, Davicci, desperate to shed his ethnic heritage and find acceptance among the WASP establishment, moved with his suspiciously blonde and brassy bride, Ethel, into a fashionable Minneapolis suburb. Under his intense pressure, and with the help of a seemingly friendly Mrs. Hancock, the naive Ethel hosts a morning coffee party for the ladies of the prestigious neighborhood, only to have the occasion ruined when Mrs. Hancock, in fact a vendor, tries to sell the guests furniture polish and a collection of pots and pans. Ethel, forlorn at what she knows will be a severe disappointment to her social-climbing husband, takes to her bed in despair. "When, toward noon, Ethel heard Ralph come into the driveway, she got out of bed, straightened the spread, and concealed the pan in the closet. She went to the window and gazed down upon the crown of his pearl-gray hat. He was carrying a big club of roses."

Powers' ear for credible dialogue was prodigious. His instinct for what was hilarious and yet at the same time poignant could hardly be matched. Nor could any contemporary writer surpass the sheer beauty of his descriptive prose. "Gauzily rain descended in a fine spray, hanging in fat berries from the wet black branches where leaves had been and buds would be, cold crystal drops" ("Lions, Harts, and Leaping Does"). "The old house always looked good to him: in spring when the locust, plum, lilacs, honeysuckle, caragana, and mock orange bloomed around it; in summer, as it was now, almost buried in green; in autumn when the yard was rolling with nuts, crashing with leaves, and the mountain-ash berries turned red; and in the winter, under snow and icicles, with its tall mullioned windows sparkling, it reminded him of an old fashioned Christmas card" ("Look How the Fish Live"). Such literary virtues, along with masterful plotting, explain why Powers' stories were published in prestigious journals, like *Partisan Review*, and *The New Yorker* during its heyday under Harold Ross. But what intrigued me and the constituency to which I belong was the author's almost eerie ability to grasp the sights and sounds and smells of the Midwestern Catholic rectory during the 1950's.

Powers spent his childhood and youth in southwestern Illinois and eastern Missouri, during which years he formed friendships with several young men who, for various reasons, came ultimately to serve with me as priests of the Archdiocese of St. Paul. Powers himself settled in Minnesota, near St. John's Abbey, some ninety miles north of the Twin Cities. I never met him, but I was acquainted with two of his priest-friends. When the stories with clerical settings began to appear, it was immediately noted that much of the detail — particularly the oddities inevitably exhibited by a group of bachelors living together — clearly had a local application. Neither I nor any of my confreres, so far as I can recall, were offended by this circumstance. Rather we marveled that this layman, whatever inside information he received from his boyhood chums, and however sensitive were his own emotional antennae, could have managed to get so many things right. Satire there was, occasionally bitter, but most priests who read the stories recognized that Powers also gave due notice, powerfully if implicitly, to "the presence of grace" — a title he used for one of his published collections.

His insights were circumscribed temporally, however. After 1964 his writing in this genre was much less successful. The explanation for this is not hard to find: in the wake of Vatican II the clerical culture Powers had captured so vividly disappeared. He tried to come to terms with this circumstance, but the results were meager. An example is "Priestly Fellowship," in which a veteran pastor tries to ingratiate himself with some younger priests; the story is too long, too meandering, too preachy. The same might be said of Powers' last publication, the novel called *Wheat That Springeth Green* (1988), a sad disappointment, which, incidentally, features a pointless and tasteless pornographic segment. Nor am I much enamored of his other novel, *Morte d'Urban* (1962), but for quite different reasons. The account of the rise of fall of Father Urban Roche, the high-powered spokesman for a third-rate religious order, displays, through a series of wonderful vignettes, Powers' accustomed magic. The trouble is that the individual scenes run off at angles from each other; transitions are weak, the denouement seems an afterthought, and the author relies too much on the infamous *deus ex machina*.

I realize that this judgment represents a minority point of view; *Morte d'Urban* won all sorts of prizes. But to me the book is really a collection of short stories strung together without a unifying theme, which, I suppose, is a not altogether surprising result, since it issued from the pen of a great teller of small tales. And there are heaps of pearls among the clerical stories. One of my favorites is "The Presence of Grace," in which a newly ordained reports to a curmudgeon of a pastor who rarely speaks to him or indeed to anybody. When the old man inadvertently spills ink on a new white vestment, he simply shrugs and, to the curate's disgust, says, " 's not ink." But when the younger man imprudently, though innocently, places himself in a compromising situation, the pastor dismisses a delegation of complaining parishioners by saying, " 's not so." Perhaps the most charming of all is "Farewell," a story about a retired bishop of a rural Minnesota diocese who, as he reluctantly eases out of a position of power and prestige, is asked to interview a farm wife who claims to have seen a vision of the Blessed Virgin in a tree. Mrs. Nagel — the bishop finds her a "perky, useful, down-to-earth type of woman, a good, average Catholic, and not some kind of nut" — has told only her husband and her confessor the message she received from the apparition, and she relents only when forced to by the ecclesiastical bureaucracy. "'KEEP MINNESOTA GREEN!' cried Monsignor Holstein, very upset. 'What about the rest of the country? Or, for that matter, the *world*?'"

But when all is said and done, Ernest Burner remains Powers' most memorable creation. He was at heart a good man and faithful to his calling, and yet he has failed to attain the only self-definition open to a secular priest, a pastorate of his own. (I was in the seminary during the 1950s when I first read this story, and I recall a professor remarking casually that the only right accorded by canon law to an assistant pastor was Christian burial.) Seventeen years a priest and still a curate — all the men ordained with him had their own parishes — Burner swerved between rage and despair at the servile state in which he continued to languish. He ate and drank a little too much, he engaged in verbal parrying with his juniors, who did not bother to disguise their contempt for him. He sought relief in hobbies and diversions, like golf and flying lessons and photography — the darkroom he set up in the basement of the rectory prompted his sardonic pastor to dub him "prince of darkness." But surely Powers meant to suggest something more than mere priestly sarcasm when he gave his tale — I almost wrote parable — this intriguing title. And, indeed, there was a darkness intruding into the soul of Ernest Burner, if not diabolical in origin, then at least of that shadowy variety that lurks nearby when youth has gone, and gone with it the bright idealism that promises a future filled with noble achievements.

Summoned to an interview with the archbishop, Father Burner, confident that his day has finally come, resolved "to show no nervousness. A trifle surprised, yes — the archbishop must have his due — but not overly affected by good fortune." He felt himself "a ball that bounced up only. He had kept faith. And now — his just reward." In fact, the occasion proved awkward, and the world-weary prelate, after some desultory conversation, rolled a piece of stationery, Father Burner's future, into his typewriter. "'Your Christian name, Father is–?' 'Ernest, your Excellency.' 'I can't call to mind a single Saint Ernest. It looks, Father, as if you have a clear field.' The archbishop pecked out a few lines, removed the paper from the machine, folded it, and put it in an envelope. 'Father, you will please not open the envelope until after your Mass tomorrow.'" The Prince of Darkness "drove a couple of blocks down the street, pulled up to the curb, opened the envelope, which had not been sealed, and read: 'You will report on August 8 to the Reverend Michael Furlong, to begin your duties on that day as his assistant. I trust that in your new appointment you will find not peace but a sword.'"

J. F. Powers did not, however, leave Father Burner in the darkness. He reappears in a story called "Defection of a Favorite," which is narrated by the rectory cat — a *tour de force* in itself. Burner is still an assistant, now to the aged, ailing and somewhat daft Father Malt, who, however, has been hospitalized, leaving Burner in what he hopes will be permanent charge of the parish. Then, unexpectedly, the old man returns. "They looked at each other, Father Malt and Father Burner, like two popes themselves not sure which one was real. The irremovable pastor stood perspiring on his crutches. As long as he lived, he had to be pastor, I [the cat] saw; his need was the greater. And Father Burner saw it, too. He went up to Father Malt and laid a strong, obedient hand on the old one that held tight to the right crutch. 'Hello, boss,' he said. 'Glad you're back.' It was his finest hour. In the past he had lacked the will to accept his setbacks with grace and had derived no merit from them. I was happy for him."

Catholic Dossier, **Volume 5, Number 4, July-August 1999, Pages 6–8**

This second piece in the "Historian and Literature" duet of essays demonstrates a professional interest in the story of beloved Catholic martyr Sir Thomas More, as told in the theatrical drama and screenplay written by Robert Bolt. Despite admiration for Bolt's play, O'Connell's commitment to sound history prompted an essay of clarification, complete with footnotes. His argument: More was not quite a "man for all seasons." – WGS

"A Man for All Seasons":
An Historian's Modest Demur

"More," wrote Robert Whittinton in 1520, "is a man of an angel's wit and singular learning. I know not his fellow. For where is the man of that gentleness, lowliness and affability? And, as time requireth, a man of marvelous mirth and pastimes, and sometime of a sad gravity. A man for all seasons."[1]

Mr. Robert Bolt found in these lines a title for his remarkable play, in which More becomes "a man with an adamantine sense of his own self, [who] knew where he began and left off, what area of himself he could yield to the encroachments of his enemies, and what to the encroachments of those he loved."[2] Such a person, with such a knowledge of and hold upon himself, must be the stuff of heroism at all times and all places — a hero bigger than life, or rather a hero whose moral sway is so prepossessing that he evokes a human response beyond any limiting considerations of time or place — and that, I suppose, is the point of Mr. Bolt's title. In the poet's vision, London of the 1530s is as good a backdrop as any against which to pose questions about the nature of law and the love of God and the demands of honor, questions which are appropriately posed at every human season, because they touch at every season the human spirit stirring to unravel the mysteries it finds itself wrapped in.

In dealing with Mr. Bolt's More, we deal with the likes of Oedipus and Faust, not with a Willy Loman, whose tale is told within the context of a narrow and specific cultural setting essentially familiar to us. There may indeed be an apt season for the death of the salesman, but surely not for the death of the lord chancellor whose *crise de conscience* is too stark, too universal, too genuinely radical to exhaust its significance in that poignant moment on Tower Hill, Tuesday, July 6, 1535, a little before nine in the morning. In dealing with More, we have to face, in Mr. Bolt's words, "the terrifying cosmos, terrifying because no laws, no sanctions, no mores obtain there; it is either empty or occupied by God and Devil nakedly at war."[3] The brilliant artistry of Mr. Bolt assures us that in watching the confrontation between More and King Henry VIII we are witnessing, as in some cosmic mirror, the seasonless struggle of our unhappy race.

Mr. Bolt's grand and moving drama now provides the standard picture of Thomas More. What is the historian's reaction to it? Initially, it disturbs him because it seems at once to say too much and too little. So pedantic and prosaic is the historian, so bound is he to the smudged and often obscure documents before him, so accustomed is he to building modest houses out of the fragments at his disposal, that he pales before this great edifice. He tends to be highly suspicious of a concept like "a man for all seasons." There is no such person, he will argue in his fussy way. Everyone has his allotted time, his season, his moment upon the stage, and then he is gone, replaced by someone else.

Look at the phrase itself. It was coined, as we have seen, by Robert Whittinton in 1520.

Whittinton was one of More's literary friends, a writer, a teacher of Latin composition, a humanist in the precise sense of that much-abused term. What did he mean by the phrase? Apparently, he meant the witty and learned More was so sensitive to the feelings of others, was so affable and gentle, that, depending on the situation, he turned mirthful or grave and thus matched his mood to whatever emotional "season" his friends were experiencing.

This at any rate is the sense of the words themselves, and they express a high compliment indeed. It is possible also, though less likely, that Whittinton intended them simply to flatter More. Possible, because More, author of *Utopia* and intimate of Erasmus, was the foremost intellectual in England, and besides that a king's councilor whose patronage might be valuable to an ambitious author. And yet less likely, because More was notoriously straightforward and impatient of humbug, so that flattery might have been expected to repel rather than attract him.

However that may be, Whittinton's "a man for all seasons" could have had nothing whatever to do with the Thomas More about whom Mr. Bolt wrote his play. In 1520, when Whittinton's book on Latin Composition appeared, More was still a year away from his knighthood and his first ministerial post, three years from the speakership of the House of Commons, nine from the chancellorship, and fifteen from the heroic ordeal which ended on Tower Hill.

Henry VIII had not yet published his *Assertio Septem Sacramentorum* against Luther. Anne Boleyn was a dark-eyed little girl of thirteen, and Thomas Cromwell was still a moneylender in London. In short, Mr. Bolt's concerns are with More the martyr who died in witness to the inviolability of the human conscience. Whittinton had nothing in mind so grandiose as that.

Well, one might say, so much the worse for Whittinton. And so much the worse for the pedant who enters such a demur. The poet's ecstasy is infinitely more valuable than fastidious chronology. This is so. And yet the poet's method in this instance has its difficulties. There never was an Oedipus or a Faust, nor even a Willy Loman. But Thomas More was a real man who lived in Chelsea, a man of medium height, with auburn hair and blue-gray eyes, who liked beef and eggs and small beer, who had a wistful way with animals, who walked with his right shoulder slightly higher than his left, who wore a hair-shirt next to his flesh.[4] He was a lawyer and a politician. He married two wives and sired several children. He was a literateur who wrote one great book and many lesser ones. He was tone-deaf and unmusical, though he regularly sang in the choir of Chelsea Church (not necessarily, it has been observed, incompatible statements).

Thomas More died at a tyrant's hands, but during the greater part of his life he labored diligently in the service of that same tyrant, so diligently indeed that he described himself on the scaffold in a phrase which neither his friends nor his enemies have attempted to rebut: he was "the king's good servant." Six years earlier, when the highest office in the land was offered to him, he accepted it as any sensible politician would have, seeing it as the culmination of his public life.[5] The evidence that he accepted the great seal of the chancery reluctantly is highly suspect, and there is no evidence at all that he demanded and received, as a prior condition for acceptance, assurances from the king that he would not be troubled over the divorce. On the contrary, what reluctance there was about the appointment seems to have arisen in the king's council and perhaps in the king's mind. It is certain at any rate that More received no assurances from the king about the divorce until after he had hung the chancellor's insignia around his neck.[6]

Thomas More was killed in defense of his conscience. He was asked, in Mr. Bolt's words, "to state that he believed what he didn't believe."[7] He refused, and he died. That he did so with courage, with a kind of whimsical gallantry which has gained him almost universal admiration since,[8] needs hardly be said. But it is particularly important to understand the principle he so loyally followed. He did not mount the scaffold in defense of freedom of conscience as such; that is to say, he never maintained, as you and I might do, that conscience is the ultimate voice, that privy place where no authority may intrude and where no abstract truth has any claim, or, as Mr. Bolt might put it, the last refuge of one's selfhood. Such may have been two centuries later Voltaire's notion of conscience,[9] and it may be ours. It was never Thomas More's. Listen to the man himself after he had been pronounced guilty, thanks to the perjured testimony of Richard Rich.

> Seeing that I see ye are determined to condemn me (God knoweth how) I will now in discharge of my conscience speak my mind plainly and freely touching my indictment and your statute withal.
>
> And forasmuch as this indictment is grounded upon an Act of Parliament directly repugnant to the laws of God and his holy Church, the supreme government of which, or of any part whereof, may no temporal prince presume by any law to take upon him, as rightfully belonging to the See of Rome, a spiritual preeminence by the mouth of our savior himself, personally present upon the earth, only to St. Peter and his successors, bishops of the same see, by special prerogative granted; it is therefore in law amongst Christian men insufficient to charge any Christian man.

The presiding judge replied by citing the bishops, universities, "and best learned of this realm" who had approved the Reformation settlement. More answered:

> For I nothing doubt but that, though not in this realm, yet in Christendom about, of these well-learned bishops and virtuous men that

are yet alive, they be not the fewer part that are of my mind therein. But if I should speak of those that are already dead, of whom many be now holy saints in heaven, I am very sure it is the far greater part of them that, all the while they lived, thought in this case that way that I think now; and therefore am I not bounden, my lord, to conform my conscience to the Council of one realm against the general council of Christendom. For of the foresaid holy bishops I have for every bishop of yours, above one hundred; and for one council or Parliament of yours (God knoweth what manner of one), I have all the councils made these thousand years. And for this one kingdom, I have all other Christian realms.[10]

These are not the words of a man for whom conscience, defined as the private grasp of the truth according to one's lights, is the supreme tribunal. Conscience for More was the right to be right, not the right to be wrong. He did not refuse to "conform" his conscience to the Act of Supremacy for private but public reasons: "For one council or Parliament of yours," he thundered at his judges, "I have all the councils made these thousand years." Similarly, in the days of his power it had been irrelevant to him that those whom he called heretics and whom he pursued relentlessly with both pen and sword had considered themselves right. In his view it was neither irrational nor cruel to take away their lives, if need be, precisely because they were in fact wrong about the public good.

They understood this conviction of his, even if we do not, because they shared it, and, like More, they were willing to die for it. They were not, any more than he was, martyrs to a pale pluralism. Indeed, the Protestants burned by Mary Tudor twenty years later, the Catholics disemboweled by Elizabeth Tudor twenty years after that, even, in their different ways, Charles I and Robespierre, John Brown and Trotsky, Sacco and Vanzetti would have understood More more readily than we do. For all of them ideology was the expression of the commonweal, and conscience was far removed from bland personal preference. For all of them ideology was a public good which was worth dying for indeed, but which was also — and this may have been harder — worth killing for.

I believe that, for More at any rate, it was harder to kill than to die, and this may help explain his otherwise incredible good humor upon the scaffold. But he did not shrink from either killing or dying. He did not hold that the state must be ideologically neutral, must be indifferent to what is ultimately true and false, right and wrong, must be content to practice the art of the possible in a less than perfect universe. It never occurred to More or his contemporaries that the state should trouble itself with problems of sanitation or urban development, any more than it occurs to us that the state should support the Christian religion because the Christian religion is true. For, we ask ourselves with a flutter of the mind, what if it is not true? More would have understood us no more easily than we understand him. For we are all humanitarians now, nineteenth-century positivists or twentieth-century libertarians or technocrats or hedonists. And conscience is a voice deep within ourselves which no one else can hear.

So there is for us something particularly beguiling about Mr. Bolt's brilliantly argued thesis in the play, that More was a martyr to the lonely existential self, "a hero of self-hood," as Mr. Bolt puts it.

> A man takes an oath only when he wants to commit himself quite exceptionally. Of course, it's much less effective now that for most of us the actual words of the oath are not much more than impressive mumbo jumbo. . . . But though few of us have anything in ourselves like an immortal soul which we regard as absolutely inviolate, yet most of us still feel something which we should prefer, on the whole, not to violate. It may be that a clear sense of the self can only crystallize around something transcendental, in which case our prospects look poor, for we are rightly committed to the rational. I think the paramount gift of our thinkers, artists, and men of science should labor to get for us is a sense of selfhood without resort to magic.11

The historian, dry and finicky, can only reply that this "hero of self-hood" and therefore this "man for all seasons" is radically different from the person so painfully, so incompletely reconstructed from the evidence that has come down to us. It is not that Mr. Bolt's presentation of More is vulgar or superficial — so often the fate of historical personages at the hands of less-skilled artists. On the contrary, Mr. Bolt's sympathy for his subject is so deep that one senses it in every lilting line he has written. If anything, the playgoer or moviegoer will find in *A Man for All Seasons* confirmation of Swift's observation that More was "the person of the greatest virtue this kingdom ever produced," and of the more recent judgment of Hugh Trevor-Roper — a contemporary historian not much given to compliments even to the dead — that More was "the first great Englishman whom we feel that we know, the most saintly of humanists, the most human of saints, the universal man of our cool northern renaissance."[12]

Nor is it that the historian is right and Mr. Bolt is wrong. Truth wears many mantles and confronts the mind from many angles. After all, the play's the thing, and there may be more to be learned in one poetic experience than in the study of a thousand worn documents. Perhaps the discrepancy lies in the vocation of the historian whose chief aim, Herbert Butterfield has said, "is the elucidation of the unlikenesses between past and present and [whose] chief function is to act in this way as the mediator between other generations and our own. It is not for him to stress and magnify the similarities between one age and another, and he is riding after a whole flock of misapprehensions if he goes to hunt the present in the past."[13] It remains a lowlier calling than the poet's, but it has its uses.

It shows us that in a very real sense Thomas More was a man of one season — that moment of golden twilight when the Middle Ages were slowly giving place to something new, to something no one yet could name, a time of bright hope and fervor, an age of certainty, when Luther stood boldly before the princes of the Empire and Loyola bent before the mystic winds at Manresa, when kings dallied on the Field of Cloth of Gold, when popes still preached crusade. It was a time when people, who had never had the chance to read Camus,[14] had no doubt of what was true and what was right. It is all gone now, whistling down the wind, and Thomas More has gone with it.

Notes

1. In the *"ad lectorem"* of the *Vulgaria*. See Beatrice White (ed.), *The Vulgaria of John Stonbridge and the Vulgaria of Robert Whittinton*, Early English Text Society (London, 1932), p. 28.
2. Robert Bolt, *A Man for All Seasons* (New York, 1962), p. 12.
3. Bolt, p. 16.

4. This is the famous description by Erasmus. See p. 5. and H. M Allen, *Opus Epistolarum Des Erasmi Roterodami* (Oxford, 1906 ff.), IV, no. 999 (July 23, 1519).
5. R. W. Chambers, *Thomas More* (London, 1935) p. 176. This is still the best biography of More.
6. For a summation of the evidence on these points, see G. R. Elton, "Sir Thomas More and the Opposition to Henry VIII," *Bulletin of the Institute of Historical Research*, 41 (1968), pp. 19–34.
7. Bolt, p. 13.
8. Not quite universal. The chronicler Edward Hall (d. 1541), the first to be permitted in England to write about the execution, thought More excessively frivolous. "I cannot tell whether I shoulde call him a foolishe wyseman or a wise foolishman." See Charles Whibley (ed.), *Henry VIII by Edward Hall* (London, 1904), p. 265.
9. Voltaire's oft-quoted remark about willingness to defend to the death the right of those with whom he disagreed to state their views freely is not to be found in his Works. It may have been a gloss by one of his female English admirers. (I owe this information to my late friend and colleague M. A. Fitzsimons.)
10. Elsie Hitchcock (ed.), *Harpsfield's Life of More*, Early English Text Society (London, 1932), pp. 193–96.
11. Bolt, pp. 13, 14.
12. *The New York Times*, December 4, 1977.
13. Herbert Butterfield, *The Whig Interpretation of History* (London, 1931), p. 10.
14. Mr. Bolt says (p. 14), "Albert Camus is a writer I admire in this connection," especially in *La Chute*.

Catholic Dossier, Volume 8, Number 2, March -April 2001, Pages 16–19

Having demonstrated a rigorous sense of responsibility to the past, present, and future, a panoramic view of factors shaping people and their journeys, and a determination to make fair and firm judgments, O'Connell emerges as an historian suited to the twenty-first century. In the essay presented here, his life experiences have led him to a set of remarkable diagnoses and recommendations about life in a Church that may galvanize today's readers.

His candid litany of challenging issues, from divorce to homosexuality to declining Church participation, prompts an urgent survival plan: Catholics must rediscover, in a kind of "ghetto," their sense of themselves and their true priorities. They must summon up their zeal, wisdom, and faith. Again, O'Connell sees historical scholarship as a resource for the Church to draw upon. – WGS

An Historical Perspective on Evangelization in the United States:
Shifting Concentration of Interest

[Editor's Note: *The following article was an address given at the Fellowship of Catholic Scholars Convention in Philadelphia in September 1990.*]

Jonathan Swift, you may recall, was the dean of St. Patrick's, the Anglican cathedral in Dublin, at the beginning of the eighteenth century. He was a waspish man by all accounts, one who did not suffer fools or Tories gladly, and many a politician and ecclesiastic — largely a distinction without a difference in his time as, unhappily, in ours — felt the sharp edge of his tongue or his pen. His strong literary suit was satire, in an age of great satirists, and he would no doubt have been chagrined had he lived long enough to have witnessed one of his most acidic treatises, *Gulliver's Travels*, considered merely a fairy tale for children. Swift, almost alone among the Irish Protestant ascendancy of penal times, earned the respect and affection of the masses of persecuted Irish Catholics, for whom he had the courage to act as advocate, not only in his writings but in his personal protestations at Dublin Castle and even at the court of St. James itself. One of the books he wrote in this continuing battle against bigotry and cruelty was a satire called *A Modest Proposal for Preventing the Children of Poor People from Being a Burden to their Parents or the Country*, in which he argued that the solution for the hunger and deprivation endured by the people of Ireland was the fattening and consequent eating of Irish babies.

An outrageous suggestion, to be sure, even from a satirist. But let me put before you an outrageous suggestion of my own, a modest proposal of my own. And let me say from the start that, unlike Swift, I do not mean to advance it in a satirical way. My modest proposal is that we American Catholics return to our ghetto. To the extent that the Catholic left — by which I mean the ideologues who have captured our once respectable learned societies and journals; the bland and fearful technocrats who govern most of our colleges and universities — to the extent, I say, that the Catholic left would pay the slightest attention to such a proposal made at a gathering like this one — but in the extreme — the reaction would be one of mock horror or, from the slightly more intelligent, a smug "I told you so." The latter assessment would be elaborated — to the limited degree, of course, that Bishop X, Professor Y, or President Zed were capable of sustained argument, a dubious proposition in itself — something akin to this: You people wonder why we have marginalized you, why we pay no attention to you, why we label you "fundamentalists" and thus equate you with the likes of Jim Bakker and Jimmy Swaggart, why we keep you away from the decision-making process at every level, why we ignore your books and, yes, make fun of your conferences. You wonder why. Well, the reason is clear: you have a ghetto-mentality, you are not open, you are insensitive, you are inflexible, you cannot adjust to the temper of the modern mind, you doubtless need counseling, preferably by an ex-priest or by a nun who wears an unfashionable mu-mu and too much eye shadow.

Since this is the kind of reaction my modest proposal would no doubt receive from the ecclesiastical powers-that-be, it is incumbent upon me to explain what I mean with great care. Let me try to do so by pointing to, in a highly schematic form, the historical roots we share with those who tyrannize over us, in order to suggest that a return to the ghetto may be the only realistic course open to the American Catholic community. While

Shakespeare posited seven ages of man, I would posit five ages of the Catholic church in the United States: the age of survival, of expansion, of assimilation, of consolidation, and, finally, in our own day, of survival once again. Everything, they say, that goes around, comes around. I intend no original dissertation here, nothing more pretentious that a survey of our shared past and of the modes of evangelization dictated by the varying imperatives of that past.

Survival

The First Age, I say, was the age of survival, begun with Lord Baltimore's colony in Maryland where, it was hoped, Catholics might find toleration for their religion which was brutally denied them in England. In exchange they offered toleration to others, only to discover — as Mary Queen of Scots had discovered when she tried to find a *modus vivendi* with John Knox — that British hatred of popery was too deep and pervasive to admit any form of accommodation: as soon as Protestant numbers in Maryland made it feasible, Catholics there were deprived of all civil rights, as was already the case in the other colonies. The Old Faith, however, though it cannot be said to have flourished along the Maryland shore, did manage to survive there, adapting to its own needs the social model of the Catholics living under the penal laws in England. A handful of wealthy families, like the Carrolls and the Spaldings, imitated their English counterparts — the Talbots, the Vauxes, the Petres — by sealing themselves and their tenants off from the rest of society, depending — much as the Amish do today — on their ability to sustain themselves in economic independence, and cultivating a variety of Catholic practice as understated and unobtrusive as possible.

This latter characteristic should by no means be considered blameworthy in these "Old Catholics" of America, as we might label them; they lived, after all, on the sword's edge, never entirely safe from overt persecution. But it must be observed also that these Marylanders, like their cousins in England, had never been allowed to experience the fruit of that great moral, intellectual, and spiritual revival of Catholicism we call the Counter-Reformation. They knew nothing of the Oratory or of Saint-Sulpice, nothing of the Spanish mystics or of the revival of Thomism, nothing of Vincent de Paul and the Sisters of Charity or of Pascal or of Alphonsus Liguori or of Daniel Papebroch. English-speaking Catholics, on either side of the

Atlantic, remained a proscribed and endangered minority, heroic indeed, but also narrow, introspective, circumscribed by the realization that only the regard of their countrymen for the sacredness of private property — a spiritual principle Albion held dearer than any other — saved them from obliteration.

In the kind of situation that prevailed among Maryland Catholics, cultural inbreeding was as inevitable as intermarriage. Their community assumed the character of its dominant families, who came to regard themselves, also inevitably, as the measure of all things Catholic. Their brave and steadfast adherence to the faith has surely earned them our plaudits, though their aristocratic hubris quickly rendered them irrelevant once other than English immigrants had arrived in any numbers. Yet the hubris, sometimes absurdly, lingered: one of their descendants was John Lancaster Spalding — note the middle name — the celebrated first bishop of Peoria, who always maintained that he was by blood a Plantagenet, sprung in a direct line from King Henry II.

The able Jesuits, who were the younger sons of the Catholic squires and who, after a spell of education in Italy or France, came back to Maryland to minister to them, were in essence domestic chaplains. Among them was John Carroll, cousin of that Charles Carroll of Carrollton who signed the Declaration of Independence. But while John was still in Europe the Society of Jesus was suppressed, and so he returned to Maryland a secular priest and, after the revolution, was selected first bishop and then archbishop of Baltimore. Given the social realities governing the tiny Catholic minority in the new United States — scarcely 25,000 souls, less than one percent of the population — the appointment to this post of a scion of the Maryland squirearchy was surely sensible. So it was that Carroll became the father of the American episcopate and, more immediately, the presider over the beginnings of the age of American Catholic expansion.

Expansion

You may think "presider" a rather bland word, and so it is, but I use it purposely. Nothing in John Carroll's antecedents or training led him to adopt the ways of a fiery missionary. Nor was he ever such. Indeed, he had enough trouble simply holding together the little pockets of Catholics strung along the Atlantic seaboard. But neither Carroll's temperament nor his Enlightenment proclivities weigh much in the balance when compared to his status as a successor of the apostles present on these shores. As St. Ignatius of Antioch had testified 1,700 years earlier, the Church is where the bishop is; and so, from the moment when John Carroll fixed the miter on his head, the Church stood in the United States of America as proud and as complete as the Church did anywhere in the world.

The expansion of Catholicism over which Carroll first presided was very modest and, no doubt, of a kind not always in tune with his aristocratic sensibilities. Native converts were few — Elizabeth Seton and Rose Hawthorne did not set any particular precedent. But nevertheless, the numbers of Catholics grew steadily, if not spectacularly, by reason of immigration. The new land, blessed with its remarkable constitution and its bill of rights, bright with the promise of economic opportunity, attracted peoples dissatisfied with the European old world, including Catholics who, thanks to the first amendment, had no hostile establishment to fear any more. Prejudice they had indeed to endure, for many generations yet to come. But prejudice, however distasteful and ignoble, is a far cry from tar-and-feathers or a knock on the door in the middle of the night.

The expansion of the nation *ipso facto* involved the expansion of Catholicism. The purchase of Louisiana and Florida, and, later, the conquest of the Spanish southwest and California, brought into the American Catholic community the venerable churches of St. Augustine and New Orleans, St. Louis and Santa Fe and Los Angeles, and with them a zestful and healthy new Latin flavor. And meanwhile, as the march of Manifest Destiny brought ever- increasing crowds of settlers across the Appalachians into the rich valleys of the Ohio and the Tennessee and finally to the banks of the Mississippi itself, the Catholics came with them: English and French at first, then more and more, the Irish and the Germans.

To be sure, many of the immigrants stayed in the great eastern cities, presenting to the new bishoprics established there immense institutional challenges. But many more pushed into Ohio and Kentucky and Michigan, and in those frontier places the difficulties were, if anything, more formidable. A late esteemed colleague of mine wrote a book about all this which he called *Cathedrals in the Wilderness*. An apt title indeed, for long after John Carroll had departed the scene his episcopal successors labored in an America he had never dreamed of; and long after the rather effete Maryland

Catholicism had been swept aside by the tide of events, its rough, bustling, lower-class, egalitarian successor — from Boston to Erie, from Mobile to Cincinnati to Detroit — had taken its place.

Assimilation

The Civil War is the great watershed in our national history, and that cataclysmic and searing experience marks also the divide between my age of expansion and age of assimilation. The division, however, was by no means a rigid one, for the expansion of Catholicism, despite the Yankee bigotry exhibited in the brief but vicious nativism of the know-nothing movement, continued apace with the huge increase, after the war, of immigration. Nor was there any significant abatement for the next fifty years. Hordes of indigent Irish, fleeing the ravages of the Great Famine, were followed by Italians, Poles, more Germans, Hungarians, Czechs, Croatians. By 1889, a century after John Carroll had begun his episcopate, there were 8,000,000 Catholics in the United States, sixty bishops, thousands of churches and schools, hospitals and foundling homes.

During these tumultuous decades, evangelization, broadly understood, meant, first of all, providing an ecclesial home for these mostly poor and uneducated masses, speaking a babel of tongues and clinging to the various customs they had brought with them from the old country. An ecclesial home: that is, a building, however, humble and simple, where the eternal sacrifice of Calvary might be fittingly celebrated; a schoolroom, however cramped and even wretched, where an immigrant child might learn about his faith without being ridiculed and proselytized by the still dominant Protestant culture.

It has become fashionable in our own day for the fastidious descendants of those immigrants to deride the so-called brick-and-mortar preoccupations of those days. But such negative criticism betrays remarkable ignorance as well as a good deal of snobbishness. Perhaps the greatest boast of the American church during the age of assimilation is precisely its achievement, won at terrible cost, of providing for itself a physical structure: a place to go to Mass, a place to go to school, a place, not too far away, where the sisters would take care of you if you were sick or old or achingly alone. It can never be said too often: ours is an incarnational religion. We are neither Docetists nor Quakers nor Christian Scientists nor any other species of spiritualists.

We depend, humanly speaking, upon the predictable cycle of feast and fast, we partake in the ordinary rhythms of human life, we divinize — if I may put it so — the rites of passage, we incorporate into our worship all human moods and all human emotions, just as our most sacred rituals rest upon the use of simple physical things — a flagon of water, a jug of oil, a crust of bread. We repudiate with equal vigor foolish Pelagian optimism and the monstrous conceit of Lutheran and Calvinist predestination.

So it is with sacred space: we cannot do without places, places that are ours. The historical record is very clear: at the time of the Reformation, when for a while it seemed that the new Protestant evangel would sweep everything before it, the Catholic faith survived only where the traditional structure survived, however deformed that structure may have been by the abuses of the time. In Poland and Bavaria and Hungary Catholicism successfully rebounded from the early Protestant assaults, because in those countries the structure of parish and convent and school was maintained; in England and Holland, by contrast, Catholicism suffocated and died during the sixteenth century, because the persecutors succeeded in depriving it of its sacred space.

Three hundred years later, during the nineteenth century, that lesson apparently had been forgotten in the European Catholic heartland, as it passed through profound demographic changes. Indeed, the old continent, in the grips of a population explosion, was experiencing something parallel to the influx of alien peoples into the United States, and that was the vast shift of the populace from the countryside to the teeming concentrations of people in the new industrial centers. The lamentable failure of the Catholic hierarchies to provide physical facilities for these men and women, and their children, who had left their village church and its embracing culture behind them, was by no means the least important reason the European working classes were lost to the Church, and remain lost to this day.

American Catholic leadership did not make this mistake, for which we must be eternally grateful. But this passion, largely realized, of immigrant Catholics in the United States to provide themselves with a solid, palpable, permanent ecclesial home brought with it another, very poignant, aspiration. Polish and Irish and Italian Catholics wanted themselves and their institutions to belong to the larger American society, and — perhaps even more important to them — to be recognized as belonging. For some of them — notably Archbishop John Ireland of St. Paul and his allies in the so-called Americanist party — this desire became almost an obsession. They pointed to the admirable American political and economic institutions which gave poor Catholics a chance to practice their religion unhindered, even as they enjoyed the chance to make a decent living. Contrast our situation, they argued cogently, with that of our co-religionists in the old countries of Europe, where almost universally the salvific work of the Church was inhibited by hostile governments, where Catholic schools were shut down and religious orders disbanded and, in Germany, bishops imprisoned, where even the pope was cabined up inside the Leonine walls, a self-proclaimed "prisoner of the Vatican."

No such enormities occurred in the land of the free and the home of the brave, where, besides, civic virtues like sobriety, self-reliance, tolerance, industriousness, and delayed gratification were duly honored and rewarded. Indeed, so impressed were the more advanced Catholic Americanists that they proposed the ecclesial structure arrived at in the United States as the model to be adopted by the universal Church.

Thus did the age of expansion evolve into the age of assimilation. There were difficulties, to be sure, not least the lingering distaste for and suspicion of popery within the overall still nominal Protestant society. Nor could one always assert unequivocal approval of America during the aptly nicknamed "Gilded Age," during the time of the "Robber Barons" and of the Trusts, during the time of seemingly endless industrial violence in the cities and similar outbreaks in frustration across the countryside, as well as the signs of a crude and aggressive imperialism marked by the irrational determination to go to war with Spain.

Witnesses as they were to these events, it is to the credit of the most enthusiastic Americanists — to Archbishop Ireland and his friends — that they qualified their call for assimilation into the American community by insisting upon a very important condition. "It is true," Ireland proclaimed in a famous speech delivered in Baltimore in 1888, "the choicest field which providence offers in the world today to the occupancy of the Church is this republic, and she welcomes with delight the signs of the times that indicate a glorious future for her beneath the starry banner. But" — and here we must pay special attention — "it is true also that the surest safeguards for her own life and prosperity the (American) republic will find in the teachings of the Catholic Church, and the more America acknowledges those teachings the more durable will (those) institutions be made." A large measure of the assimilation of immigrant Catholics into American culture was, of course, made inevitable by the simple passage of time. Prelates like Ireland and Michael Augustine Corrigan of New York quarreled indecorously for a generation over the pace of that amalgamation, but the process went relentlessly forward without, in the end, being much affected by their feuding. The children of the immigrants spoke English and played baseball and joined labor unions, and not a few of them sailed off with "Black Jack" Pershing to fight in France in 1917. Then, after the war, restrictive legislation reduced the flow of immigration from Europe to a trickle. The age of consolidation for American Catholics had come.

Consolidation

I speak now of an era in which I myself grew up and which, therefore, I may be tempted to romanticize as "the good old days." This is a temptation that must be stoutly resisted, all the more so because historical memory is so easily confused with nostalgia. But certain generalizations, I think, can be safely made without the intrusion of any sentimentality. The five decades or so between the first world war and the Second Council of the Vatican witnessed to a degree the realization of the hopes of the Americanists. Catholics assumed an ever more comfortable place in American life, and clearly came to be accepted as partners in the national scheme of things. Not equal partners, to be sure; not in the board rooms of the great corporations, nor in the smart country clubs, nor in the academic establishment — remember the shrewd aphorism, that "anti-Catholicism is the anti-Semitism of the intellectuals" — nor in the arena of national politics, of which the presidential campaign of 1928 remains a sour symbol. Nevertheless, Catholics, a solid twenty percent of the population (and much higher than that outside the deep south and inside the big cities), exercised a real influence within the larger American society, influence felt particularly within the labor movement, in urban youth work, and in mildly leftist programs of social amelioration. If the whole truth be told, the aching desire of Catholics for acceptance was often expressed in trivial ways, like Notre Dame football or the success of Catholic film stars — I remember how my sixth grade teacher, Sister Kathleen, was bursting with pride as she told us how a very young Gregory Peck, by reason of his knowledge of some obscure rubrical details, had won the role of the priest in the movie version of A. J. Cronin's *The Keys of the Kingdom*. "Give that man," Sister Kathleen quoted the producer as saying, "give that man a collar, a cassock, and a contract."

What strikes me as particularly remarkable about that period of Catholic consolidation was the perhaps grudging but nevertheless genuine and widespread admiration for the Catholic community's adherence to certain ethical standards — especially sexual and familial ones — which other Americans, most of them by then cut off from any seriously dogmatic religion, vaguely regretted to see slipping away. There was as well in the public consciousness enormous respect for the priesthood and the religious life, and particularly for the various Catholic sisterhoods. The sacrifices cheerfully borne by the teaching and nursing nuns — and by their cloistered sisters as well — were no doubt only partially understood by non-Catholic Americans — and indeed the popular depiction of these women, by the likes of Ingrid Bergman and Loretta Young, was often embarrassingly mawkish — yet admiration for them was universal, so much so that the savage attacks and the snide caricatures directed against the nuns of the last generation — a staple now of stage, screen, and nightclub comedy — shocks an old fogie like me as little else can.

One characteristic of this age of consolidation, as I have dubbed it, appears to me to explain its ethos and, perhaps, much of its success. The Americanists' dream of the integration of Catholics into secular society was fulfilled only partially. American habits of daily life, American ideals, American civic and economic values: all these Catholics embraced as ardently as any other group. Indeed, when America went to war, Catholics rallied to the grand old flag perhaps even more ardently than others. Even so, the Catholic community, taking advantage of the genius of the American dream, continued to insist on making its contribution to American life, not by merging into some common secular consensus, but by asserting, freely and responsibly, its own uniqueness. Let me, for lack of a more satisfactory term, label this, analogously, a [kind] of federalism. Catholics of my vintage vigorously denied that their differences from the secular mainstream — moral and ideological differences of the greatest moment — denied that such differences somehow made them less American. Quite to the contrary. What is America, they asked more than rhetorically, if not a vast concourse of peoples, sprung from every race and clime, and representing divergent points of view, who have entered a constitutional compact to live in harmony and mutual respect with each other? Federalism is an American ideal, they might have argued, that goes beyond the merely political arrangement between the states and the central government. *Vive les différences!*

This conviction took on its most concrete expression in one issue, or perhaps I should say in one institution: the Catholic school. Catholics of the age of consolidation stubbornly defended the principle that the Church should be directly involved in the education of their children. In doing so they were following the mandate, laid down in 1888 by the fathers of the third plenary council of Baltimore, who decreed that every parish must have its own school. This ideal proved, of course, physically impossible of complete fulfillment, but the ideal remained in place, and by the eve of the Second Council of the Vatican there were millions of children enrolled in parochial grammar and secondary schools, as well as an elaborate catechetical apparatus to service those who, for whatever reason, could not attend them. Add to this remarkable system more than five hundred Catholic colleges and universities, and you have some quantitative measure of what a cohesive and idealistic Catholic community could achieve.

But here was a matter upon which the otherwise tolerant secular majority took continuing umbrage. It may have been because of all its accomplishments the American citizenry was proudest, understandably so, of the establishment of a system of free, compulsory, universal, non-sectarian education. The existence of a lively rival to the romanticized little red schoolhouse seemed to most Americans to be a kind of reproach, and it certainly was an irritant. So, unlike every other developed nation, the United States has consistently refused to offer support for the confessional schools to be found within its borders, which has meant, with few exceptions, Catholic schools. On this crucial question, however much accommodation there may have been on other, less sensitive fronts, the twain between the secular majority and the Catholic minority did not meet. Consolidation and federalism for American Catholics involved the maintenance, at enormous sacrifice, of their own schools. And their pride rightly paralleled that taken by their secular neighbors in the public schools: never in the 2,000-year history of the Church has any group of Catholics anywhere created anything approaching the educations system American Catholics built and supported during the age of consolidation.

The Second Age of Survival

And it is all gone now, or practically so. Even the most affluent parishes have difficulty keeping a school open now, and, except for a handful, Catholic colleges and universities, as they scramble to become as comprehensively mediocre as most of their secular counterparts, have ceased to stand for anything distinctive. We American Catholics have arrived at the fifth age in our collective history, another age of survival. We who are proud to call ourselves Catholic scholars naturally focus our attention upon the collapse of our institutions of learning, and, to tell the truth, upon the very shriveling up of learning itself within our community. Can anything be more deplorable than the state of the science of theology in this American place and time, when, for example, Matthew Fox and his coven of witches are taken seriously? Can anyone estimate the long-term damage being done at this very moment by the pop-psychologists and pop-sociologists — the real savants of this dreary age — who edit our journals, control our seminaries and novitiates, and teach our children that values, undefined and indeed undefinable, are to be preferred to virtues?

But it is not only within the limited parameters of the intellectual life that we find plentiful evidence of decay. Let me cite some instances quite at random. The liturgical renewal, which held such promise on the eve of the Council, has degenerated in many places into idiosyncrasy and irrelevance and, sometimes, into a vulgarity bordering on blasphemy. All too often people who simply want to pray the Mass are afflicted with the silly self-aggrandizing of the preening priest, for whom eye-contact with the front pew is more important than the meaning of the memorial of Christ's passion that he is celebrating. Preaching, which was not very good before, is even worse now due to that same kind of self-indulgence and, of course, due also to the woeful level of training offered by most seminaries.

The scandal of the Catholic divorce mills continues unabated. An officer of an archdiocesan tribunal told me not long ago that he and his colleagues are now convinced that no marriage is valid and binding, because nobody is mature enough to make a permanent commitment. I dare say his opinion was shaped to some degree by the fact that he was in the process of deserting his wife of thirty-six years, the mother of his six children (themselves all married in Catholic ceremonies, presumably invalidly), because he had finally found true love in the person of Patty, a woman twenty-five years his junior, whom he was "counseling" due to her troubled marriage. When confronted recently by a five-year-old granddaughter who asked, "Why do you make mommy and grandma cry?", he replied, "Honey, God sent Patty to me, to make up for all the unhappiness I've had in my life." Now I need hardly say that lust in old men is hardly a novelty; witness Susannah and the elders in the book of Daniel. What does seem to me to be novel in this instance, and what has become unhappily commonplace in our second age of survival, is that people who no longer want to abide by the Catholic moral code or to accept Catholic dogmatic teaching are not content to go their way to do their thing. Instead they seek, indeed they demand, your approval and mine, and the sanction of the Church. The same unsavory characteristic of course marks the conduct of many men who have defected from the priesthood.

The failure of our leadership to face straightforwardly the issue of feminism, and specifically the question of women's ordination, presents us with a crisis of another kind. One prelate, though a frivolous and ill-educated fellow, has put his sensitive political finger on the central problem: the relation between decision-making within the Church and the sacrament of Orders. It is a question of power. But by that very fact it is also a question of hormones; it remains, however, much though our anointed leaders wish it were otherwise, a question of sexuality. Blurring that reality serves no purpose. Nor does blaming the present pope, as so many American bishops do in hopes that the militant feminists will leave them, the bishops, alone. Another prelate has said publicly that no resolution to the problem of women's ordination — by which of course he means surrender to the agenda of the most extreme feminists — will be possible during the present pontificate. By which he implies that no benighted Pole could be expected to accede to women's legitimate claims but that in the future a more enlightened occupant of the throne of St. Peter will put things right. He might as well have said, *Apres moi, le deluge.*

Why could he not say that Jesus chose only males as the vehicles for the transmission of his revelation to the world, not simply as a matter of the acculturation, long since passed away, of the first century, but because of the physiological and emotional differences between the sexes of which we have more than sufficient experience and which in any case have been revealed to us in the scriptures. Let us not beat about the bush: sexual equality, as affirmed in the most ancient revelation God has deigned to give us, does not mean sexual activity. One cannot blithely accept the first chapter of Genesis and ignore the third chapter. Nor can one fail to see that the functional difference between the active and the passive, between physical assertion on the one hand and acceptance on the other in the most intimate of human relationships, is bound to have social and indeed political consequences.

Perhaps the prelate I cite did not say all this because he is too delicate. Or — the evidence is rather stronger on this side — perhaps he is too ignorant. For he did say that a useful compromise might be to ordain women as deacons, which proposal displays a breathtaking ignorance of the developed theology of Holy Orders. Indeed, I am convinced that our radical problem is intellectual. Granted, knowledge is not virtue. Granted that the recent bizarre events in Atlanta and at Covenant House in New York are not without precedent. But surely one might argue, for example, that the depressingly widespread incidence of homosexuality within the priesthood, and the dreadful instance of pederasty, are attributable, to some degree at least, to the ambiguity of recent Catholic teaching on sex. I do not mean the magisterial teaching, of course; I do mean the sort of mush, now so prevalent in our diocesan press, that insists upon honoring "alternate lifestyles," and that seems more concerned to demonstrate compassion for the victims of AIDS than to instruct young Catholics on how to avoid contracting AIDS.

It seems to me we have entered a period of sharp decline. Even the numbers are disheartening. We have now considerably more than 300 bishops, at least a hundred more than we need. And how many of them have recently ventured into the highways and byways, or hoisted themselves onto the rooftops, to proclaim, "Repent! The Kingdom of God is at hand." We have bloated bureaucracies, growing all the time and sucking up our diminishing resources, at the national and diocesan and even parochial levels. The only numbers that have fallen, and they precipitously, are those of practicing Catholics. You may recall last spring when the archdiocese of Chicago closed fifty parishes for financial reasons, there were many protests and even one appeal to the Vatican. To justify its actions the diocese released some statistics, the most arresting of which had to do with Mass attendance and therefore contributions: of the 2.4 million nominal Catholics living in the diocese of Chicago, about 600,000 go to Mass on Sunday. Twenty-five percent, or about the same as in Italy, much less than in Alsace or Brittany, light years less than in Poland or Ireland or in the young churches of Africa and Asia.

And so I recommend, as the evangelization proper to these unhappy times, a return to the ghetto, by which I mean something quite precise. I think we need to recapture a sense of ourselves, who we are, how we differ from the consumerist world around us, what it is in contemporary American society that we admire and what we despise. We need to find again that spirit of community and fellowship we have lost. Those of us dedicated to the intellectual life have, it seems to me, a special call: through our often lonely and unappreciated scholarly endeavors we need to rediscover that Catholic tradition which has nourished our forebears across nearly two millennia and which, once we have found it, has to be shared with our brothers and sisters in Christ. The road will be long and narrow and rutted, the signposts few, the hazards many. To reach the goal we shall need something of the stubborn loyalty to the faith of the old Maryland Catholics: something also of the missionary zeal that gloriously lit up the years of our expansion here in this new land; and something of the wisdom of our immediate ancestors who looked sharply at America, loved it for its goodness, and heartily worked to make it even better.

Toward the end of his long life, the chronicles tell us, Dean Swift, a lonely widower, grew more and more whimsical and capricious, morbidly suspicious and crotchety. He was struck down, finally, by paralysis, and it became necessary to appoint guardians of his person and estate. Learned physicians debated over the causes of the dementia which afflicted him just before he died and which caused, as they put it, "the automatic utterance of words ungoverned by intention." Yet, despite all his frailties, despite even this curiously unchecked rush of speech, the same doctors testified that their patient "never talked nonsense or said a foolish thing."

May the same be said of me, and of my modest proposal.

Lay Witness, Volume 12, Number 9, May 1991, Pages 1–8

O'Connell sees history as a resource to tap into, partly because the Catholic faith, which is under grave attack from ephemeral but powerful forces of modernism, is inseparable from human history.

He has spent a lifetime valuing truth and using facts to differentiate the meaningful from the vacuous. O'Connell warns against a worldview of abstract ideas — a world of atomistic individuals misusing words and defining their own realities. He says the standards he has applied as an historian can help today's truth-seekers contending with ideas, good and bad. – WGS

Modernism — An Historical Sketch

In the debates that inevitably arise within any cultivated society, not all the words used are equal. If, for instance you are able to invoke "reform" or any of its variants on behalf of your position, you immediately secure an advantage over your adversaries. This is because, in ordinary parlance, "reform," no matter in what context you employ it, automatically puts you on the moral high ground, makes you an advocate of "improvement" and an enemy of corruption. A proposal to reform the Church or the state, to reform education or athletics or health-care, will give you a leg-up in any argument you care to take on. Your opponents will then find themselves forced to protest that they too are for improvement of whatever institution is under discussion, and so, instead of stating their case effectively, they will waste their energies in insisting that their brand of reform is better than yours.

The absurdity to which this dialectical device can lead was demonstrated some years ago when the mayor of New York City was reelected by campaigning as a reformer; he promised, that is, to eliminate the corrupt administration he had himself created. The classic example of its effectiveness, however, remains the enshrinement in our language of the term "Reformation" to describe the religious revolt of the sixteenth century. The presumption continues to this day that the Protestant Reformers "improved" the Christian Church and cleansed it of its alleged decadence. Never mind that the root definition of "reform" has nothing whatever to do with improvement, that to "re-form" means simply to "re-shape," to give something a different structure from what it had before.

Of course, it is true that in this proper etymological sense "reformation" is an appropriate word to characterize what Luther, Calvin, and their ilk brought about: The Church was indeed reshaped as a result of the doctrines they preached. Improvement, however, is surely quite a different matter. Our Catholic ancestors, in any event, long ago lost this particular terminological battle; the improvements they secured within the Church to which they remained faithful have been largely dismissed as "reactionary" ploys and consigned to that oddest and most offensive of historical designations, the "Counter-Reformation."

And we may be in danger of losing a verbal battle of our own. The word "modern" reverberates as seductively and uncritically as does "reform." "Modern" is in itself a neutral and innocuous word that merely signifies the recent in time, the up-to-date, the fashions of the moment. Modern appliances, modern styles of dress, modern modes of transport and communication — none of these is in the least objectionable. Quite to the contrary: they are boons to humankind. Nobody at the end of the twentieth century thinks it a virtue to wash clothes on a rock by a riverside, or to wear a hoop-skirt, or to listen to a crystal-set.

But there has crept into the commonly accepted meaning of "modern," as is the case with "reform," a connotation entirely improper, one which introduces, in defiance of etymology, an element of moral superiority. What is modern must be better than anything that has gone before. If central heating is an improvement over potbellied wood-stoves, it does not follow that situation ethics, also a "modern" advancement, must be preferred to the Decalogue. If the internet brings us more information than smoke-signals, we do not for that reason become wiser than Socrates.

This distinction is especially important for us Christians whose religion is rooted in certain historical facts that occurred two thousand years ago. The Sermon on the Mount, the Beatitudes, the Lord's Prayer: none of these is "modern" except in the sense that they are universally applicable. They are for all times, and all places, and all peoples.

Nearly ninety years ago the pope of that day, St. Pius X, issued an encyclical in which he condemned the "Modernists (as they are commonly and rightly called)," these "most pernicious of all the adversaries of the Church, who lay the axe not to the branches and shoots but to the very root, and thus disseminate poison through the whole tree, so that there is no part of Catholic truth they do not strive to corrupt." The rather awkwardly mixed metaphor of axe and poison suggests how intense were the pope's feelings of revulsion toward those he conceived to be conspiring against Catholic truth. Nor did he relax his heated rhetoric: "None is more skillful than they in the employment of a thousand noxious arts, all calculated to lead the unwary into error. And, what almost destroys all hope of cure, their very doctrines have given such a bent to their minds that they disdain all authority and brook no restraint; and relying upon a false conscience, they attempt to ascribe to love of truth that which is in reality the result of pride and obstinacy. Can anybody who takes a survey of the whole system be surprised that we should define it as the synthesis of all heresies?"

The encyclical, titled *Pascendi Dominici Gregis* from the opening words of the Latin text, was dated September 8, 1907. What provoked such a fierce papal denunciation — so different in tone from the Vatican pronouncements we are accustomed to reading — was a small collection of intellectuals, most of them French, English, and Italian, with an insignificant smattering of Germans and Americans. They were historians and philosophers, philologists and political thinkers, novelists and literary critics. Though they formed a group too varied, too far-flung, too little in touch with one another to provide an entirely consistent pattern, yet they were all in their different ways enthusiastic representatives of the modernity prized by their generation. They were the uninhibited children of the nineteenth century. Science had taught them secrets of nature which for millennia had been locked up in myth and fable. They had evidence at hand of what industrialization, free trade, and the extension of the franchise could accomplish. They cheerfully and confidently bore the white man's burden around the world in this uniquely European century.

Those whom *Pascendi* called Modernists sang out lustily their unbending confidence in progress and enlightenment. Humanity on the march to utopia may sound to us now like a strange, hollow theme, played against the background of genocide and terrorism and seemingly endless war. Not so then. What an opportunity the Modernists saw for the Christian Church if it would sweep away the conventions of yesterday, the dead theories and spent systems, good enough perhaps for the benighted ages of the past but mere debris around the Proud Tower of 1900.

But of course the battle of Catholic Modernism was to be fought out on more specific ground. The many intellectual faces of modernity were to show themselves one by one. Thus, the Modernists assumed the correctness of Darwinian evolution as applied to societies and institutions as well as to organisms. They took it for granted that Immanuel Kant had forever demonstrated the inadequacy of the human intellect to penetrate beyond itself to objectively real phenomena. But they judged this to be a liberation, not a hindrance; a liberation from formulas and legalisms that grew out of lifeless philosophical realism. A realist metaphysics, they liked to say, was not only foolish but perverse, because it encouraged illusion just as it thwarted the inward drive toward godliness. For Kant had also taught them that the stern voice of conscience within gives assurance of truths which the intellect is powerless to establish.

So they espoused what they called the "Philosophy of Action," under-standing "action" in the widest sense of the word, disdaining the dead end of useless speculation, and arguing that, since the will directs life and produces action, and since the will cannot satisfy itself with the finite, the very existence of God can be accepted only because of one's deep and natural longing for him. So they developed "Moral Dogmatism," which sets aside the impotent intellect and seeks the definition of the divine out of "all the activities of life." Empty dialectics can then give place to something vital and complete which provides a sure base for the fundamental truths of religion and the dogmas of Christianity.

The Modernists habitually contrasted Christian reality with Greek theory, the concrete with the abstract, and since for them the individual experience, welling up from inside oneself was the Christian reality, the eternal verity, it followed that all creeds and traditions and sacred books needed constant reinterpretation if they were to be relevant to the individual Christian in an ever-changing, ever-evolving life. Modern thought, they argued, has a deep aversion to the Catholic faith and especially to the Catholic notion of dogma. The idea of an immutable and authoritative statement of religious truth is unthinkable. A secure apologetic, therefore, for modern men and women can be reached only by reversing the conventional order. Instead of seeing dogma as a speculative proposition which has impact upon moral conduct, rather, the Modernists insisted, regard dogma as the minimum affirmation necessary to justify conduct.

Thus, for instance, the dogma of the Real Presence in the Eucharist would mean treating the altar-bread as though it were the Body of Jesus.

This philosophical approach, which *Pascendi* called, quite appropriately, "immanentism," stood as one of the two pillars supporting the Modernist edifice. The second was the so-called "higher criticism" as applied to the Sacred Scriptures. This discipline had emerged out of the linguistic and historical scholarship of the eighteenth-century Enlightenment. It flourished first in German universities and then spread gradually through the whole of European academe. The basic assertion of the higher critics was that the truth of the Bible depended solely upon reading it in the light of the literary sources of its authors, studying it, that is, as any other piece of ancient literature is properly studied. The notion of divine inspiration must give way, in this scenario, to the insights of the linguistic critic. As one of the leading Modernists put it, "The idea of God as author of a book is more contradictory, more absurd than the idea of a toad-man or a snake-woman. This is an infantile myth, as infantile as the formation of the first man out of clay and of the first woman out of Adam's rib."

The acceptance of this theory was a devastating blow to conventional Protestantism, but the Roman Church took the line — much too smug as things turned out — that the higher criticism could not challenge its positions, because Catholics had never accepted the view that the Bible authenticates itself or interprets itself. Apologetics demonstrates the divine foundation of the Church, and then the Church guarantees the Scriptures. But before long that conviction came under severe attack as the higher critics shifted their attention from the Old to the New Testament. A Catholic might accept placidly enough the depiction of the patriarch Abraham as a desert sheikh, but what if Jesus is reduced to an amiable Jewish reformer with no moral or supernatural significance?

The ultimate Modernist assault was indeed launched against the very concept of the supernatural. The gospel, proclaimed the Modernists, is Jesus' preaching of the messianic kingdom, with its call to penance as an eschatological warning of imminent destruction — a message entirely characteristic of the Judaism of the first century. The Church continues this function, but always in a way subject to the conditions of the time, just as Jesus' own preaching was conditioned. So come the successive formulas, creeds, hierarchical institutions, sacraments — all in a kind of rational flux, pressing forward, ever refining themselves, just as the evolving universe does. Nothing stands permanent; nothing that has been said will not be unsaid. "Jesus and the Church," said the Modernist critic quoted above, "lift their eyes to the same symbol of hope. The dogmatic formulas are in the same condition as the words of the Savior: their value is in the sense that one attaches to them."

What in essence Pius X discerned, and what called forth the condemnation in *Pascendi* of this "synthesis of all heresies," was the striking of a bargain between the Modernist philosophers and the Modernist higher critics. Criticism stripped away the objective foundations of the Christian religion, but immanentism stepped in to fill the gap. The historical personage named Jesus may be permanently elusive; the evangelical miracles may be fairy tales; the dogmas of the Incarnation and the Resurrection may not be factually true. But never mind. Religious truth is not something which comes out of a proclamation from outside yourself. Religious truth wells up from within you and reflects your deepest needs and longings. Religious truth is what you, caught in the flux of time, make it.

The sketch that I have tried to draw here does not do justice to the complexity of the events associated with the Modernist crisis of a century ago. Nor does it describe the poignancy of the drama. For, despite the regrettable invective of *Pascendi*, the Catholic Modernists, with a notable exception or two, were men and women of great probity, and several of them were persons of genuine holiness of life. Not all those whom the encyclical categorized as Modernists subscribed to the extreme elements of the theory, and most of them, with much soul-searching to be sure, accepted the Church's judgment. But *Pascendi* was by no means all invective and sarcasm. If the encyclical overstated the conspiratorial nature of Modernism, it nevertheless captured the essence of the movement and its radical destructiveness, a fact which even the most outspoken of the Modernists reluctantly acknowledged.

Modernism was very much an elitist program, which had at the time no impact upon ordinary Catholics. But, as the old saying goes, "Ideas have consequences," and, since the ideas brought forward by the Modernists impinge upon the very heart of Catholic belief, it is no surprise — the strictures of *Pascendi* notwithstanding — that they come to be debated again and again and that in the long run they affect the men and women in the pew. In saying this, however, I do not refer to the effusions of those who today are sometimes called Neo-Modernists, who with utter foolishness and effrontery maintain that the decrees of Vatican II reflect the insights of historical Modernism. Such persons in any event are obsessed with superficial arguments about, say, gender and political power in the Church, arguments which self-respecting Modernists — who, whatever their shortcomings, were genuinely thoughtful people — would have despised.

Ideas indeed have consequences — ideas embodied in words like "reform" and "modern." As long as the pilgrim Church toils along on its hard trek toward its patria, its supernatural homeland, ideas must be contended with. Which, despite moments of gloom and crisis, may be seen as a sign [of] God's profound respect for those whom he has made in his image and likeness.

Catholic Dossier, Volume 2, Number 1, Jan.–Feb. 1996, Pages 4–7

Now turning inward after observing the world with the rigorous standards of an academic discipline, O'Connell observes his own past as an historian — how the seeds of that vocation were planted not through discipline, but delight. In this lecture, presented to the American Catholic Historical Association in Houston in 1996, he calls himself "an old man" and expresses gratitude to teachers who kindled his sense of wonder.

He looks back over the power of the printed word as a source of excitement and panoramic experience. Notably, this master of story-telling with insight into people, their circumstances, and their lives of change points out that his love of history was first nurtured by the genre of historical fiction. O'Connell describes historians as "practitioners of the humblest of the sciences but the grandest of the arts." – WGS

How History Came to Be . . . My Passion

Last summer, right on schedule, I received a Medicare card. A humdrum, routine sort of event to you perhaps, but for me it was fraught with unprecedented gloom. The fact is that, despite any illusions I might continue to entertain to the contrary, I am now an old man, formally declared to be so by the omni-competent state. Euphemisms are of course ready at hand — senior citizen, grey panther, denizen of the golden years, a comrade of Browning's Rabbi Ben Ezra: "Grow old along with me!/ The best is yet to be,/ The last of life for which the first was made." I must say I don't much care for that phrase "the last of life," but I cannot avoid its significance. Old is old no matter what one calls it, and I have discovered already that its somber touch brings with it, among other things, stiffness in the joints, shortness of breath, an overwhelming desire to sleep in the middle of the afternoon, and — for the male of the species — an ever-increasing interest in the functioning of the prostate gland.

You may recall the lines from the Book of Joel, that young men shall see visions and old men shall dream dreams. I've never been quite sure what exactly the Prophet had in mind — but then there are many among the sacred texts whose meaning has eluded me. Not that my lack of complete understanding will keep me from theorizing about this particular prophetic adage. In doing so I find myself in good company. After all, our esteemed colleagues, the Scripture scholars, earn their bread by teasing the rest of us as to the explanation of this or that cryptic biblical passage. Perhaps it is not too much to suggest that at least since the time of Tertullian they have dignified obscurity as though it were the mother of their science.

It strikes me at any rate as possible that the dreaming in which, according to the Prophet, the old indulge may very well be a species of memory. Selective memory, to be sure, embellished inevitably by a measure of self-service, the triumphs of the past more vivid than the defeats, the injuries and slights received more keenly recalled than those delivered, the hard edges crusted upon the years gone by softened by all the poignant might-have-beens and should- have-beens. I find such an interpretation consoling, both personally and professionally, because I speak to you as an historian to historians, and we, as practitioners of our craft, have presumed to present ourselves to our contemporaries as guardians of the collective memory of our race.

More than that, history, whatever its scientific trappings, remains an art, and we are artists. Existentially the past is gone beyond recall; whatever reality it possesses depends upon us who think about it and write about it. Caesar crossing the Rubicon; Luther fixing his Ninety-five Theses on Indulgences to the door of the castle-church in Wittenberg; Rose Hawthorne caring for incurable cancer patients in a New York tenement; none of these events or personages has actuality except to the extent that we give it to them. Therefore, as it seems to me, the personal remembrance of things past merges with the professional. The dreams we ourselves have dreamt, the memories we still cherish, the variety of experiences that has uniquely stamped us as individuals, has also shaped us as historians. So let me take shameful advantage of my grey hairs and impose on you, a captive audience, an account of how history came to be not only my profession but my passion.

"Hurrah for Polk and the annexation,/ Down with Clay and high taxation." This bit of doggerel, a species, I suppose, of negative advertising employed during the presidential campaign of 1844, is my oldest historical memory. It comes from the fourth-grade classroom of Sister Benedicta in the Immaculate Conception School of Charles City, Iowa, 1939. Sister

Benedicta — a tall, lanky woman with sunken cheeks and piercing black eyes — was a hard taskmistress, but she had a way with her, an ability to create in a child a sense of excitement over events long past, at the prospect, in this instance, of Texas being brought into the union. What, I recall precociously asking myself, what would the United States be like if Texas were not part of it? I don't know that Sister Benedicta answered this question, but I do know that, despite some very bad teachers at various times, I was overall blessed by mentors who possessed something of her magic. The two most notable that come to mind now after all these years were luminaries of the American Catholic Historical Association: Patrick Henry Ahern, one of the bright jewels in the crown of John Tracy Ellis, and an adopted member of the Association; and the Englishman, Philip Hughes. I can best testify to the debt I owe to the benign and critical guidance of the latter by saying how pleased I was when a reviewer of my most recent book referred to me as a student of "the incomparable Philip Hughes." He it was who plunged me into the maelstrom of Elizabethan history by sending me directly to the treasure trove of Catholic recusant literature.

And yet, despite all that I owe Sister Benedicta, Father Ahern, and Monsignor Hughes — the three of them now, I am confident, resting in the bosom of Abraham — I owe still more to the world of the printed word. I have been told by some of my progressive colleagues that the era of the book and the journal is over, that the technological revolution has rendered such old-fashioned means of communication obsolete, that from now on the Internet and the Worldwide Web and Windows Ninety-five will define the intellectual development of humankind. Presumably the film — a word uttered these days with much solemnity to describe what we used to call movies — will do the same for emotional development. In an ironic sense I find these predictions consoling, because, if they are correct, I can confront the relentless approach of dotage with some composure. For I am a man of print, unabashed and unashamed, and no one can expect me to alter my eccentric habits at this late date.

Saying this I do not mean to denigrate manuscript research. Indeed, I don't believe there is any thrill an historian experiences to match holding in his hand, as I have been privileged to do, a holograph letter to Pius IX headed "*Mon cher saint Pere*" and signed "Bernadette Soubirous"; or the dispatch sent from Washington to Cardinal Rampolla by John Ireland confessing that the archbishop of St. Paul's efforts to avert the Spanish War of 1898 had failed: "I am going home now," the document concludes; or the poignant lines addressed by John Keble to John Henry Newman when Keble learned his friend was departing Canterbury for Rome: "I feel as though the spring has gone out of my year"; or — on a much less elevated plane — the report of the papal nuncio in Paris describing the inoffensive Felix Klein as "*il famoso Americanista*" and suggesting that Klein enjoyed the favors of a ballerina; or the doleful communique sent to the Roman curia by Patrick Riordan of San Francisco providing proof that the brilliant and enigmatic John Lancaster Spalding, Riordan's episcopal colleague and lifelong friend, was indeed a fornicator.

These occasions of sifting the dust gathered on the documents themselves have no parallel, nor would I for a moment suggest otherwise. Even so, to make sense of them demands a context, and this can only be supplied by the printed sources and by the commentaries of learned researchers. I could never have understood John Ireland's term as chaplain to the fifth regiment, Minnesota volunteer infantry, and his participation in the Corinth campaign of 1862, had I not been able to consult the relevant volumes of the monumental *Official Records of the Union and Confederate Armies*. The documents I found in the Vatican archives relating to the Dreyfus Affair in France during the early years of the century would have had little meaning for me had I not had at my disposal the printed exegesis of Jean Jaures on one side of the quarrel and of Maurice Barres on the other. The countless hours I spent in the great domed reading room of the British Library in London, and in archives at Oxford and Birmingham, stand golden in my memory, but the nagging question remains: would any of the unpublished papers I studied in those places, in hopes of unraveling the internal history of the Oxford Movement, have meant anything to me without the support I could count upon from the printed reminiscences of Richard Church, Thomas Mozley, J. A. Froude, even Matthew Arnold? Most of those papers are now indeed in the public forum, many of them found in the 31 volumes of Newman's *Letters and Diaries*. And Gladstone's diaries have been published too. I am struggling just now with the literary remains of Blaise Pascal, very little of which — with the notable exception of the *Provincial Letters* — was published during the author's brief lifetime. Now, when much of the manuscript material has disappeared, this precious testament is available in several handsome editions, the fruit of three centuries of dedicated scholarship.

So I return to my fundamental assertion: I have been a man of books. There have been so many of them, but let me mention a few that have meant most to me. Believe it or not, I look back with special gratitude to Aristotle's *Prior and Posterior Analytics*, which taught me inestimable lessons about the division of sciences and about the inner methodological light that illuminates each of them, history included. From Christopher Dawson's *The Age of the Gods* I was able finally to make sense out of the relationship between mind and nature, between physical and psychic reality, that underlay the accomplishments of classical Greek civilization. Thanks to Dawson I could appreciate something of the grandeur of Homer and the pathos of Sophocles. Bruce Vawter's *A Pathway through Genesis*, with its explication of literary forms, liberated me from the illusions of biblical fundamentalism, while at the same time made me able to assert confidently — as I do today — that everything written in the Judeo-Christian Scriptures is literally true. *The Valois Tapestries* by Frances Yates opened up for me the riches of the intellectual and aesthetic spirit of the sixteenth century as no other study ever did.

Personal reminiscences, necessary and intriguing as they often are, I have nevertheless found to be largely suspect, because they tend to be, understandably, self-serving. Alfred Loisy, the Modernist biblical scholar, wrote three of the most beguiling volumes of memoirs ever published, but woe to the reader who does not seek corroboration from other sources. Cardinal O'Connell of Boston — no relation, I'm pleased to say — told so many lies in his autobiography that it has taken sixty years to expose them all. Yet I have imbibed much heady exhilaration from the wines aged in the cellars of Bertrand Russell, Benvenuto Cellini, General Grant, Robert Graves, William Allen White. As for critical biography, a genre which has come into its own during our time, I would suggest that you read first James Joyce's *Dubliners* and *Ulysses*, and then, if you still want to know something about literary Ireland and all that that meant at the turn of the century — and all that it means now, in these unhappy times of renewed violence — take up Richard Ellmann's monumental *Life* of Joyce. Dumas on Jefferson, Southall Freeman on Lee, Meriol Trevor on Newman, Gilbert on Churchill — these are works that deserve the serious attention of any historian.

But there is another category of literary work that cannot be set lightly aside. My own career at any rate, for what it may be worth, testifies to the import of historical fiction. I do not of course refer to those imaginary adventures which are hardly anything more than contemporary commentary dressed up in antiquated clothing — *Forever Amber*, for example, or *Prince of Foxes*, which were popular when I was a young man. Such books assumed twentieth century secular values, much as the novels of Alexandre Dumas, *pere* and *fils*, assumed those of the nineteenth. On another plane altogether are Hilda Prescott's *The Man on a Donkey* and Sigrid Undset's *Kristin Lavransdatter*, both of which are based upon the kind of profound research that any academic historian could be proud of. Indeed, I have declared to several generations of students in my courses on the history of Tudor England that they could learn more about the reign of Henry VIII from Prescott than they could from any number of textbooks. The skill with which *The Man on a Donkey* is written — a fictional account, and yet rooted in the sources, of the Pilgrimage of Grace, the rebellion of 1536 which attempted to reverse the impetus of the English Reformation — remains a tribute to the acumen as well as to the artistry of the author. It goes without saying that women — Gertrude Himmelfarb and Caroline Bynum come immediately to mind — have achieved the same stature in our profession as their male counterparts. But why women compose historical fiction so much better than men remains a puzzle to me. Coincidentally it might be observed that they also write the superior thrillers and detective mysteries to which I am addicted. The roll call clearly is sounded: Agatha Christie, Dorothy Sayers, Elizabeth George, P. D. James, Ruth Rendell, Martha Grimes.

It was fiction, as a matter of fact, that first induced me to want to be an historian. I wonder how many of you here recognize the name Joseph Altsheller. If I were as good a Christian as I ought to be, I would light a candle regularly to Altsheller's memory. I was an only child who grew up in small towns in southern Minnesota and northern Iowa during the depression of the late 'thirties. I don't think I was particularly peculiar: though as a new boy in school — five different ones over the course of my eight grades — I had to prove myself by awkward fights in the playground. I always ended up with plenty of friends with whom I could share the usual diversions of masculine childhood. But I also discovered the wonders of the local public library — God reward the shade of Andrew Carnegie — and there I was introduced to the *opera* of Joseph Altsheller. I dare say he would have been embarrassed by the use of the fancy word *opera*, though I cannot be sure because to this day I really know nothing about him. Except that he wrote wondrous tales about the American past that fascinated me to a degree that I have never forgotten. The first of his books I read was called *Horsemen of the Plains*, a story about trappers and buffalo-hunters who ultimately had to confront the warriors of the Cheyenne nation. He wrote also several series of six or eight novels with continuing characters, one about colonial America and another about the Civil War — *The Guns of Bull Run, The Night Shades at Shiloh, The Rock of Chickamauga*. To be sure, Altsheller romanticized the gore and horror of those great battles, but, despite this evident defect, he also taught me at a tender age — though I did not recognize it until many years later — that anybody who would peer into the human past and hope to understand it must do so in terms of vicarious experience. Indeed, I did not even know the definition of "vicarious" until long after I had outgrown Altsheller's juvenile stories. But I realize for a certainty now that it is this characteristic of the historian's enterprise — perhaps I may go so far as to term it the poetic sensitivity which genuine history demands — that made it possible for me to remove myself for a moment from the strictures of contemporary life and to share something of the triumph of Alessandro Farnese and his scruffy, ill-paid, ill-fed soldiers who against all odds captured Antwerp in 1584; something of the anguish of Maurice Blondel at the publication of Pius X's condemnation of Modernism — "the synthesis of all heresies" — in 1907; something of the thrill of anticipation that passed through the Church of St. Mary the Virgin in Oxford on late Sunday afternoons during the 1830s when John Henry Newman emerged out of the half-light of the chancel and ascended the pulpit; something of John Ireland's exaltation when he learned that the pope had endorsed the Faribault school plan in 1892: "My crowning victory," he cried. "The Jesuits never in this century received such a blow."

May I inflict upon your patience one last stop along the lane of dreams and memories? When I was twelve or thirteen, I received as a Christmas gift a book titled *George Washington's World*. It was a pretty hefty volume, I recall, but its detailed contents and even the name of its author have, alas, long since gone whistling down the wind. Its structure, however, taught a lesson I never forgot and one that affected me as much as that sense of vicariousness aroused by Altsheller's novels. The Father of our country lived between 1732 and 1799. My new book described the persons and events that flourished outside America during those same years. It was, in short, an attempt to provide for adolescents of my generation an integrated history of the eighteenth century. *George Washington's World* succeeded with one young reader at least to this extent, that however often and egregiously I have failed to live up to it, my ideal has always been to see the past, and to reconstruct it, as an integral whole, with all the interrelationships and complexities that that involves.

Indeed, how can one do otherwise if one truly seeks to chronicle that tangle of mind and emotion, of pride and passion and sentimentality, of providence and chance, of cruelty and compassion, of the good and the bad, that has been the human story? We dare not let Shakespeare's Prospero have the last word: "The cloud-capped towers, the gorgeous palaces,/ The solemn temples, the great globe itself,/ Yea, all which it inherit, shall dissolve/ And like this insubstantial pageant faded,/ Leave not a rack behind." No, we historians, practitioners of the humblest of the sciences but the grandest of the arts, shall not let the great globe of the past dissolve, even if rueful agreement must be accorded to the rest of Prospero's siren-song: "We are such stuff/ As dreams are made on, and our little life/ Is rounded with a sleep."

Lecture, American Catholic Historical Association, Houston, March 1996

O'Connell's contributions as an historian must never overshadow the value, for him and for countless others, derived from his life as a Catholic priest. Part of his love for the stories of people — and his intuitions about the depths and contexts of those stories — must have been cultivated by his years of service in parishes, his roles as a leader of worship and prayer, and his ability to embrace gifts of revelation. In this funeral homily, he assesses those gifts in another's life; he preached this at the funeral of Dr. James E. Ward in Sacred Heart Church in Notre Dame, Indiana, on July 17, 1978.

"The historian is midwife to our faith," O'Connell says, "because without him, without the facts which he relentlessly thrusts at us, our faith is stillborn." This aligns with his dedication to truth and reality, based on a recognition of Christianity's links to the passage of time and the ongoing influence of God and people throughout each life. – WGS

The Faith of an Historian

It is the peculiar character of Christian religion that it bases its claims to our attention and adherence upon historical facts. Philosophers may enlighten us about our faith, theologians may give us stunning insights into its meaning, social scientists may instruct us as to how its principles can be usefully applied to a certain set of circumstances.

But in the end we keep coming back to the same nagging question: Is the Christian religion *true*? And that question remains essentially an historical one. Aquinas on the Trinity and Schillebeeckx on the Eucharist have only indulged in flights of fancy unless their arguments are rooted in concrete, particular events which took place once for all a long time ago. If, as St. Paul solemnly reminds us, if Christ did not *in fact* rise from the dead, then our faith is a vain and foolish thing, and we are the most unhappy of men. We are as a believing people confronted at every turn in the road by a challenge to our intellects which is radically historical. Of course we move along the front edge of time, constantly probing into the future, but behind us trail those past facts — some of them highly uncomfortable to our damaged natures — which determine the kind of people we are and shall be. It is a trial, sometimes, to be burdened as we are by the baggage of the past.

We hanker as much as other people do to join the "Now Generation," but, alas, we cannot do it. The Christian religion is not something that we find within ourselves or something we generate out of our sense of need. The Christian religion is a revelation, an objective fact, exterior to us and independent of us. And God has chosen to reveal himself to us not in the beauties of flowers and sunsets, nor in signs and visions — indeed, "it is a sinful and adulterous generation that asks for signs." He has chosen to reveal himself in an historical person who, at a particular time and in a particular place, went from town to town doing good, who was like us in all things save sin. "Show us the Father," the apostle Philip said, "and it will be enough for us." "Phillip," Jesus replied, "when you have seen me, you have seen the Father."

The Christian religion must be a thing of the mind before it can become a thing of the emotions. Indeed, for many believers it never does engage the emotions in any steady or regular way. And if the Christian religion is to be a thing of the mind, for us who, unlike Philip, never saw Jesus in the flesh, it can be so only through history. We can reach the Jesus of this Eucharist, we can reach the Jesus who sits now at the right hand of the Father, only through the Jesus who was born in Bethlehem of Judah in the days of King Herod.

History therefore has a special role in the life of the Christian people, and so does the historian. Yes, the historian, that humdrum fellow who stirs the dust on broken-down monuments and rattles the bones on long-forgotten battle fields. The historian is midwife to our faith, because without him, without the facts which he relentlessly thrusts at us our faith is stillborn. Voltaire's oft-quoted remark that if there were not a God we should have to invent one, is clever and memorable and even plausible. But it is a lie, or at least, in the Christian context, it is unintelligible. What monsters of selfishness we should invent were we to make gods for ourselves. The historian saves us from such a calamity, because his obsession with objective facts saves us from the cloying self-consciousness and sentimentality to which religion is all too easily reduced.

The life of Christ is extended into the life of his people the Church. So the Christian historian who practices his craft with sensitivity is about a business which is at once humane and divine.

Sermon, preached at the funeral of Dr. James E. Ward, Sacred Heart Church, Notre Dame, Indiana, July 17, 1978

Addendum

This essay is not written by O'Connell. It was written by Ralph McInerny, the legendary philosophy scholar and prolific author who taught at the University of Notre Dame from 1955 to 2009. McInerny, who died in 2010, had been O'Connell's friend for nearly 70 years. They understood each other, sharing a number of traits such as the love of both non-fiction and fiction. In this tribute, O'Connell is dubbed "Clio's Cleric" — a reference to the muse of history in Greek mythology, the proclaimer of great deeds. — WGS

A Friend's Tribute: "Clio's Cleric"

"This is the worst novel I've read all the way through." Thus began a review by Father Marvin O'Connell some years back. Woe to the sloppy writer who has such a reader — luckily the work in question was not mine. O'Connell has not devoted much time to such ephemeral productions, his own or others. His Irish ire has limited the occasions for it. Years ago he reviewed Paul Johnson's book *The Jews* for us, and Michael Novak asked for a few changes. He has never written for *Crisis* since. An editor at *Notre Dame Magazine* presumed to cut a commissioned article in half. He will never again appear in those benighted pages. He is, in a word, Irish. He is also, far and away, the best historian we have.

As a newly ordained priest, Marvin O'Connell came to Notre Dame to study with the acclaimed Church historian Philip Hughes. Another recipient of a Lingard fellowship that year was the now Monsignor Eugene V. Clark. The two have been close friends ever since. O'Connell's graduate work bore fruit in a book on the Counter-Reformation figure Thomas Stapleton (Yale, 1964). He was assigned to teach history at St. Thomas College, and he spent fifteen years there. His teaching became legendary, his rectorship of a residence hall was draconian, his weekend work was pastoral. These were the years when things fell apart, the center did not hold. Priests went over the wall like lemmings or disappeared on unexplained leaves. Imagine the annoyance this faithful priest, doing three jobs, felt toward such self-indulgence. When the call to Notre Dame came and his archbishop gave the go-ahead, Marvin O'Connell entered into what were to be his golden years.

Shortly before making the academic move, *The Oxford Conspirators* appeared (MacMillan, 1969). Those who thought they had understood Newman and the Oxford Movement were given a fresh and deeper look at both. When, in 1980, the novel *McElroy* appeared, I and many others read it all the way through with profound pleasure. This was O'Connell's only venture outside history, but it revealed a talent that those who had known him since schooldays were well aware of. Fellow Minnesotans professed to see Eugene McCarthy as the inspiration of the main character, but O'Connell remained appropriately mum.

In the major works that have since appeared, O'Connell found his mature style as an historian. Few writers have the ability to locate the reader more surely in place and time, to give a sense of the human beings whose deeds and antics are the stuff of history. The historian dotes on the particular; the great historian makes it shine with a more than particular import. An historian like O'Connell becomes perforce a bit of a biographer, and there is always a *soupçon* of the novelist in his style now.

John Ireland, the life of the great churchman, archbishop of St. Paul, appeared in 1988. It is neither hagiography nor demythologizing, putting the man and the times and the issues before the reader's unblinkered eyes. Ireland might have winced a bit in reading it, but in the end would know he had fallen into good hands. Next came what is to date O'Connell's finest work, *Critics on Trial: Introduction to the Catholic Modernist Crisis* (Catholic University Press, 1994). Anyone wanting to know how we got to where we are must understand the theological turmoil and dissent at the beginning of the century. The modernists have been lionized by some and demonized by others; O'Connell gives them to us as almost sympathetic figures. Rare is the writer who can combine compassion for his subjects and judgment on what they did and said. There will never be a better book on the modernist crisis.

Last year, as if to exhibit yet another string in his bow, O'Connell published *Blaise Pascal: Reasons of the Heart* (Eerdmans, 1997). As a subject, Pascal is perfectly adapted to O'Connell's strengths as a writer. The frail and troubled prodigy, whose conversion experience was written out in the Memorial he always carried with him, as Descartes carried the record of a similar experience; Mere Angelique, all the figures at Port-Royal and beyond; the Jesuits; the spiritual and theological issues; the delicate dialectic of heart and mind — has anyone ever handled these with such deftness and authority as Marvin O'Connell?

We wait now for his next major work, the life of Edward Sorin, founder of Notre Dame. He is proceeding with the same sure and deliberate pace with which he has written all his books. Luncheon previews whet the appetite; dinner table asides make one impatient for the book. Much has been written about Notre Dame and his founder, but O'Connell's life promises to be worthy of its subject and, dare I say, vice versa too.

There are those who may attribute my high estimate of Marvin O'Connell to the fact that we have been friends since boyhood. The Irish answer to that is, *although* I have known him since boyhood, I regard him as the premier Catholic historian of our time — and as my oldest friend in every sense. *Ad multos annos.*

Ralph McInerny, *Crisis*, March 1998

Afterword

On May 5, 2011, an academic conference entitled "Marvin R. O'Connell: Telling Stories that Matter" was held in honor of Father Marvin R. O'Connell. It was convened by Fr. Wilson Miscamble, CSC, Professor of History, and facilitated by Greer Hannan, of the Notre Dame Center for Ethics and Culture. There were three sessions: Marvin O'Connell and the Reformation/Counter Reformation; Marvin O'Connell and 19th-Century European Christianity; and Marvin O'Connell and American Catholic History. Professor David Solomon gave the after-dinner address at the banquet that concluded the conference. These remarks are David Solomon's tribute to his friend. –WGS

"O'Connell of Notre Dame"

This evening is, among other things, the fulfillment of a promise that Father Bill Miscamble and I made to Ralph McInerny before his death last year. Ralph had for years been planning an event like this for Marvin. He was an enormous admirer of Marvin's as well as his best friend for over 65 years. Ralph should be standing here giving this talk right now — and I feel my utter inadequacy to fill that role which is rightfully his. Ralph had been very taken with the celebration of his own career, given for him on the occasion of his 50th year as a member of the Notre Dame faculty. After Ralph became ill, one of the things he fretted most about — and he didn't fret about much — was his failure to organize a similar celebration for the career of his best friend, Marvin O'Connell.

On the occasion of Ralph's event, Marvin was the one standing in my place giving, as many of you may recall, a marvelous evocation of what it was like to be young and Catholic and intellectually alive in the years of their early manhood. His after-dinner talk, at the banquet closing the conference to honor Ralph, covered Ralph's life and early friendship with Marvin from roughly 1944 to 1950. To the casual listener it might have appeared that, according to Marvin's account, Ralph simply disappeared from history on the eve of Eisenhower's election to the presidency: a shooting star who shot across the sky with his literary buddy Marvin O'Connell and who, like some Midwestern Keats, burned out like a candle.

I was sitting next to Connie McInerny, Ralph's wife, during Marvin's talk and noticed that she seemed a little upset. At one point she leaned over to me and said, "Would you slip a note to Father O'Connell and remind him that Ralph did later marry and have seven children and twenty-two grandchildren — and that they are all in the audience. I thought historians were supposed to pay attention to such details."

Details, indeed. Marvin's memory of those days was, one might say, a bit selective. No one in the room, however, (except possibly Connie) could have resisted the opportunity to be alive with Ralph McInerny and Marvin O'Connell in 1950 when everything seemed to be going their way. Robert Lowell had become a Catholic, the Catholic literary revival was at full tide, and Thomas Merton was leading legions of monks into Gethsemane. Maritain, Gilson, and Simon stood astride the world of philosophy. Even the secular University of Chicago was kneeling at the altar of Thomas Aquinas. And Marvin and Ralph were two Minnesota Catholic boys, aspiring to be Catholic intellectuals, at a moment in history when their side was winning.

Well, it is now sixty years later and here we are.

My remarks this evening will not be a sober reflection on Marvin's historical scholarship — and that is no idle boast, as Ralph said on an earlier occasion like this. I am, of course, not qualified to make such an assessment, though I will say something a bit later about what I have taken away from Marvin's marvelous series of books, all of which I have read, and continue to reread, with great pleasure. My talk is rather a series of rambling remarks about a now 35-year friendship. I know some of you in this room have known Marvin much longer than that, but a lot has been packed into those 35 years, certainly much more than I can touch on this evening. I have spent all of today listening to learned historians, colleagues, and friends of Marvin's, say how wonderful and perceptive he is. It is surely time to pull back the veil (at least a bit) and talk about the real Marvin. History demands that the truth be told.

I came to know Marvin well in the late 1970s, though I had first met him when he returned to the Notre Dame history department, where he had earlier been a graduate student. He joined the Notre Dame history faculty in the early 1970s after teaching for some years at the University of St. Thomas. I, in the meantime, had joined the Notre Dame philosophy faculty in 1968. Ralph McInerny and I had become close friends and through our friendship I had first become acquainted with Marvin.

After returning to Notre Dame from a two-year post-doc at Boston University in the fall of 1977, my family and I moved into the McInerny house on Portage Avenue while the McInernys were headed to Rome for a sabbatical year. Part of the deal was that we were to "look after" three of the older McInerny daughters, Mary, Cathy, and Ann, all of whom were undergrads at Notre Dame. With "responsibility" for the daughters came Ralph's suggestion that if there were any problems in our taking possession of the house we were to consult his best friend, family counselor, and consiglieri, Father O'Connell.

Now I had met Father O'Connell on a number of occasions, but like many others, especially callow junior faculty members, I was intimidated by him — to be perfectly honest, I was scared to death of him. I had for many years shared an office with my philosophy colleague, and later Dean of the Arts and Letters College at Notre Dame, Mike Loux (back in the good old days when we all shared offices until tenure). Mike had been a student of Marvin's while an undergraduate at St. Thomas. He had regaled me with stories of Marvin picking up students bodily and throwing them into the hallway. (Indeed, this was a kind of refrain when Marvin's name was mentioned in those days — "that's the guy who throws them out of class — no, I mean really throws them out of class.") When I asked Mike what these students had done to deserve such clerical reprobation, he told me that they might have been caught not taking notes or, even worse, they might have had the temerity to don a baseball cap in Father O'Connell's lecture. These were the days, of course, when Marvin had what one can only call an aggressive flat-top haircut, looking a little like a cross between a Marine drill sergeant and one of those character actors who played the villains in the old westerns — a kind of pudgy Clint Eastwood wannabe.

Ralph also told me that Marvin might stop by occasionally during our stay on Portage Avenue to check on us and see if we needed any advice on how to manage the house — (this advice to be given by a priest who lived in a dormitory until he was forty). It turned out that Marvin did drop by most evenings about dinner time for a pre-prandial Scotch or two, and he stayed for a while — at least through the dessert course. It was a wonderful year in which our friendship blossomed — and Marvin ate very well. Not exactly a Stanley and Livingston story, but the origin of our friendship.

We all know Marvin to be a writer of beautiful English prose, limpid, elegant, and expressive. And Marvin, of course, is not unaware of his gifts in this regard. Indeed, he is not bashful generally about his virtues. As he once told me, "you might fear that, in a conference like this celebrating my career, you might praise me too much. You have no reason to fear that — it is impossible." And so I suspect it is.

Marvin was also well known for his unwillingness to be edited. Some of his most beautiful prose pieces are still unpublished for this reason — editors who dared to shorten, by so much as a line or two, his perfectly crafted prose felt the sting of Clio's tongue.

Marvin is also well known for his allegiance to the "scientific" character of historical research. Those of us who work in more speculative fields like philosophy often have had to suffer little lectures from Marvin about how the humble discipline of history is simply the "reconstruction of the past from sources." Purely objective, indeed scientific. No point of view, no ideology, no cooking the books. Marvin is famous for never writing about a location that he has not seen — if it still exists and can be seen, and if he can afford to get there (first class if the budget allows). He has traveled widely to be able to see exactly what the South Downs would have looked like on one of Newman's walks, or exactly what Archbishop Ireland might have seen while walking down a back street of Rome or a Left Bank street in Paris. It is quite remarkable how frequently, however, these places he must see are close to very fine restaurants, usually French, where the earnest but humble historian must retire for a little repast, after his strenuous scientific observations. Perhaps future humble historians, reconstructing the past from sources in telling their story of Father O'Connell's career, will note how frequently this coincidence occurs.

I had the opportunity on one occasion (and one for which I have always been enormously grateful) to observe the humble historian at work in his scientific observation. I was teaching in London when Marvin came for a visit while working on his Modernism book, *Critics on Trial*. He wanted to visit one or two sites of some importance to his narrative, and he wanted, in particular, to see the burial site of the great Irish modernist, Father George Tyrrell, buried near a small village south of London. I offered to be his chauffeur for this odyssey of scientific observation. After searching through a maze of country lanes south of London (where we were lost for much of the morning) we finally, with the help of a sturdy and knowledge-able local librarian, found the cemetery. With the help of an equally sturdy and knowledgeable vicar, whom we found tidying the graves in the ceme-tery, we found Father Tyrrell's grave. Now the time had come for the appli-cation of scientific method. I, out of respect for reason, stepped back to leave the scientist alone. As I watched, transfixed, Marvin, standing near the grave of Father Tyrell, took out a tiny notebook and opened it to a blank page. Looking around at the sky and trees, but barely glancing at the grave, he scratched one or two lines of notes, then turned to me and, in a portentous tone, said, "Do you think we can find any lunch?" And we did. It turned out, best of luck, that Father Tyrell was buried just down the street from one of the best pubs in the south of England.

Ralph McInerny, though Marvin's ardent admirer and best friend, was not always as respectful as he no doubt should have been of Marvin's pursuit of scientific history. Ralph's idea of history was that it should be engaged, it should render a verdict, and, when necessary, it should send down a thun-derbolt. While Marvin regarded it as one of his greatest compliments that William Langer (editor of the Rise of Modern Europe Series) said of his book on the Counter Reformation that it was impossible to tell whether the author was a Catholic or a Protestant — Ralph regarded this as no less than letting down the side. Given a chance to really give it to those Protes-tants, Ralph thought Marvin flinched.

Ralph, however, was particularly excited when Marvin undertook his Modernism project, hoping that, in spite of Marvin's aspiration to be ob-jective, indeed scientific, he would use the book to make up for his lapse in the Counter Reformation book and hammer Ralph's intellectual opponents in contemporary Catholic theology. Having forgone the opportunity to bash Protestants, maybe he would now make use of this opportunity to bash (the wrong kind of) Catholics. As Ralph said to me on more than one occasion, "O'Connell will show that they are all modernists — every one of them." Well, O'Connell didn't show that; he steered well clear of any real contact with post-Vatican II Catholic theology. Ralph held out hope for a long time that, if one read between the lines of the Modernism book, Marvin might have implied it — or at least insinuated it. But, alas, Marvin's conception of objective history won the day — with his Modernism book, as with every one of his books, he strenuously reconstructed the past from sources. What sources he had in the Modernism book, however, and what a reconstruction!

While Marvin has been careful and controlled, however, courting objectivity on every page of his big books, he has shown himself to have a more combative spirit in other literary genres. For all of Marvin's close friends, it was worth getting into trouble with some established authority just on the off chance that Marvin might write a letter defending you. One never felt so vindicated as when Marvin chose to rise to one's defense. When Ralph was, as all of us confidently believed, unjustly removed as the director of the Medieval Institute at Notre Dame in the early 1980s, Marvin was first in line to defend him — and thunderbolts did rain down from the sky. Those editors who dared sully Marvin's manuscript pages with their red pens also provided more than one occasion for his pen to be put to use.

But perhaps the genre in which Marvin's combative side was most effectively deployed was in the book review. One must say, however, that Marvin's book review technique displayed consistently one quite serious weakness: he tended to blow all of his dynamite in the first sentence, leaving the rest of the review a kind of afterthought. The first shot indeed tended to end the skirmish. But just as he is surely the master of the "indignant letter," he has had no equal in the quality of his first lines in book reviews. Who can forget, "This is the worst book I have ever read all the way through." And shouldn't a writer with the audacity to title his book *Caesar's Coin* know that Marvin could not resist titling his review, "*Caesar's Coin* is A Bad Penny"?

Marvin was the center of a circle of treasured friends who took up a certain insouciant, indeed irreverent, attitude toward some of the more hallowed aspects of Notre Dame life. My wife and I were privileged to live on the fringe of this group in its mature years — we were indeed among the younger members of it and regularly attended their celebrations. The rites and rituals involved birthday parties, celebrations of national holidays —

the Fourth of July, a special favorite of Ralph's and Marvin's — and dinners out. Among the central players on these occasions were the inimitable Liz Christman, the delicate flower; Tom Stritch, the basso profundo; Ralph McInerny, the chronicler and the balladeer; and Marvin, the straw that stirred the drink. His house in darkest Winding Brook was the scene for many of the frivolities of this group. His dinner parties were occasions to be treasured. Rumor had it that Marvin had only one recipe in his kitchen — his famous pork chop recipe. But others in this room can attest to the fact that he had in fact two — his coleslaw recipe as well. His original vocal compositions performed after dinner on these occasions remain things of legend.

The high point of the yearly activities was the "alternative president's dinner." A veil of secrecy has been drawn across the activities of this group, though there are those in this room who could say much if plied by appropriate liquid refreshment. Secreted in the archives, with a 25-year ban on any snooping, are the carefully recorded chronicles of this dinner — its poetry, its speeches, its annual prizes, its citations for scholarly excellence. What wouldn't you give to know, for example, who won the Ed Fisher Award for Slow Walking in 1988? The files are in good order and accompanied by copious photographic evidence of the penchant of Marvin O'Connell for high silliness — photographs carefully organized by the official photographer of the group, Connie McInerny. We await the time when the ban is lifted and an eager young historian reconstructs that past from those sources.

It has been wonderful for me to sit through the talks today and to hear from real historians why I should love the books that I have already learned to love. I did not need to be taught why I should love the man who wrote them. I am in a slightly different position at this conference from most of you. I attend as Marvin's friend and his fan — not as a fellow historian, nor as a former student — though in some ways I have been his student as well as his friend for the last 35 years. He has certainly taught me a lot. As my own interests in philosophy have shifted in directions that engage more directly the Catholic intellectual tradition, Marvin's books and conversations have been for me a kind of *vade mecum* to that tradition.

It is easy to be struck by the diversity of Marvin's scholarly productions, but what is much more significant about his work is surely its close-knit unity. His books comprise a veritable history of the major engagements of the Catholic Church with culture and intellectual life, from the religious turmoil of early modernity to the cultural turmoil of the 1960's. The Counter-Reformation books, together with his study of Blaise Pascal, cover the early modern period; *The Oxford Conspirators* and *Critics on Trial* reflect the major developments in nineteenth- and early twentieth-century European Catholicism; his magnificent trilogy — the biography of Archbishop Ireland, *Sorin*, and *Pilgrims to the Northland* — focuses on the great developments in the American Catholic church since 1850; and *McElroy*, Marvin's only venture into fiction, captures the ferment and spirit of change that followed the Second Vatican Council. What an achievement!

Each of these books is a significant achievement in itself, but taken together, as a series, it is a comprehensive history of the Catholic church in the modern world, told with a single voice, expressed in brilliant prose, inspiring its readers to follow the examples of its often flawed but heroic characters — Ireland, Sorin, Newman, Tyrell, and Loisy among others. It is a magnificent accomplishment. It is that accomplishment and the man who brought it about that we are gathered here today to celebrate. Let us lift our glasses to Father Marvin O'Connell — O'Connell of Notre Dame.

David Solomon, May 5, 2011

Index